PENGUIN CANADA

THE RETIREMENT TIME BOMB

GORDON PAPE is Canada's best-known financial author and the publisher of four investment newsletters, including *The Income Investor, Mutual Funds Update,* and the *Internet Wealth Builder.* He has authored or co-authored over 40 books and has spoken at hundreds of seminars in Canada and the United States. He is frequently quoted in the media and is a popular guest on radio and television shows. His website is located at www.buildingwealth.ca.

Also by Gordon Pape

INVESTMENT ADVICE

Get Control of Your Money

6 Steps to $1 Million

Retiring Wealthy in the 21st Century

The Complete Guide to RRIFs and LIFs
(with David Tafler)

*Gordon Pape's 2004 Buyer's
Guide to Mutual Funds*
(with Eric Kirzner)

*Gordon Pape's 2004
Buyer's Guide to RRSPs*

Secrets of Successful Investing
(with Eric Kirzner)

Making Money in Mutual Funds

The Canadian Mortgage Book
(with Bruce McDougall)

The Best of Pape's Notes

Head Start
(with Frank Jones)

Building Wealth in the '90s

Low-Risk Investing in the '90s

CONSUMER ADVICE

*Gordon Pape's International
Shopping Guide*
(with Deborah Kerbel)

HUMOUR

The $50,000 Stove Handle

FICTION
(with Tony Aspler)

Chain Reaction

The Scorpion Sanction

The Music Wars

NON-FICTION

Quizmas: Christmas Trivia Family Fun
(with Deborah Kerbel)

Montreal at the Crossroads
(with Donna Gabeline
and Dane Lanken)

VISIT GORDON PAPE'S WEBSITES

Building Wealth on the Net
www.buildingwealth.ca
Investing commentaries
Financial news and views
Gordon Pape's email newsletters
Answers to your financial questions
On-line Buyer's Guide to Mutual Funds
Net Worth Calculator
Family Budget Planner
Book excerpts
and much more!

Quizmas
www.quizmas.net
Christmas trivia for the whole family
Readers' Christmas memories
Quizmas contests

THE RETIREMENT TIME BOMB

HOW TO ACHIEVE
FINANCIAL INDEPENDENCE
IN A CHANGING WORLD

GORDON PAPE

PENGUIN
CANADA

PENGUIN CANADA

Published by the Penguin Group

Penguin Group (Canada), 90 Eglinton Avenue East, Suite 700, Toronto, Ontario, Canada M4P 2Y3
(a division of Pearson Penguin Canada Inc.)

Penguin Group (USA) Inc., 375 Hudson Street, New York, New York 10014, U.S.A.
Penguin Books Ltd, 80 Strand, London WC2R 0RL, England
Penguin Ireland, 25 St Stephen's Green, Dublin 2, Ireland (a division of Penguin Books Ltd)
Penguin Group (Australia), 250 Camberwell Road, Camberwell, Victoria 3124, Australia
(a division of Pearson Australia Group Pty Ltd)
Penguin Books India Pvt Ltd, 11 Community Centre, Panchsheel Park, New Delhi – 110 017, India
Penguin Group (NZ), cnr Airborne and Rosedale Roads, Albany, Auckland 1310, New Zealand
(a division of Pearson New Zealand Ltd)
Penguin Books (South Africa) (Pty) Ltd, 24 Sturdee Avenue, Rosebank, Johannesburg 2196, South Africa

Penguin Books Ltd, Registered Offices: 80 Strand, London WC2R 0RL, England

First published 2006

1 2 3 4 5 6 7 8 9 10 (WEB)

Copyright © Gordon Pape Enterprises Ltd., 2006

Excerpts from Richard Shillington's report "New Poverty Traps: Means-Testing and
Modest-Income Seniors," located on pp. 112–13, are reproduced courtesy of the C.D. Howe Institute.

Manufactured in Canada.

LIBRARY AND ARCHIVES CANADA CATALOGUING IN PUBLICATION

Pape, Gordon, 1936–
The retirement time bomb : achieving financial independence in a changing world / Gordon Pape.

Includes index.
ISBN 0-14-305073-7

1. Retirement income—Canada—Planning. I. Title.

HD7129.P37 2006   332.024'01   C2005-904956-1

Visit the Penguin Group (Canada) website at **www.penguin.ca**

To the memories of David Tafler, Bob Nelles, Bruce Smith,
Shirley Smith, Herb Sanders, Carl Kaye, and Stu Strebel.
You are greatly missed by us all.

CONTENTS

ACKNOWLEDGMENTS

Being an author is a lonely job in many ways. No one else can write the words for you; it's a task that must be done alone and which sometimes requires shutting out the rest of the world for hours or even days on end.

But that does not mean that a book is a one-person accomplishment. There are many people who play important roles in making everything come together and their hard work deserves recognition.

To begin with, I want to thank my daughter Deborah Kerbel for her assistance in the research of this book, which she amazingly found time to do while writing a series of children's novels of her own.

I would like to thank my editor-in-chief, Andrea Crozier of Penguin Canada, who has been a constant source of support, encouragement, and skilful guidance for many years. I would also like to thank Lisa Berland, my copy editor on this book, and Eliza Marciniak, the production editor, who looked after the myriad details that transformed my words from computer files to the book you are holding in your hand. As well, my thanks to all of the other folks at Penguin Canada who played important roles in the design, promotion, and marketing of *The Retirement Time Bomb*.

And finally, thank you to all of my faithful readers over the years. I have received letters and emails from many of you saying that my books have helped you reach your financial goals and attain a better lifestyle for yourselves and your families. Your words have meant a great deal to me and I very much appreciate the fact that you took the time to tell me that, in some small way, I made a difference.

Gordon Pape

INTRODUCTION

The Speed of Change

The only constant in life is change, and that is particularly true when it comes to retirement planning. Assumptions that seemed valid 10 years ago have been turned upside down in the intervening years and an entire new set of dynamics has come into play. Consider:

- A decade ago, people were worried that the Canada Pension Plan would run out of money and would not be there to support them when the time came to draw benefits. Today, only the most pessimistic fret about the solvency of the CPP. If the actuaries are right, Canada has one of the most stable public pension systems in the world.

- A decade ago, every Canadian with an employer pension plan believed that it would be the mainstay of their financial well-being in retirement. Today, the stability of the whole private pension system is in question. Financially stressed companies seek to reduce pension benefits that were once taken for granted. In a few cases, plans have actually collapsed into insolvency, leaving people who contributed to them for years with virtually nothing.

- A decade ago, the stock market was seen as the primary source of future retirement wealth. The big gains of the 1990s created an expectation that the good times would roll forever, boosting the assets of RRSPs and pension plans with annual returns of 10 percent and more. Today, after the Millennium Crash, rampant optimism has given way to sober realism. Few people talk of 10 percent returns from stocks any longer.

Nor should they; in April 2005 the chief institutional strategist of RBC Capital Markets, Myles Zyblock, published an analysis that predicted annual returns of only 2.9 percent at best from the Toronto Stock Exchange over the next 10 years.

- A decade ago, guaranteed investment certificates and government bonds were seen as the cornerstones of a retirement income program. Today, after years of ultra-low interest rates, financially strapped retirees are looking elsewhere for cash flow, and income trusts, which were virtually unknown in the 1990s, have become the hottest growth sector on the TSX.

- A decade ago, almost everyone wanted to retire early. London Life's "Freedom 55" slogan became a national mantra. Today, more people than ever are working past 65, often quite willingly, and mandatory retirement laws are falling by the wayside.

Nothing lasts forever. You can't take anything for granted when it comes to planning for your future. You must be aware of new developments and evolving attitudes and adjust your strategies to deal with them as they occur. That's the message of this book. The principles I outline in these pages are timeless, but the means by which you go about implementing them will need constant review and adjustment as the years go by. As you read through the chapters, keep in mind the following 10 basic guidelines to successful retirement planning. Treat them as a checklist, to be reviewed periodically (at least once every three years) to ensure that you are still on track.

Guideline #1: Have a plan. You can't get there if you don't start. Procrastination only makes the ultimate goal more difficult to achieve. Create a realistic retirement plan based on your age and financial situation and start implementing it.

Guideline #2: Control risk. Never let greed dominate prudence in managing your retirement assets. A few years of big losses will take a long time to recoup.

Guideline #3: Be realistic. Set achievable targets. Don't overreach. As athletes like to say: stay within yourself. An average annual return of 6 percent will produce a healthy nest egg after 30 or 40 years.

Guideline #4: Know the status of your pension plan, if you have one.
Don't assume the money will be waiting for you when you retire. Find out how your plan works, read the financial reports, attend meetings. If the plan looks like it is running into trouble, ask hard questions of the administrators. It's your future happiness that's at stake, so be aggressive.

Guideline #5: Keep tabs on government programs. As this book is written, the CPP appears to be on solid ground. But that was not always the case and may not be so in the future. If the politicians start talking about raising the retirement age or fiddling with the benefits, adjust your income projections accordingly. Ditto with Old Age Security.

Guideline #6: Review your personal timetable. Right now your plan may be to retire at 60. In 10 years, you may have adjusted that to 65. Or poor health may require you to exit the workforce at an earlier time. Your retirement date is a critical component in the entire planning process. The more years you work, the greater the RRSP capital and pension credits you will accumulate and the fewer years you will need to draw on them. If your retirement plans change, revisit all your projections. They will most certainly be affected.

Guideline #7: Watch the economic climate. The events in the world around you will play a large role in determining which types of investments are most appropriate at any given time. When economic growth is weakening, bonds will normally be a good place for your money. When the economy begins to emerge from a prolonged slump, stocks should surge. Be sensitive to the cycles and you will prosper.

Guideline #8: Monitor performance. I am constantly amazed by how people can discard the financial statements they receive every month without giving them more than a cursory glance. Treat these as your sentinel trees. If they appear sickly, apply treatment fast. If your assets do not grow at least 6 percent in any given year (excluding new contributions) do a complete analysis to find out why.

Guideline #9: Know the tax laws. You can save yourself a lot of money both in your savings years and after retirement by understanding the tax laws and using them to your advantage. But remember, they keep changing. You have to stay up to date or use an advisor who will do so.

Guideline #10: Don't despair. Despite the best-laid plans, things won't always go right. There will be setbacks; it's just the way of the world. Do your best to minimize the damage when they do happen and prepare an action plan to get back on track. Don't, under any circumstances, allow yourself to fall into a deep funk and let matters continue to slide. Like everything else in life, the winners are those who learn from adversity and fight through it. It's the same with your retirement plan.

Following these guidelines will seem difficult at times, especially in the early years when retirement seems a long way off. But the rewards at the end of the day are more than worth it. Although I have not yet retired (I like what I do too much), we spend our winters in Florida. Every day I meet older people who are living life to the fullest: playing golf, walking the beaches, watching the sunset from a restaurant patio, fishing, boating, painting landscapes, photographing birds, and doing a million other things that they had always dreamed of. Some of these people live in expensive gated communities, some in condominiums, some in mobile homes and recreational vehicles, some own, some rent. Whatever their level of accommodation and their way of life, they are fulfilling a dream.

Your personal dreams may be quite different. It doesn't matter. The important thing is to make them happen. If this book helps you achieve that in some small way, then my work has all been worth it.

1

The Retirement Time Bomb

It was April 2004 in New York City. Canada's finance minister of the day, Ralph Goodale, was in town for a conference with his G8 counterparts. As part of his pre-meeting itinerary, he was the featured speaker at a luncheon given by the Canadian Society of New York. His speech and others that followed highlighted a quiet but growing threat to the fabric of Canadian society, a danger he would subsequently refer to as a "demographic time bomb." In his New York address, Mr. Goodale spoke of the "greying of the baby boomer generation" and the impact it will have on Canada and other nations within a relatively short time. It was a theme that clearly concerned him greatly.

So it should. The demographic challenges we are facing have huge consequences for governments throughout the developed world if they fail to take action to meet the coming societal changes. These challenges also have serious financial implications for all Canadians—and not only the baby boomers. Everyone from workforce entrants to retirees will be affected by the powerful forces that are already in motion.

Mr. Goodale told his New York audience that Canada will see a major demographic shift after 2010 that will have a dramatic effect on the nature of our population and the composition of the workforce. As the baby boomers reach retirement age, the ratio of employed people to retirees will decline by about 50 percent, from five to one to two and a half to one.

"This will have at least two profound effects on our society. There will be greater demand for the social programs we value, particularly health care, and at the same time there will be fewer people working and therefore contributing to those same programs," the minister said.

Later in an interview he added: "This is not never-never land. This is just around the corner and we'd all better be ready for it."

More than a year later, in June 2005, he was still hammering away at the subject. Speaking to the Economic Club of Toronto, he said:

> The fact of the matter is our country is facing a demographic time bomb. As members of the baby boom generation begin to retire in large numbers over the next 5 to 10 years, the remaining members of the workforce will be supporting an expanding population of seniors—there will be more and more reliance upon health care, pensions and other age-related social programs, with fewer people coming along in the following generation to finance all that.

The only way to fill this gap, he said, is to improve our national productivity. "We must invest in the areas that drive productivity growth—our physical capital, human capital and innovation."

With the first wave of baby boomers turning 60 in 2006, the fuse of the time bomb to which Mr. Goodale referred is not only lit but is burning quickly. The federal government recognizes the danger and is trying to deal with the problem on a macro basis with millions of dollars in new money being poured into education, infrastructure, skills training, and research.

But how should individual Canadians prepare for the sea change in our society that is on the doorstep? That's what this book is all about.

A Blissful Unawareness

Most Canadians have only a vague idea of what lies ahead. That's not surprising when you consider that many people have problems planning for next month, much less for developments that will occur years from now and over which they feel they have little or no control.

Moreover, there seems to be a blissful unawareness of the potential harsh retirement years that await the unprepared. A poll conducted for Manulife Financial by Maritz Research in December 2004 found that almost two-thirds of respondents were confident they would be able to achieve their retirement goals. If the reality is anywhere near as rosy, it will be a tremendous accomplishment and a tribute to the foresight of individual Canadians. Unfortunately, the prospects are for a far different outcome.

A study done for the Canadian Labour Congress by Vector Research in March 2004 comes closer to what I believe the true picture to be. It found that 73 percent of those questioned were worried they would not have adequate income in retirement. That was up an astonishing 19 percentage points from two years earlier. The worry about retirement income was topped only by concerns over health care, which were voiced by 82 percent. The results prompted CLC officials to complain to the federal government that retirement security was not getting enough attention.

Mr. Goodale addressed those concerns in a minor way in his 2005 budget speech by raising the maximum contribution limit for RRSPs, but the way in which he did it will benefit only high-income people. That's because he chose to raise the dollar limit on maximum annual contributions, which helps only Canadians with income in excess of $100,000. Had Mr. Goodale increased the percentage of earned income that may be contributed from the current 18 percent to, say, 20 percent, every working person could have put more aside for retirement.

The reality is that there is just so much that Ottawa and the provinces can do, and many of the changes already in the works are really designed to throw the burden back onto individual Canadians. The trend toward ending mandatory retirement is an example, and one which the labour unions strongly oppose. Advances in health care have resulted in longer, more productive lives. Many people want to use the extra years to remain in the workforce, either because they like their job or through economic necessity. Indeed, one of the most significant changes in the next decade will be in the number of people over 65 who are still working either full- or part-time. This is not the type of change that much of organized labour is likely to ever welcome. But it is part of the new reality.

Private Pension Crisis

When I wrote *Retiring Wealthy in the 21st Century* in 1999, some critics castigated me for being overly alarmist. In one aspect, they were right. At the time, I was very concerned about the future of Canada's two cornerstone income support systems for retirees, the Canada Pension Plan and Old Age Security. Since then, changes have been implemented to put both programs on a much firmer footing and to make them fairer to those who depend on them. So on that count, we're in better shape now than we were then.

Offsetting that, however, is a crisis in the private pension industry that threatens to undermine the stability of one of the main sources of retirement income for employees. Experts disagree on exactly how serious this crisis actually is, but no one pretends that we don't have a problem.

Nor is the crisis confined to Canada. The United States is wrestling with how to cope with the biggest private pension plan deficit in its history. Great Britain is also in trouble, as a cartoon that appeared in the October 17, 2004, edition of the *Financial Times* of London demonstrated. It showed a muscular man trying to carry a gigantic elephant labelled "The Pension Crisis," on the back of which dozens of workers clung to a precarious perch. The point was crystal clear: the whole system was on the verge of collapse. In an article in *Investment Executive* that same month, writer Monica Townson quantified the extent of Britain's problem by reporting that the government estimates that about 65,000 people will lose part or all of their pensions because of the wind-up of underfunded plans since 1997. I'll explore the pension crisis in more depth in Chapter 3.

The Health Care Crunch

Perhaps the biggest danger in the ticking time bomb is health care. If the costs seem high now, just wait until the baby boomers move into their retirement years. In the words of the great Jimmy Durante, "You ain't seen nuttin' yet!"

The American public is rapidly becoming sensitized to the dimensions of the problem as an offshoot of the Social Security debate now raging in that country. In testimony before the U.S. Congress in early 2005, Federal Reserve Board Chairman Alan Greenspan warned that health care costs will far outstrip Social Security expenses within a relatively short time. A report released about the same time by the U.S. Centers for Medicare and Medicaid Services estimated that by 2014, health care expenses in the U.S. could reach $3.6 trillion, almost 19 percent of total American economic output, even though the rate of increase in percentage terms will gradually decline. Prominent economists say devoting that large a percentage of GNP to health care is simply not sustainable.

In a subsequent editorial, the country's largest-circulation newspaper, *USA Today*, wrote:

> Imagine a government that has stopped providing national defense, halted criminal prosecutions, canceled mail delivery, and abandoned its highways and parklands. This government, in fact, does nothing but write benefits checks and pay interest on its debts—and still runs a deficit.
>
> Sound farfetched? Actually, that prospect is just three decades off if U.S. government benefit programs grow at current rates and the size of the government relative to the economy stays constant. Social Security is partly to blame for this dire outlook ... but by far the biggest culprit is the exploding cost of health care....

Perhaps surprisingly, we are not hearing similar alarm bells in Canada. Everyone knows that health care costs are a problem that must be dealt with, but we have not reached the stage—at least not yet—at which dire warnings are being issued about the possibility that our governments will sink under the weight of the burden.

Even the highly touted and much-praised Commission on the Future of Health Care in Canada, which was headed by former Saskatchewan premier Roy Romanow, confined itself largely to the short-term dimensions of the problem. The commission's final report, which was released in the fall of 2002, projected combined public and private health care costs only out to the 2005–2006 fiscal year, at which point they were expected to reach $122.7 billion. The commission did not offer a forecast of how much of that amount would be spent by governments, but using their overall percentage increase projections the figure will be in the range of $87.5 billion.

Population forecasts tell us what to expect after that. In 2001, not quite 17 percent of Canadians were over age 60. By 2011, that figure will be over 20 percent and a decade later it will top 25 percent. By 2041, almost 30 percent of Canadians will be 60 and over. More disconcerting from a health expenditure perspective, almost 18 percent will be 70 and older.

In his 2005 budget speech, Mr. Goodale said that federal transfers to the provinces and territories for health care will total $19.6 billion in the 2006–2007 fiscal year and will reach $30.5 billion in 2013–2014. All that money will have to come from somewhere.

During his final illness in the winter of 2005, the late Pope John Paul II suggested that too much of the world's resources are being diverted to health care costs by affluent Western nations. The implication seemed to be that older people should be prepared to accept some suffering as a normal part of the aging process. The Pope's message may have been well intended but it is not going to have much resonance in Canada and the United States. No one wants to be incapacitated in their later years if medical science can prevent or alleviate the condition. The demand for high-quality health care will continue to grow and the costs will inevitably escalate as the population ages.

The macro decisions of how to deal with this situation will obviously be in the hands of governments. But individuals would be wise to prepare for what appears to be a virtually inevitable hand-off of some government-sponsored health programs to the private sector over time. Because of the politically charged nature of the issue the changes will come gradually, but they most assuredly will come. Therefore, you'd be wise to prepare to pay a higher proportion of health care expenses out of your own pocket in future years, either directly or in the form of insurance premiums. Factor this into your retirement planning forecasts.

Laying the Groundwork

According to Statistics Canada, almost 20 percent of our population classified as "near retirement" in 2002, and the number goes up every year. These people cannot allow themselves to become dependent on others to ensure that their retirement years are lived in comfort—nor can any of us. We must put our own personal foundation in place. If governments and employers are able to add some bricks to the structure later, so much the better. But it's up to each one of us to lay the groundwork.

The purpose of this book is to help you do this. We'll look at the problems created by the retirement time bomb from both macro and micro perspectives. The purpose is not to alarm you but rather to make you aware of the reality of what lies ahead so that you can properly prepare. It may be that events will conspire to ease many of the concerns that are being raised today. But even if they don't, you'll be ready to cope with whatever awaits you down the road.

2

The Bear Market Trauma

The long bear market of 2000 to 2002 was a shocking wake-up call for millions of Canadians. Most had never experienced anything like it. In fact, all things considered, it was the worst period for investors since the Great Depression. Those grim two and a half years left deep psychological scars that persist to this day. Worse, they threw into chaos the retirement plans of many people and left some pension plans teetering on the brink of insolvency.

The shock was magnified by the fact that few people saw it coming as the world prematurely celebrated the dawn of a new millennium on New Year's Eve, 1999 (although technically, the twenty-first century began on January 1, 2001). As fireworks lit the sky from Sydney Harbour to Times Square, people were generally feeling pretty good about their personal financial situation and the economy in general.

And why not? North American stock markets were on a record roll. Over the previous 12 months the Nasdaq Composite Index had moved from 2,193 to 4,069, an incredible advance of 85.5 percent in a single year. Internet frenzy had gripped investors and high-tech stocks were being bid to the sky. Few people paid any attention to small details like the fact that virtually none of the companies could show a penny of profit.

Nasdaq went on to reach a closing high of 5,049 on March 10, 2000. The collapse that followed came with dizzying suddenness. By the end of that month, the index had plunged 476 points, to 4,573. That represented a 9.4 percent decline, but it was only the beginning. By the time April was over, the Nasdaq Composite stood at 3,861, down 23.5 percent from its March 10 high point. Investors scrambled for the exits, and it turned out to be just as well that they did. After a summer rally, the index resumed its free fall. By the time 2000 came to a close, it was down to 2,471, representing a 51 percent plunge in less than 10 months. That precipitous drop rivalled the Crash of 1929 in its severity and depth.

The carnage still wasn't over. By the end of 2001, the Nasdaq Composite was down to 1,950. It hit rock bottom on October 9, 2002, when it ended the day at 1,114. The 31-month bear market had cost Nasdaq investors 88 percent of the market value of their shares by the time all was said and done. Billions of dollars had vanished into limbo. On the financial version of the Richter scale it was almost as bad as the collapse of the Dow Jones Industrial Average between September 1929 and July 1932, when it fell 89 percent.

The other major U.S. indexes were slower to react and the damage wasn't quite as severe, although it was bad enough. The Standard & Poor's 500 Index, which tracks the performance of the biggest American corporations, lost only slightly more than 10 percent in 2000. That was seen as a modest, and expected, correction, and conventional wisdom was that the meltdown was going to be confined to the high-tech sector. But the slide accelerated in 2001, exacerbated by the 9/11 attacks, and the S&P gave up another 13 percent to finish the year at 1,148. Things were starting to look serious, and indeed they were. The following year, 2002, saw the blue chips tumble another 33 percent to reach a low of 769 in October before the final selling spree was done. Between March 2000 and October 2002, America's biggest and proudest companies, core holdings in many public and personal pension plans, lost slightly more than half of their market value. In Canada, the crunch started a few months later than in the States but by the time it ended in the fall of 2002, the S&P/TSX Composite Index had fallen about 60 percent. There was simply no place to hide!

Devastation and Demoralization

Individual investors were devastated and demoralized. Few had any advance inclination of what was coming. Many had been seduced by the siren call of financial experts who spoke glowingly of a "new golden age" and a "new paradigm" that would see stock markets rise for at least a decade on the strength of the tech revolution. It was like Hollywood in the early days of the film industry. What people forgot was that most of the companies that pioneered the birth of movies weren't around long enough to reap the profits.

By early 2000, even conservative investors were scrambling to get on the bandwagon after seeing some science and technology mutual funds post triple-digit gains in the prior year. I still remember talking to a woman after a seminar I gave in St. Catharines, Ontario, in February of that year. She was bound and determined that she was going to shift her entire RRSP into a Nasdaq Index fund. I argued strongly against it, telling her that such a move would be extremely risky and counter to all retirement planning common sense. I could tell when we parted that she was not convinced. I only hope that she had the good sense to reconsider the idea later.

A few brave money managers had the courage to stand up to the general consensus that all was well, laying their reputations on the line in the process. One such was Francis Chou, who a few years later, in December 2004, was named Manager of the Decade by the mutual funds industry. Few thought of him in those terms, however, when he wrote the following in his 1999 annual report:

> Let's not play a fool's game by thinking that a stock can be bought at 100 times revenues and then proceed to hope, against hope, that someone who is carried away by emotion, and is unaware of the risk involved, will buy it at 200 times revenues the following week. When the urge hits to make such a leap, take a cold shower until the inclination passes.

Because he refused to play the high-tech game and stuck to his value principles, both of Mr. Chou's funds lost money in 1999 while almost every other stock fund in the business was scoring huge gains. But he had the last laugh. While stock markets tumbled from 2000 to 2002, his Chou RRSP Fund scored double-digit gains in every single year, culminating in a 32 percent advance in 2002!

Hardest hit by the bear market were those poor souls who heeded the advice of some so-called experts and mortgaged their homes to the hilt in order to buy equity mutual funds in 1998 and 1999. Leveraging, as this strategy is called, is a two-edged sword, as they discovered. When stocks are strong, it magnifies gains significantly. But in a market swoon, the losses mount up at a rapid pace. Many of these people saw the equity in their home erode dramatically and then compounded the problem by bailing out just as the bear market reached its culmination, thereby locking in their losses. It was a painful lesson in the harsh realities of the financial world.

Low Interest Rates Compound the Problem

The effect of the stock market collapse was made worse for many investors by the interest rate scenario that accompanied it. For decades, Canadians had found a safe haven from the turmoil of stocks in their beloved guaranteed investment certificates (GICs). These securities fit the Canadian persona perfectly. The principal and interest is guaranteed by the issuing financial institution and in the event it should ever run into difficulty the Canada Deposit Insurance Corporation (CDIC) would jump in to save the day. What better place to put your retirement money?

The early years of the twenty-first century changed all that. Interest rates had been sliding for some time but when the extent of the stock market carnage became clear, the central banks knocked them down to levels unseen since the end of the Second World War. In the United States, the federal funds rate was slashed all the way to 1 percent as the Federal Reserve Board tried to inject life into an economy that had been shattered first by the stock market crash and later by the terrorist attack on the World Trade Center. In Ottawa, the Bank of Canada took a similar, if not quite as drastic, course by reducing its key overnight rate to as low as 2 percent in early 2002.

The result of this rate-slashing was to take GICs off the table as a viable option for many investors. The safety factor was still there but the returns being offered were so low that only diehards were interested. That left people in a quandary. Stocks were too risky. GICs were too stingy. Economists were saying that bonds were overpriced and due for a fall. What to do? Where to go? Mattresses had never looked so good.

What happened was the worst of all possible scenarios. Many people, paralyzed by fear and uncertainty, did nothing. They turned their backs on their investment portfolios, hoping that things would soon turn for the better. When that didn't happen, they started throwing their monthly statements into the wastebasket, unread, because they couldn't deal with the losses. The newspapers began to publish stories about folks who had been forced to postpone their retirement because of the damage to their finances. Those who had already retired often found themselves in a cash crunch as falling interest rates reduced the returns on their investments. It was the worst of all possible worlds for the retired and the about-to-retire.

Meanwhile, professional pension managers were tearing their hair out. They were caught by the same market forces that were buffeting individual investors. However, in their case the implications were much more serious. Pension plans, at least the defined benefit type, represent an obligation by the plan sponsor to pay a specified level of income to retirees. The plans are governed by actuaries, who determine what level of investment return is needed to meet the obligations and whether the funding is adequate to fulfill those requirements. A pension plan that has the assets to pay its members in full is said to have a "solvency ratio" of 100 percent. According to a Bank of Canada report released in 2004, the majority of defined benefit pension plans were below that mark.

The bear market and plunging interest rates combined to create what pension expert Keith Ambachtsheer described as a "perfect storm" for plan managers. The result was to drive many plans from a surplus position into deficit. For example, Paul Haggis, the CEO of the giant Ontario Municipal Employees Retirement Board, told a conference in June 2004 that their pension fund, the third largest in Canada, saw a $5 billion surplus turn into a $3 billion deficit in just three years. That's an $8 billion swing! Many other plans, large and small, suffered a similar fate although their absolute numbers weren't as large.

All told, the Certified General Accountants Association of Canada estimated in mid-2004 that about $160 billion was needed to cover the collective shortfall in private pension funding. In a report, they said it would take special contributions of $15 billion a year for five years from corporations to make up the deficit. That is very unlikely to happen. We'll look at the implications of this crisis in the next chapter.

A Financial Hurricane

The New Millennium Crash left a trail of financial chaos in its wake that might be compared to the passage of a hurricane. We are still feeling the effects of it today and we will continue to do so for years to come.

The only positive thing to come out of it is that, hopefully, it shook us out of our collective lethargy and forced us to take a fresh look at our personal finances and our plans for the future. Things that we used to take for granted, such as a pension plan, have been thrown into doubt. Unrealistic investment expectations, fed by the heady days of the 1990s, have been brought down to earth. The casual attitude many Canadians had toward retirement planning has been challenged, especially among the baby boomers, who have suddenly become aware that the future is almost upon them.

It all adds up to the need for a new approach to preparing for our retirement years. When I wrote *Retiring Wealthy in the 21st Century*, I emphasized the need for greater self-reliance and reduced dependence upon others in planning for the day when we stop work. As a result of the bear market, that self-reliance has become even more important today. It's time to get over the trauma of the crash and start taking charge. We can't change the past. But we can learn from it and change the future.

3

The Pension Mess

Just about everyone agrees that the North American pension industry is going through a state of crisis. But there is a wide divergence of opinion on just how serious that crisis is and how, or if, it will be resolved. The basic issue is very simple: Will private defined benefit pension plans be able to make good on their obligations to retired workers? Or will an unacceptably high percentage of these plans be forced to reduce benefits or even, in a worst-case scenario, default on them entirely? The answers to those questions will have a huge impact on the retirement income of millions of people and may mean the difference between affluence and borderline subsistence in their later years.

Let's be very clear about one point at the outset. Not all employer and union pension plans are in trouble. Some are in good financial shape, despite the ravages of the 2000–2002 bear market. But others are hurting and a few have actually gone under, leaving their participants angry, frustrated, and helpless.

Former employees of the St. Anne Nackawic Pulp Company in the small community of Nackawic in New Brunswick's Saint John River valley west of Fredericton were shocked to find themselves in exactly that position in late 2004. CTV News reported that the mill went into bankruptcy in September of that year, throwing half the town's population out of work. But that was just the first blow. Later came the news that the company's pension plan had run up a deficit that the Canadian Auto Workers union said could be as much as $25 million. As a result, all employees under 55 years of age were expected to lose their pension benefits while older workers would experience cuts. The grim faces of ex-employees shown on the CTV National News told the whole story. Their lives had been devastated, their futures were unknown, and there seemed to be nowhere to turn for help.

It's not a scene that anyone wants to see re-enacted ever again. Unfortunately, it has happened elsewhere and could become a common occurrence if the worst fears of the pension Cassandras are realized. Financially troubled U.S. Airways was forced to cut pension benefits for its pilots by as much as 70 percent. Other major American airlines have sought to do the same, as did Air Canada while it was under creditor protection (it didn't succeed). Bethlehem Steel went into bankruptcy, leaving behind US$3.6 billion in unpaid obligations to its plan. And the list grows every year.

It's not just pension plans that are at risk. So are a variety of other benefits that retirees receive from former employers, such as ongoing extended health insurance, dental coverage, and life insurance. A study conducted by Watson Wyatt, an international human resources consulting firm, found that 71 of Canada's largest employers were carrying a total of $16 billion in retirement benefit liabilities at the end of 2003. One of the firm's consultants, Gregory Durant, called the issue "a sleeping giant."

The issue of pensions and benefits has become a hot button for the executives of some of the continent's largest companies. Gary Cowger, president of the North American operations of General Motors, went so far as to characterize it as going to the very core of U.S. competitiveness. His company paid out US$3.6 billion in 2004 on health care benefits for retirees, according to General Motors CEO Rick Wagoner. All told, the Big Three U.S. automakers were hit with a US$10 billion bill in 2004 for health care benefits for active and retired workers. They claim that adds US$2,000 to US$2,500 to the sticker price of a car, making it difficult for them to compete with imports.

Some Canadian companies, such as Suncor, have already moved to reduce future obligations by introducing flex plans that allow retirees to choose from a menu of benefits, with a limit on the amount that can be spent.

It's one thing to prepare workers in advance for reduced benefits in retirement. It's quite another to slash them after the fact. That's what happened to some retired Ontario public servants who were informed by letter in 2002 that their health insurance program was being cut. The outrage that resulted ended up in the courts with a class action suit filed against the Government of Ontario. The case had not been heard at the time of writing.

The growing tendency of financially strapped corporations to look to their pension plans and benefits programs for relief will probably result in more court battles. Although the case did not arise from a troubled company seeking bankruptcy protection, a decision handed down in July 2004 by the Supreme Court of Canada is seen as a landmark ruling that could have a significant impact on corporate pension plans going forward. The Court unanimously ruled that workers who had been laid off by Monsanto Canada in 1997 and 1998 were entitled to receive a portion of the pension plan's surplus, which was over $19 million at the time, resulting in a partial wind-up of the program. In a report issued subsequent to the ruling, Watson Wyatt said the decision "will further weaken Canada's already-troubled private-sector defined benefit pension system" by causing many sponsors to make changes to their plan's design as well as funding and investment policies. "The decision could ultimately lead to the further reduction of private-sector pension coverage in Canada," the company warned in a press release. Ian Markham, the company's director of pension innovation, called on governments "to take decisive action to address the problems of a regulatory environment that can only be described as hostile to sponsors of [defined benefit] plans, lest the pension system be thrown into crisis."

The CGA Report on Pensions

So just how serious is this whole problem? It depends on whose interpretation you believe to be most accurate. The Certified General Accountants

Association of Canada warned of a "looming social and economic crisis" in a 2004 report on the health of the country's defined benefit pension plans. Titled *Addressing the Pensions Dilemma in Canada,* the survey of 847 plans, which uses data and research provided by Mercer Human Resource Consulting, concluded that 59 percent of defined benefit plans were in deficit with the total amount owed by employers being a staggering $160 billion.

In the report, the CGA fingered the bear market and low interest rates as being the proximate causes of the crisis but warned of "deeper systemic problems which require redressing." It urged that the financial difficulties arising from market conditions be seen as "a wake-up call" that will "create a foundation from which to explore reform." Commented Anthony Ariganello, the organization's president: "The Canadian pension landscape is changing. Where previously, many large and well-established employers provided generous pension plans and employees fully expected to receive their benefits as a matter of course, we are now faced with a fluid and shifting environment."

Fluid and shifting indeed! And what, exactly, is the leading edge of the baby boomers now approaching retirement supposed to make of that statement? That nothing is certain—*nothing*! We can't take anything for granted. The whole retirement universe is in a state of overhaul and it will be years before everything gets sorted out.

The Conference Board Report

A less pessimistic view was contained in a report published by the Conference Board of Canada in November 2004, in collaboration with Watson Wyatt Worldwide and Financial Executives International Canada. It surveyed chief financial officers (CFOs) in 68 organizations, representing 20 percent of private sector pension plan assets. Its main conclusions, as stated in the document:

1. Sponsors of large plans do not expect the crisis to last.
2. There appears to be a desire to increase the amount of contributions above the minimum level, but regulatory barriers are getting in the way.

3. Emerging trends include a movement to DC (defined contribution) plans and cuts in DB (defined benefits) plans and other post-retirement benefits.

4. The flow of pension information within organizations, to board members, and to plan members has increased substantially over the past two years.

5. Many organizations are examining their pension liability structure when assessing investment decisions, but most do not appear to be changing their investment strategies.

Although the overall thrust of the Conference Board report is that the problems can be dealt with, some of their conclusions have to raise concerns for retirees, present and future. Consider point 3, for example. What the Conference Board is saying here is that defined benefits plans are gradually being phased out, replaced by defined contribution plans. There is evidence to support this conclusion. According to Statistics Canada, just under 40 percent of workers were pension plan members at the start of 2003. Of those, 82 percent were in defined benefits plans, while only 15 percent belonged to defined contribution plans. But in percentage terms, the number of DB plan members almost doubled over the previous year. "The number of [defined contribution plan] members rose sharply to more than 830,000 in 2002, some 1.8 times higher than in 1992" StatsCan said in a daily commentary published in September 2004. (For details about the differences between defined contribution and defined benefit plans, see Chapter 4.)

The implications of this trend are huge. Defined benefit pension plans theoretically guarantee a certain level of income at retirement, usually based on a formula that takes into account income and years of service. Assuming that the plans are able to fulfill their commitments, they provide a basic level of income security for retirees, the more so if the plan is indexed. However, such plans are very expensive and have come to represent a major liability on the balance sheets of corporations.

Defined contribution plans put much less financial pressure on the sponsor but offer no guarantee of any kind to the retiree. The income you receive when you stop work will be based primarily on the amount of money you and the employer contributed to the plan over the years and the return that was generated by the invested capital. These plans are capable of producing some big-time shocks, as happened during the bear market when equity-based securities were clobbered. People who were due to retire toward the end of that period may have found that the amount of their pension was much less than they had expected.

Point 5 of the summary is also worth noting. At the core, it seems to be saying that while sponsors are taking a close look at their pension plans, few are doing anything to change the investment strategy that has brought them to their present state. There are exceptions, however. Paul Haggis, chief executive officer of the big Ontario Municipal Employees Retirement Board (OMERS), was quoted in *The Globe and Mail* in June 2004 as saying that the time had come for a change in direction in the way the almost $40 billion fund invests its money. He said that measuring results against stock market indexes only results in the plans going "off the cliff together" when markets crash. The answer, he feels, is a shift to more direct corporate ownership and real estate assets that will transform the fund into "more of a holding company with an enormous treasury department."

It remains to be seen whether this is a long-term solution to the problem—real estate can go through bust periods too. But at least OMERS is giving serious thought as to what needs to be done to protect the interests of plan members.

Governments Won't Help

If pension plan managers can't find a solution, will governments step in? Perhaps. In May 2005, the federal Department of Finance issued a consultation paper in which it called for public input on several key issues relating to pension plan governance, administration, and funding. One of the issues raised was whether this country should create a government-sponsored pension guaranteed income fund that would come to the rescue of workers whose plans were unable to meet their commitments. Right now, there is no federal support program in such situations and the politicians and bureaucrats will probably think long and hard before going that route, given the experience of the United States in this regard. That country's Pension Benefit Guaranty Corporation (PBGC), a federal agency that is supposed to insure the pension benefits of some 44 million Americans, lost US$12 billion in 2004 after stepping in to support almost 200 plans during the year, including those operated by such high-profile companies as Kaiser Aluminum. The PBGC is facing long-term liabilities totalling US$62 billion as a result of being forced to provide financial assistance when plan sponsors reneged on commitments. Some observers believe that only a large-scale bailout by the U.S. Congress can keep the agency solvent.

In Canada, the Province of Ontario is currently the only jurisdiction to provide any sort of protection for pensioners, but its program is very limited in scope.

Apart from the huge liability potential, there are other serious concerns about creating such a national program. Some of these were outlined in the Finance Department's consultation paper, such as the potential incentive a bailout plan would create for financially troubled employers to simply throw in the towel.

Unless there is a huge public groundswell of support for the idea, it will likely quietly disappear. At the end of the day, you will have to protect yourself against the possibility that the pension income you expect may not be there, in whole or in part, when the time comes to start collecting your cheques. In the next chapter, we'll look at some of the steps you need to take right now to reduce the chances of retirement shock.

4

Take the Offensive

There's an old saying in sports that the best defence is a good offence. It's a strategy that should be applied to retirement planning as well. By that I mean that you can no longer afford to simply react as best you can to whatever life throws at you. You need to take the initiative and make things happen. That means knowing exactly where you stand at all times and not placing yourself in a vulnerable position where "unexpected" events can compromise or even destroy your dreams.

If you have an employer pension plan, that should be your starting point. It is supposed to form the foundation of your retirement income but, as we saw in the previous chapter, in some cases that foundation is showing cracks.

When a company runs into financial trouble, one of the first places they look for relief is the pension plan. Hamilton-based steel manufacturer Stelco Inc. is a classic example. When the company sought creditor protection while it reorganized, management persuaded the Ontario government to give it a pension holiday, which meant it did not have to make contributions to its pension plan. That holiday, which lasted several years, saved Stelco hundreds of millions of dollars. But those savings came at a cost to plan members; at the end of 2004 the plan was looking at a deficit of $1.3 billion!

That raised alarm bells at Queen's Park, the seat of the Ontario government. So in February 2005, Stelco was told that the holiday was over. The company and whoever emerged victorious for the bidding war that was taking place for it at the time would be required to make up that deficit over a period to be determined.

Ontario's move demonstrates that governments are becoming increasingly nervous about the financial pressures being placed on defined benefit pension plans and the potential social problems that may arise down the road if some of the big ones are forced to reduce benefits or even, in a worst-case scenario, default on their obligations. It serves notice that pension contribution holidays will not be granted lightly in the future and that if and when they are the company should expect that it will have to make up any deficiency that results.

Of course, there is little a government can do if a company goes belly up and leaves behind a pension plan with a huge shortfall. Any employee caught in this unhappy situation should not expect a bailout from their provincial legislators or Ottawa. No government would want to establish that kind of precedent at a time when revenue is tight and demographics make it inevitable that the financial demands for providing services to seniors will increase exponentially.

This leaves employees in a difficult position since they have no direct control over how their pension plan is administered. However, plan members aren't completely helpless. If you are concerned about the financial position of your pension plan, it's time to use the best-defence-is-a-good-offence strategy. But first, you need to understand exactly what type of plan you have and how it works.

Types of Plans

The first step to understanding your pension plan is to know what type it is. Without that basic piece of information, you're flying blind. Here are the most common types of plans.

Defined Benefit (DB) Plans

In a typical defined benefit plan, each employee contributes a percentage of income to the plan and the employer provides the "top-up" needed to ensure the program meets actuarial requirements, which is the amount of money a plan must have in order to meet its obligations. This can sometimes mean that an employer can go for years paying nothing into a plan if the return on invested capital is particularly good. Most of the private pension plans in Canada are in this group, although the percentage is diminishing.

Defined benefit plans guarantee a specific income at retirement, according to a formula that can vary from one plan to another. Typically, this formula is based on the number of years of service plus an income factor. More generous plans define income as the average of your best three or five years' earnings. Others may use your final three or five years (which may not necessarily be the peak earnings years), while some base the pension on your average career earnings. Obviously, the latter formula is the least desirable from the pensioner's point of view because the final payout will be based in part on your early years with the employer, when your salary was lower.

A typical formula for calculating a pension in a plan based on your best earnings years would be:

$$(2\% \times \text{Years of service}) \times \text{Average of best five years of income}$$
$$= \text{Annual pension income}$$

So if you had been with your employer for 25 years and your best five years averaged out to an annual income of \$60,000, your pension entitlement would be:

$$(2\% \times 25) \times \$60,000 = 50\% \times \$60,000$$
$$= \$30,000$$

That amount would be guaranteed, assuming the pension fund remained solvent.

There are many variations on these basic approaches so it's important to find out which one your plan employs. Ask for a calculation of your projected pension at retirement using different income hypotheses to see what you might expect. Of course, the closer you are to retiring, the more accurate the projection will be.

Defined Contribution (DC) Plans

Defined contribution plans used to be known as money purchase plans, but that term has now virtually disappeared. In some ways it was more accurate, however, because these programs do not carry any income guarantees. Instead, contributions made by you and your employer are invested on your behalf and the final pension is based on the total value of your pension credits when you retire. In other words, the amount of your pension will be whatever the money in the plan can purchase on your behalf.

Members of defined contribution plans are increasingly required to be their own pension plan managers. They have to decide how their money will be invested from a menu provided by the plan administrator that may include everything from guaranteed investment certificates to equity mutual funds. This puts a tremendous onus for maximizing returns on each individual. Plan members must decide on the amount of risk they're prepared to accept, the asset mix they want, and the rate of return they'd like. If they know nothing about investing, the potential for trouble is obvious.

The pension that's eventually paid will be based on the end value of the account at retirement and how the money is invested after that. The greater the principal that is accumulated, the more cash you'll have to live on when you stop work. Conversely, if the fund does poorly, you'll suffer the financial consequences and face a reduction in your retirement standard of living. The following table illustrates the end value of a plan, based on an annual combined contribution of $5,000 from employer and employee.

VALUE OF DEFINED CONTRIBUTION PLAN

Years	Average Annual Rate of Return			
	5%	6%	7%	8%
10	$ 62,889	$ 65,904	$ 69,082	$ 72,433
20	165,330	183,928	204,977	228,810
30	332,194	395,291	472,304	566,416
40	603,999	773,810	998,176	1,295,283

Some readers may wonder why the projected rates of return are low. The answer is simple: because in the current environment I feel that 8 percent is the maximum annual return you should aim for in a pension plan. Anticipating more is unrealistic and will expose your investments to far more risk than is suitable in a retirement plan.

As you can see from the table, the end value of the plan varies greatly with the annual rate of return and the number of years you participate. But what do those numbers actually mean in terms of your retirement income? Let's assume that the $5,000 average annual contribution represented 5 percent of your income, so you were earning an average of $100,000 annually (of course few people will be this fortunate). If you worked for the employer for 30 years and realized an average annual return of 6 percent on the pension money (the number I believe to be most realistic in this table), your plan would have about $395,000 in capital at retirement. If you were to invest that money in a bond portfolio yielding 5 percent, the annual income generated would be not quite $20,000. That's one-fifth of your average annual income! And this after 30 years! If you didn't learn this until a few years before retirement and had made no other provisions, the normal reaction would be sheer panic!

You could increase your cash flow by investing in more risky securities. A portfolio of income trusts could be put together that would yield about 8 percent, which would bring your pension income up to $31,600. That's a lot better, but still probably short of what you expected when you began contributing to the plan 30 years earlier.

The length of time you participate in a defined contribution plan is very important. Look at the difference if you have contributed for 40 years.

In this case, the pension fund at retirement is about $774,000 (again assuming a 6 percent average annual return). A 5 percent bond portfolio would produce annual cash flow of $38,700. Moving to income trusts at 8 percent would increase your income to $61,920 and you may decide that the extra risk is worth it. With supplements from the Canada Pension Plan and Old Age Security you should be able to live comfortably. A little extra money from investments certainly wouldn't hurt, however.

Group RRSPs

As an alternative to defined contribution plans, more employers are making use of group RRSPs (sometimes abbreviated as GRSPs) because they are cheaper to operate and are not subject to the same oppressive governmental restrictions that have made pension plans so unwieldy. Administrators of GRSPs are not obliged to file a seemingly endless array of returns and reports or pay actuarial and accounting fees. That translates into lower costs and greater efficiency.

GRSPs are similar to defined contribution plans in the way in which they're funded and managed. Here again, the end value will depend on a combination of contributions, average rate of return, and length of participation. The actual pension that will be paid cannot be predicted with accuracy until you're close to retirement.

However, there are some important differences between a defined contribution pension plan and a group RRSP. In fact, technically, there is no such thing as a group RRSP. Every RRSP is registered in the name of a single individual. A group plan simply involves bundling many individual plans together under the same set of rules. Under current tax law, only the owner of an RRSP can make contributions to it. This means that, unlike defined contribution plans, your employer may not pay money directly into your GRSP. However, some companies get around this by raising an employee's salary and then deducting an equal amount from each paycheque, which is contributed to the GRSP. The contribution offsets the pay increase so there is no difference in withholding tax.

In some cases, a group RRSP may be a better choice than a defined contribution plan because it provides greater flexibility. For example, you can withdraw money from a group RRSP if you need it for a cash emergency (although you may require permission from your employer to do so). You can't do that with a defined contribution pension plan, which is owned collectively by all the participants. You can continue to contribute to the GRSP until the end of the year in which you turn 69, which may be long after you stop work. Also, you have more options at retirement. With a defined contribution plan, you can only choose between an annuity, a life income fund (LIF), or a life retirement income fund (LRIF), which is not available in all provinces. A GRSP allows you to open a RRIF, which has fewer constraints than a LIF or LRIF, buy an annuity, or even take the money in a lump-sum payment if you prefer.

The differences in the definition of contribution limits can be important in certain circumstances. For example, alimony and maintenance payments are deducted from earned income for purposes of determining a GRSP contribution limit. A person with large annual alimony/maintenance obligations might find more retirement contribution room in a defined contribution plan, which is based strictly on salary.

Deferred Profit Sharing Plans

Deferred profit sharing plans, known as DPSPs, allow employees to participate in the profits of a company for retirement purposes. They operate in a similar way to defined contribution plans, but the employer contribution limit is only half as much. No employee contributions are allowed.

A DPSP offers a number of choices when you retire or resign, including taking the money in the plan as a lump-sum cash payment. Alternatively, you can opt for an instalment plan in which the money is withdrawn over a 10-year period.

Comparing and Choosing Plans

From all this it should be obvious that the type of pension plan you belong to will have an important bearing on your retirement income projections. In most cases, you won't have any choice; however, a few companies offer employees a selection of retirement programs. You might also want to give some serious thought to the retirement plan of a company you're considering joining. For most people, the pension plan is way down on their priority scale when they look at the pros and cons of a new position. In fact, it should rank close to the top of the list if you're at all concerned about the future.

If you find yourself with a choice of what type of pension plan to take (lucky you!), you'll have to weigh several factors. A defined benefit plan offers the greatest level of security and is generally the best choice. Your pension is guaranteed (always assuming the plan can meet its obligations when you retire) and can be calculated based on your income level and years of service. On the other hand, defined contribution plans and, especially, group RRSPs tend to be more portable, an important consideration in our mobile society. And if the investments perform well, the payout could be higher than from a defined benefit plan that uses a career average approach. There's a lot to think about!

Know Your Plan

If you have an employer pension plan, it is essential that you understand it thoroughly and have a good idea of how much it will pay when you retire. As we have already noted in this chapter, many people know woefully little about their pension plans. The more information you have, the better position you'll be in to plan your retirement. Here are some questions to ask your plan's administrator:

What is our benefits formula? If career average is used, probe more deeply. Some companies will upgrade career earnings to reflect inflation. The answer you'd prefer, however, is a formula based on your best three years of earnings.

When am I vested in the plan? Vesting simply means you gain entitlement to the contributions the employer has made on your behalf. If you leave the company before you're vested, all you're likely to receive is a refund of your premiums plus some modest interest. If you're vested, you're guaranteed some retirement benefits, although they may be very modest. In most provinces, an RPP is considered to be vested after two years.

If you're vested and leave to go elsewhere, you're usually given three choices.

1. You may leave the money in the plan and draw a benefit at retirement. In this case, ask some hard questions about how the benefit will be calculated and how much it is likely to be. Compare that with the income that will likely be generated by the other two options.

2. Switch the money into a locked-in RRSP, also known as a locked-in retirement account, or LIRA. These plans function in most respects like an ordinary RRSP; however, you cannot withdraw the money before retirement and your income options when you stop work are restricted to an annuity, a life income fund (LIF), or a life retirement income fund (LRIF) in provinces that have approved them. You can't transfer funds from a LIRA to a registered retirement income fund (RRIF) and withdrawals from these plans are only allowed in special circumstances under rules determined by each province.

3. Have the money transferred to the pension plan at your new place of employment if there is a plan and if such a transfer is permitted.

If you leave your job, you may be entitled to a pension adjustment reversal (PAR). This concept was introduced in the 1997 budget as a way of restoring lost RRSP contribution room to people who lose pension plan benefits because they leave their employment, or for other reasons. If you think you may be eligible for a PAR, get hold of a copy of the Canada Revenue Agency's booklet titled *Pension Adjustment Reversal Guide*. You can obtain it from your local taxation office or download it from the Canada Revenue Agency website at **www.cra-arc.gc.ca**.

What is my plan invested in and what return is it earning? This is a "nice-to-know" piece of information if you're in a plan over which you have no control. It's essential information if you're required to make decisions on what type of securities your pension money is invested in, as is increasingly the case with defined contribution plans and group RRSPs. If the returns are not meeting your expectations, find out why and consider alternatives.

Is the plan fully funded? Given what has happened in recent years, it's important to know whether your pension plan has adequate resources to meet its obligations. You may find this information on the plan's annual report, but if it is not there ask questions. If the plan has a deficiency, request an explanation and find out how serious the underfunding is and what is being done about it. It's not only corporate plans that are encountering problems—multiple-employer plans that cover a specific industry such as construction also may be at risk.

Is my plan integrated with the CPP? Integration with the CPP means the benefits paid by the plan will be adjusted to reflect payments you receive under the Canada Pension Plan. The argument is that the employer also contributed to the CPP and this should be recognized in the payments made to you. Most private pension plans are integrated with the CPP.

When can I retire? Provisions for retiring on a full pension can vary widely. Some plans allow for retirement after a certain number of years of service, others on reaching a specific age. A formula now being used more often involves adding age to years of service; if the total is equal to or greater than a target number (for example, 90), you may retire with full benefits.

Can I retire early? Find out whether the plan has a set formula for early retirement and, if so, how it works. Ask especially about bridging arrangements, which provide for extra benefits until your CPP and OAS payments kick in. Normally if you choose to retire early the amount of your pension will be reduced.

What happens if I die? You should know what benefits your spouse and children can expect to receive from your pension plan if you're not around to collect. Make sure you understand the difference between survivor benefits if you should die before retirement and the amounts payable after you begin drawing a pension.

Am I allowed to make past service contributions and, if I do, what effect will they have on my pension? If you're allowed to make contributions for previous years of service (for example, you were with the company but hadn't joined the pension plan), it may be in your interest to do so. But find out how much your benefits will increase as a result. Also, the government has tightened up in recent years on the tax deductibility of past service contributions, so find out what you're allowed to claim before going ahead. For a full explanation of the rules, obtain a copy of the current edition of the CRA's guide titled *RRSPs and Other Registered Plans for Retirement.*

What happens to any pension surplus? Surpluses can build over time if the pension fund investments perform better than the actuaries allowed for. Some employers use any surpluses to improve benefits, but this is certainly not a universal practice. A great debate continues to rage over who owns pension surpluses, the employees or the employer. If your company has a firm policy in this regard, or if your province has passed legislation on this question, you should know about it.

Are benefits indexed and, if so, are there any limits? This is one of the most important questions you can ask. An unindexed pension plan (which most of them are) can put you in a vulnerable financial position as you grow older and the buying power of your pension cheque erodes. It's better to find out the bad news up front and plan accordingly rather than be hit with it at retirement. If the plan is indexed, count yourself lucky; very few Canadian pension plans offer this desirable but very expensive feature and they are mainly in the public sector.

How often are benefits improved? Some employers upgrade their pension plans every two or three years to keep pace with changes in salaries, economic conditions, inflation, etc. Others keep their plans in what amounts to the Dark Ages. Find out about the track record of your employer.

Who pays what? The employee contribution to the pension plan is usually clearly defined. The employer's may be more ambiguous. Find out whether the company is on the hook for a certain percentage of salaries each year or whether the only obligation is to contribute just enough to bring the plan's assets into line with the anticipated future benefits.

What kind of reports do I get? A well-managed pension plan will provide a benefits report at least once a year which will contain details of your current status and outline your entitlements. If you're not receiving such a report, ask why.

When you know as much as possible about your pension plan, you'll be in a better position to assess how significant the income it produces will be in your total retirement financial plan. You'll also have a better handle on how much additional income you'll have to generate from sources over which you have more control, such as your RRSPs and non-registered investments.

A Desperate Need for Knowledge

Everyone agrees that most members simply don't understand their pension plans and that something needs to be done about it. In its 2004 report titled *Addressing the Pensions Dilemma in Canada,* the Certified General Accountants' Association of Canada stressed the importance of empowering plan members "to attain increased understanding of their pension arrangements; intrinsic risks, entitlements and expectations; and the actions which they might pursue in planning for retirement." The report recommended,

> Towards this end, pension arrangements need to be well articulated and communicated with accentuation on the roles and responsibilities of the numerous participants. Pension advisory committees and pension committees, working in harmony with Human Resources departments, are likely the most suitable candidates to take up this duty and should be relied upon to promote understanding of the cost and value of this noteworthy compensation component.

That's a lot of verbiage that translates into the basic principle that employers have a responsibility to educate their pension plan members. Sadly, they don't seem to be doing a very good job of it. A survey conducted in August 2004 by Decima Research on behalf of the Investor Education Fund (IEF), which is funded by the Ontario Securities Commission, produced some worrisome results. It found that while two-thirds of the plan members who responded believe that their pension income will be critical for them in retirement, almost half did not understand the terminology of their plan or how it worked. The primary reasons given were that there is too much financial jargon to cut through and that investing is a dull subject.

"A company pension plan can make a significant difference to the quality of someone's retirement years," said IEF president Terri Williams. "Members can be missing out on the potential rewards of their plan unless they thoroughly understand it and the impact their pension decisions can make."

Such knowledge is particularly important in cases where employees have to make investment decisions, such as defined contribution plans and group RRSPs. Employers who offer such programs (a growing number as we saw in the last chapter) have a responsibility to ensure plan members are given the tools they need to make informed decisions; however, the survey found that smaller companies with fewer than 500 employees often are derelict in providing such guidance. Since such companies are more likely to have group RRSPs and defined contribution plans that fact is particularly troublesome, especially when you consider that only 16 percent of pension plan members rated their investment knowledge as "good to excellent."

Another study, this one published by SEI Investments Canada in November 2004, found that 39 percent of defined contribution plan members did not know whether their plan was compulsory and more than half weren't aware whether they could make personal contributions. "People don't even know the most basic, black-and-white facts about their own plan," said SEI's chief executive officer, Patrick Walsh.

The comprehensive survey of over 2,000 employees in 17 plans, completed in conjunction with Richard Deaves, professor of Finance at the Michael G. DeGroote School of Business at McMaster University in Hamilton, Ontario, identified what it described as five types of "plan member mindsets":

- *Smart guys.* This group comprised 13 percent of the survey participants. SEI concluded that they knew a lot about their plans but "exhibit the highest levels of overconfidence—opening them to the costly habit of frequent trading" in their self-managed accounts.

- *Participators.* Almost one-quarter of the respondents were placed in this category. SEI described them as being just about as well informed as the first group and about as prone to overconfidence. The difference was a desire for employer-provided education. "These members are too comfortable about the future and lack focus on long-term risks and needs," SEI concluded.

- *The disengaged.* The study found that 15 percent of the participants had real problems with their plans and lacked the motivation to do anything about it. "These people … tend to use the default investment option more than other groups."

- *The needy.* This was the largest group, with 26 percent of the survey participants, just slightly more than the "participators." SEI said their main problem was confusion. "These people … are the least comfortable in managing their plans," the investment firm concluded.

- *The seekers.* This group made up 22 percent of the survey respondents. SEI described them as being worried and wanting support. "They have an insatiable appetite for education and advice," the company said. "Their knowledge level falls in the middle, but they are least comfortable with the ability of the pension plan to provide for retirement."

Commenting on the findings, Patrick Walsh said: "An overhaul of the design and structure of communication programs, incorporating psychographic profiles towards education, advice, confidence and comfort in pension plans and investment decision-making is the key to ward off potential disaster."

Perhaps "disaster" is too strong a word to use in this context but there seems to be no doubt that, unless pension plan members take greater control of their own destinies with appropriate help from employers, many will face serious financial problems in later years.

Lawsuits a Concern

One of the big stumbling blocks to more financial guidance from employers appears to be the fear of being sued if the advice doesn't work out. That was the conclusion of yet another study, this one done for Sun Life Financial by *Benefits Canada* magazine. About 60 percent of the companies surveyed said that providing financial advice to members of defined contribution plans is important but many of them are hesitant about doing so.

"The risk of litigation is a significant barrier," Sun Life vice-president Lori Bak told Advisor.ca. "But a real conundrum exists for employers—fully half of plan sponsors surveyed said that providing members with access to good solid financial advice will actually reduce their liability."

Faced with this dilemma, companies seem to be doing the predictable—hedging their bets. Rather than taking the initiative to provide investment advice to members of pension programs that require individual decision making, many are contenting themselves with repeatedly encouraging their employees to get expert help—but on their own. That's clearly a cop-out, but as matters now stand it's all the guidance many people are receiving.

In an effort to at least partially fill the void the IEF has created an online resource titled "Focus On ... Pension Decisions," which can be found on their website at **www.investorED.ca**. It's a useful primer that covers a wide range of issues, from the different types of pension plans to job loss and early retirement. If you are one of those plan members whose knowledge of the subject falls into the "fair to poor" range, it is must-read material.

A Limit on Your Pension

Most people don't realize that the amount of the pension they receive from a private plan is limited by federal government legislation. If you are in a higher-income bracket, you may be affected by this little-known rule, which is called the pension cap.

The pension cap has been in existence for decades, but for many years very few people noticed because it kicked in only at salary levels that were at the highest end of the scale. The idea of the cap was to limit the amount of tax assistance that Ottawa would provide for private pension plans to prevent companies from using tax-deductible contributions to fund outrageously high benefits for senior employees. By introducing a pension cap, the government was able to impose a limit on the amount of money a pensioner could receive.

Recently, however, the cap has come to represent a problem for some people. After years of wage inflation, the situation reached the point where middle-income earners at the higher end of the range were bumping up against it. This created a barrier in putting together a retirement plan that would provide an appropriate level of income when they stopped work, usually defined as about 80 percent of pre-retirement income.

This problem happened because of indifference in Ottawa and the failure of advocacy groups to clearly understand the implications of the cap for future retirees. As a result, until the 2003 budget, the pension cap had not been changed in any meaningful way since 1977. Since it was not indexed to inflation, this meant that more retiring Canadians were affected by the ceiling each year.

In 2003, the finance minister of the day, John Manley, announced that the cap would be increased from $1,722 per year of service to $1,833 in 2004 and $2,000 in 2005. That was certainly an improvement but it didn't come anywhere near providing adequate redress for the 27 years that the cap remained unchanged while inflation steadily eroded the purchasing power of pensions. In his February 2005 budget, Ralph Goodale, who assumed the mantle of finance minister when Paul Martin took power, finally took action to deal with the issue in a serious way. He proposed gradually escalating the pension cap over several years until it would become fully indexed in 2010.

As a result of this initiative, only high-income people will feel any impact from the cap in future years. Here is what the planned scale will look like, assuming 30 years of pension plan eligibility in all cases.

THE EFFECT OF THE PENSION CAP

Tax Year	Cap Limit	Maximum Pension
2005	$2,000	$60,000
2006	2,111	63,330
2007	2,222	66,660
2008	2,333	69,990
2009	2,444	73,320

Your pension may exceed these limits in subsequent years if your plan provides for indexing. Government rules allowed for indexing of

up to 4 percent a year or the increase in the consumer price index (CPI), whichever is greater, for most plans. Individual pension plans may only be indexed to the CPI if the beneficiary is receiving the maximum allowable payment.

Retirement Compensation Arrangements (RCAs)

If the pension cap becomes a problem for you, there are ways around it. Some companies have set up supplementary retirement plans for higher-income employees. These are paid for with after-tax dollars, sometimes totally by the employer, sometimes with joint contributions, and the income they earn is taxed. They're known as retirement compensation arrangements (RCAs) for tax purposes. Payments into these plans are held by a designated custodian, who uses the money to supplement the employee's income after retirement.

From a tax perspective, RCAs are expensive. The government assesses a 50 percent tax on all employer contributions to the plan as well as on investment income earned within the RCA. However, this is a refundable tax. When the time comes to distribute money from the plan, half the amount paid out is refunded to the custodian by the Canada Revenue Agency. The advantage to the government is that it has the use of the money for many years in the interim and the refunds are made in inflation-devalued dollars. Moreover, Ottawa pays no interest on the money.

These disadvantages are offset by the additional pension flexibility provided by an RCA, flexible withdrawal options, and the fact that RCA contributions do not reduce RRSP contribution room. Withdrawals from an RCA are considered taxable income to the beneficiary in the year received.

For more information, consult the *Retirement Compensation Arrangements Guide* published by the Canada Revenue Agency.

The Pension Adjustment

One of the technical aspects of pensions that gives people fits is the pension adjustment (PA). This figure is supposed to reflect the value of the future retirement benefits you receive from your plan each year. For

defined contribution plans and deferred profit sharing plans, the PA is simply the total amount of money contributed on your behalf annually. The calculation for defined benefit plans is more complicated and takes into account the formula under which benefits will eventually be paid.

Your PA is important because it determines how much room you have left to contribute to an RRSP each year. You'll find it in box 52 on the T4 slip you receive from your employer at tax time. To calculate your RRSP limit, multiply your earned income for the previous year by 18 percent (maximum $16,500 in 2005 rising to $22,000 in 2010 if the provisions of the February 2005 budget are passed). Subtract the PA from the result. The difference is your RRSP entitlement.

To illustrate, suppose your earned income was $50,000 and your PA for the year was $6,000. The following calculation shows your RRSP limit:

$$\$50,000 \times 18\% = \$9,000 \quad \text{(Retirement savings limit)}$$
$$- \$6,000 \quad \text{(Pension adjustment)}$$
$$= \$3,000 \quad \text{(RRSP limit)}$$

In determining the PA, there is an "offset" of $600 that is used in the calculation. This can have the effect of increasing your RRSP limit in some cases. The offset is to help compensate for any inequities that may occur over the years, such as frequent job changes. However, it does not apply to defined contribution or deferred profit sharing plans.

What You Can Do

You now have all the basic information that you need to understand how your pension plan functions. Now it's up to you to take the initiative to find out the state of your plan's financial health and, if there is a problem, to have it addressed on a priority basis. Here are some suggestions about how to take the initiative.

Involve the union. If you belong to a trade union, your starting point should be a meeting with the officer of your local who is responsible for pension matters. Get his or her opinion on whether there is a funding problem and find out what steps the union is taking to have it dealt with promptly.

Organize a meeting. If there is no union, organize a meeting of pension plan members and ask that the plan administrator or a senior officer of the company be in attendance. Ask questions and insist on hard answers about the financial health of the plan. Don't accept vague responses along the lines of "everything is okay." If the plan is in a deficit position, ask what is being done to remedy the situation. If there is no remedial plan, ask for a commitment that one will be put into place within a specific time frame. Arrange for a meeting at that time to assess progress. If management balks, remember that this is *your* plan. It is your money that is being paid in and you have a right to expect full accountability.

Increase your personal savings. In most cases, your plan will be there for you when you retire. But it never hurts to have some extra money in reserve, just in case. If you don't need it to retain your lifestyle, great—you can splurge on a cruise or a new car.

Hopefully, the crisis situation that arose in the first five years of this century will pass. A strong bull market, similar to that of the 1990s, along with rising interest rates, would likely boost pension plan returns to the point where most deficits would disappear within a few years. However, no one is predicting that combination of events any time soon. The general consensus at the time this book was written was that stock market returns would be modest (low single-digit) over the next decade while interest rates will stay relatively low by historic standards.

The bottom line is that you should not view the pension world through rose-coloured glasses. The difficulties that were brought to the surface by the bear market are systemic and need to be addressed on several levels. That is going to take time and some people are going to be hurt in the process. You need to do everything possible to be sure you are not one of them.

5

Your Life Stages

Most people realize intuitively that they need to change their investing strategies as they get older. Unfortunately, many fail to put theory into practice, sometimes with serious results. A good financial advisor should provide the impetus to keep you on track. But in this era of discount brokers, many Canadians prefer to save money by making their own decisions.

To help you set targets and remain on course, here is an investment timetable that can guide your decisions after age 50. Keep in mind that these are general rules; you should adjust the portfolio weightings according to your specific needs. I assume retirement at age 65, so if your plans are different make the necessary adjustments.

Age 50–60: The Preservation Years

Until age 50, your investment emphasis should be on growth, which basically means stocks. When you're young, the stock market is your friend because, over time, it usually offers the highest potential returns. For example, a software program called Your Retirement Planner, which was developed for Canadians by Ativa Interactive, calculates that over the 50 years from 1954 to 2003, stocks generated an average annual compound rate of return of 10.3 percent, compared to 7.8 percent for bonds. A portfolio that was 80 percent invested in equities would have grown by almost $660,000 more over that time compared to one that had a balance of 40 percent stocks, 40 percent bonds, and 20 percent cash.

But in the shorter term, stocks can endanger your financial health. During the bear market of August 2000 to September 2002, stocks lost 43.2 percent of their value, according to Your Retirement Planner. A stocks-only portfolio worth $100,000 at the start of the bear market would have fallen, on average, to $56,800 by the time it was all over. Many Canadians, including some much older then age 50, experienced losses of that magnitude or worse, which forced some to postpone their retirement. However, those with more balanced portfolios fared better. An asset allocation of 60 percent bonds, 30 percent stocks, and 10 percent cash would have resulted in an overall loss of less than $500 during that rough period. That's because the profits generated by bonds almost completely offset any stock losses.

Therein lies the lesson for the 50 to 60 age group—reduce your equity weighting and build your bond/cash weightings over this period so as to preserve earlier profits and reduce the risk that another bear market could wreak havoc on your retirement plans. This doesn't have to be done all at once. Consider it to be a 10-year project, although most of the movement should take place in the first five years, from age 50 to 55, assuming economic and market conditions are favourable.

The first step is to do a complete portfolio review at age 50. Start with your asset allocation: how is your portfolio divided between stocks, bonds, and cash? (See Chapter 9 for more details.) The higher the equity weighting, the more urgent it is that you begin to reduce it as soon as possible. A portfolio that is 85 percent invested in the stock market is far more vulnerable than one with a 60 percent equity weighting.

Step two is to identify the securities that are prime candidates for early sale. These may include stocks in which you have accumulated significant profits, stocks with a high risk factor, and stocks that do not have strong near-term prospects, whether you have made money in them or not. If you own mutual funds, consider exiting any that focus on a specific sector of the economy, such as health care or energy. These tend to be more volatile than broadly diversified funds. At this stage, it's essential to consider the tax consequences of your sales if the securities are in a non-registered portfolio. If you plan to sell big winners, see if you can offset the capital gains to some extent by selling some losers as well. If this is not possible, you may wish to spread out the sales over several years to minimize the tax impact.

Step three is to decide what you are going to buy to replace the equities that have been sold. Since we are now in the preservation stage, you want to keep your risk minimal. Unless you're smart, however, that can mean unacceptably low returns. One compromise is to invest some of the assets in high-quality corporate bonds (e.g., bank issues) that mature during the five-year period leading up to your retirement. These will generate a higher return than government bonds of comparable maturities, with relatively little extra risk. The market price of the bonds will rise or fall depending on interest rate movements, but if you hold them until maturity you'll collect the full face value. If possible, try to buy bonds that are trading at par ($100) or slightly below so that you won't suffer a capital loss at maturity. If you have a broker, ask him or her to alert you when new issues rated A or higher appear. You'll find more details about bonds in Chapter 13.

Age 60–65: The Conversion Years

You don't have to convert your RRSP to a RRIF until December 31 of the year in which you turn 69. However, some people choose to do it sooner (although I don't advise it). So the conversion years will vary, depending on the individual. Whatever the time frame, you should start planning five years before the conversion will actually take place. Leaving it to the last minute can cost you money, perhaps a lot of it.

Many people don't realize that a post-retirement investment portfolio should look very different from a pre-retirement portfolio. When you were younger, your focus was on growth and then, as we have seen, on preservation. Now the emphasis shifts to income. You are about to start benefiting from all those years of saving. That requires an entirely different mindset and portfolio composition. During this period, the goal is to reposition your assets so that they will generate the cash flow you need when the time comes to start collecting. The five-year window that I recommend will give you the flexibility to achieve this by making your purchases at the most advantageous times.

Here's an example of why this is important. In recent years, income trusts have emerged from obscurity to become an integral part of many retirement portfolios. The reason is simple: they offered steady income at much higher rates of return than were available from traditional retirement favourites like GICs and government bonds. Their popularity, combined with low interest rates, drove the market prices of many of the trusts to unsustainable levels. Between November 2002 and April 2005, the price of Davis + Henderson Income Fund, an income trust that produces cheques for the clients of all of Canada's major banks, soared from $11 to more than $22 a share. Investors who bought at the low end of the trading range were enjoying a cash yield of 13.1 percent in spring 2005 on monthly distributions of 12 cents per unit. Those who bought at $22 or more were receiving only 6.5 percent on their money.

So timing is everything when it comes to converting your portfolio. If you select the securities that you want to own at an early stage, you should be able to buy them at decent prices over a five-year period. But if you do it in the space of a few months, chances are you will pay too much for at least some of them.

Tax considerations are also important in the conversion phase. If you have both registered and non-registered portfolios, be selective about which securities you buy for each. For example, some (but not all) income trusts offer tax advantages if they are held in a non-registered portfolio. The best tax breaks are usually found in oil and gas trusts and real estate investment trusts (REITs). In 2004, investors in RioCan, Canada's largest REIT, received 46 percent of their distributions in the form of tax-deferred return of capital. That means that no tax was payable at the time, nor will it be unless the units are sold or the adjusted cost base falls below zero. Clearly, this is a security that is better held in a non-registered portfolio.

On the other hand, interest paid on bonds, GICs, and similar securities is fully taxed. So where possible, hold these assets inside a registered plan where the income will be tax sheltered.

Age 65+: The Income Years

This is the point at which you start to draw money from your retirement savings to live on. As mentioned earlier, I recommend not converting your RRSP to a RRIF until you need to. Once you convert to a RRIF, LIF, or LRIF, you are required by law to withdraw a certain amount of money each year. However, there are no minimum withdrawal requirements for RRSPs. If you don't need the cash, you can allow the assets to grow tax sheltered until the mandatory conversion date. If you need some money but it is less than the RRIF minimum, you can withdraw the required amount from the RRSP and no more, thereby minimizing the tax payable.

Once you make the conversion to a RRIF or other registered income fund, you must pay close attention to the return your investments are generating. Unless they at least match the minimum withdrawal requirement, you will have to draw down capital. When interest rates are low, earning 7 percent or more on your money can be difficult, especially if you want to keep risk within reasonable levels. The solution is to adjust your portfolio over time to meet the minimum withdrawal requirements. Here's how that might work.

Let's assume that you convert to a RRIF at 65. Your plan is worth $100,000 on January 1 of the following year and you are still 65 on that date. The minimum withdrawal would be $4,000. This should create no problem; there are lots of good-quality bonds that will produce that kind of return. Let's say the value of your plan remains at $100,000 (we'll keep that constant throughout for purposes of this illustration). By age 70, your minimum annual withdrawal is up to 5 percent, or $5,000. You should still be able to manage that by using lower-risk securities.

But at age 71, the minimum withdrawal jumps to $7,380. By 75, it is up to $7,850 (7.85 percent). At age 77, it passes 8 percent and continues to move higher. Unless interest rates return to levels unseen since the 1980s, there is no way that bonds or GICs are going to produce the cash flow you will require. This is why you need to shift your asset base as the years pass if you want to avoid depleting your capital. In one sense, this means you will have to incur more risk because you'll need to invest in higher-yielding securities like income trusts and/or equity-based systematic withdrawal plans. But look at it this way: if you don't do this, then you face the certainty of seeing your capital base decline.

It's not an all-or-nothing situation. Rather, it's a matter of adjusting your asset mix to meet the changing requirements. For example, a 71-year-old could generate cash flow of 7.4 percent from a RRIF portfolio with an asset mix like this:

- Ten-year Government of Canada bonds—15 percent. At the time of writing, the yield on these benchmark bonds was 4.15 percent.
- Corporate bonds rated "A" or better—15 percent. Issues maturing in seven years were yielding around 4.5 percent.
- High-yield bond funds—20 percent. Most of these bond funds make monthly or quarterly distributions. At the time of writing, the popular TD High Yield Income Fund was generating a cash yield of about 9.2 percent annually, but that is on the high side. We'll use a 7.5 percent average.
- Medium-risk income trusts—25 percent. These would include REITs; trusts such as Davis + Henderson, Yellow Pages, Aeroplan, and TransCanada Power; and closed-end funds specializing in income trusts. When this was written, these securities were generating cash yields in the 6 percent to 8 percent range. We'll use 7.5 percent as an average.
- Higher-risk income trusts—25 percent. Included in this group would be the energy trusts, restaurant trusts, and numerous business trusts. In some cases, yields were running at 12 percent or higher (e.g., Pengrowth, PrimeWest, EnerVest), but we'll use an average return of 11 percent to allow for diversification.

The cash flow from this sample portfolio would be $7,422 per $100,000 invested—slightly more than needed to meet the minimum withdrawal requirement at age 71. Of course, the actual numbers will vary from year to year depending on conditions, so don't simply emulate this model. It is an illustration only. My point is that even when you reach the income years, you can't simply invest your money and forget it. Your needs will continue to change as time passes, and your portfolio must change as well.

Change and flexibility—those are the twin keys to a lifetime of investing success. Now, keeping these life stages in mind, let's explore the details of how to reach your goals.

6

The Secrets of Success

According to an international survey carried out in the fall of 2004, Canadians are among the most optimistic and realistic people in the world when it comes to retirement. The study, done on behalf of insurance company AXA Financial Inc., found that 70 percent of working Canadians have begun the process of saving for retirement, ranking us number two behind only the United States in that department. It also found that 78 percent of retired Canadians say their standard of living has stayed the same or improved since they left the workforce and that 94 percent of retirees described themselves as happy. The fact that Canada ranked number one in terms of retirement income with an average monthly net income of $3,020 probably has a lot to do with that very high satisfaction level.

"Canadians are among the most progressive in the world in terms of their view of and attitude toward this stage in life," commented Rejane Legault, Vice President, Communication, of AXA in Canada.

So what's the secret of Canada's success? There are some clues in the details of the report.

Start Early

We start planning much earlier than the folks in most other countries. Those already retired began at age 38, while people who are still working are starting even younger, at 34. An early start is absolutely essential if you're going to build a retirement fund of adequate size to provide the income you want after you stop work.

Here is some insight into just how important an early start can be. Suppose you were to save only $100 a month for your retirement, depositing the money in an RRSP at the end of each month starting at age 25. If your average annual compound rate of return was 6 percent, you would have $190,768 in your plan at age 65. However, if you delay just five years, to age 30, and save the same amount each month, your RRSP will be worth only $137,360 at retirement. Your total contribution to the plan will have been reduced by $6,000, but that's not the main reason that you end up with more than $53,000 less. It's those lost five years of compound growth. They account for $47,408 of the shortfall, even at a modest 6 percent annual return. If you hold off your savings program until age 35, your RRSP will be worth only about half what it would have been if you had started 10 years before.

As you can see from the table that follows, the greater the return within the RRSP the bigger the impact of delaying. If you can average 8 percent a year, a five-year delay from age 25 to age 30 will cost you a breathtaking $107,851. A 10-year delay will reduce the final value of the RRSP by $181,253. If you begin your savings program later, you can partially make up the loss from the delay by holding off retirement until age 69 (the last year in which you're allowed to have an RRSP). A 30-year-old who did that would have a plan worth $178,807 at retirement, just $12,000 short of the 25-year-old at age 65. But the price you pay is four more years in the workforce!

RRSP VALUE AT AGE 65

Starting Age	Annual Rate of Return		
	6%	7%	8%
25	$190,768	$247,154	$322,108
30	137,360	171,141	214,257
35	97,451	116,945	140,855
40	67,629	78,304	90,899
45	45,344	50,754	56,900

Note: You can do your own projections by using the retirement calculators available in the Money section at www.50plus.com.

Be Knowledgeable

AXA Retirement Scope showed that retired Canadians are quite well informed about their financial situation, which may be one of the reasons why they have fared so well. However, the study also found that those still in the workforce don't know as much about their prospects for retirement as they should. Only 45 percent knew the date of their retirement and barely more than a third (36 percent) had any idea of what their pension would be. By comparison, 49 percent of Americans knew how much they would get.

As we saw in Chapter 4, if you have an employer pension plan it is essential that you find out as much about it as possible. It appears from the AXA study that most Canadians are waiting until after they retire to figure out what to expect in the way of pension income. That's too late to do anything about it.

Open an RRSP

We live in a highly taxed country. However, we have a major advantage over many other nations: one of the most generous tax-sheltered retirement programs in the world. The federal government allows us to put aside large amounts of money for our retirement every year in the form of pension contributions, deferred profit sharing plans, and RRSPs. To encourage us to make use of this program, we're offered two valuable tax benefits: immediate tax deductibility and future income growth in a tax-sheltered environment.

These programs are classified as "registered" investments. That simply means the plan is registered with the Canada Revenue Agency and is subject to certain terms and conditions. All other investments which you make are said to be "non-registered." The tax benefits associated with registered plans are so attractive that you'd think most adult Canadians would want to take advantage of them (the plans aren't right for everyone, as we'll see in a later chapter). But that's not the case. AXA Retirement Scope found that 66 percent of working Canadians have contributed to an RRSP at one time or another. That means one-third of the workforce has not put a penny into a plan. Among retired people, 73 percent said they had opened an RRSP during their working life, which makes these plans one of the secrets of their success.

In a heavily taxed country, it's a good idea for anyone with a marginal rate over 30 percent to use every break they can get. Registered investments are accessible to everyone with earned income. Take advantage of them.

Make a Commitment

The overwhelming majority of working Canadians (87 percent according to AXA) believe that every individual has a responsibility to provide for his or her retirement through personal savings. But only 64 percent say they have actually started to put money aside for this purpose.

One of the problems with retirement saving is that it ranks well down on the scale of immediate financial priorities for many people, particularly those who are younger. It appears a lot of people are paying lip service to the idea without really doing anything about it. We've already seen the importance of starting early, but it's equally important to make a serious commitment to the process.

AXA Retirement Scope found that the average working Canadian with income around the mean national average is saving $281 a month for retirement. Some of that will be in the form of pension plan contributions, including CPP. But to demonstrate how large an RRSP you could build with this amount of money, let's revisit the previous table.

All factors remain the same except in this case the end-of-month contribution is $281.

Starting Age	Annual Rate of Return		
	6%	7%	8%
25	$536,057	$694,503	$905,123
30	385,983	480,907	602,061
35	273,838	328,616	395,803
40	190,037	220,035	255,426
45	127,416	142,618	159,889

Look at the difference! The additional $181 a month adds more than $345,000 to the final value of the RRSP of the person who starts at 25, earns 6 percent a year, and retires at 65.

There's another important point to take from this chart. For people who begin saving later in life, increasing the amount of the contribution can help to make up for the lost years. The 40-year-old in this table will finish with almost exactly the same RRSP capital as the 25-year-old who puts aside only $100 a month. The bottom line is that the greater your commitment to saving for retirement, the better off you will be at the end of the day.

Success Secrets

AXA Retirement Scope did not probe the financial minutiae of retirees (which would have been fascinating), but based on my experience and observation these are some of the Success Secrets that would be common to a majority of well-off people.

Little or No Debt

Ideally, you should begin your retirement years debt free, or as close to it as possible. That means discharging any remaining mortgages on property you own, paying off all credit cards, retiring investment loans, and getting rid of any consumer loans (e.g., a car loan) that you may still be carrying.

Not owing any money when you begin your retirement will give you a huge financial advantage, for four reasons.

- First, interest payments are a drain on what will likely be a reduced income flow once you retire. If you have to put aside a large chunk of money every month to service old debts, you may find yourself having to compensate by reducing your living standard.

- Second, loans are more difficult to pay off after you retire. If your income drops, you'll find it harder to put money aside to reduce your outstanding principal. Nor will there be any windfalls, such as an annual bonus, that can be put towards reducing debt.

- Third, carrying debt into retirement puts you at risk. Interest rates have been low in recent years, but any sharp upward move would increase your monthly costs. That would put an additional strain on your retirement budget.

- Fourth, being debt free, and, especially, mortgage free, gives you greater financial flexibility. For example, if you need more income as the years pass and inflation takes its toll, you can use the equity in your home to generate additional cash flow. More on this in Chapter 22.

So part of your retirement program should be directed toward debt elimination. Set up a repayment plan that will ensure that all your loans are paid off by the time you plan to stop work (even sooner, if at all possible).

Your first priority should be the non-tax-deductible debt that carries the highest interest rate. For most Canadians, that means credit card balances. Unpaid credit card bills are one of the most expensive forms of consumer loans, and the interest rates charged by the card companies tend to remain high even when rates generally are low. So pay off those credit card balances as soon as possible, and make it a point not to allow them to run up in future. Use the money that has been freed up by paying off your cards to attack other high-interest outstanding loans. A car loan, if you have one, should probably be next on your list.

RRSP loans come next. More people are using RRSP catch-up loans to pick up carry-forward credits, and these can take as long as 10 years to repay. Unlike other investment loans, interest on RRSP loans is not tax-deductible, so paying down the balance should rank high on your priority list.

You should also consider repaying as soon as possible any loans from your RRSP under the Home Buyers' Plan or the Lifelong Learning Plan. Although you don't pay any interest on these loans, they can cost your RRSP dearly in terms of lost earnings. Governments won't like to read this, but student loan repayment beyond the required annual amounts should rank fairly low on your priority list. That's because there is tax relief for the interest costs of these loans.

Once all your non-deductible consumer loans have been retired, go after your mortgage. Take advantage of any prepayment clauses in your contract to make the maximum penalty-free payments that you can afford. Remember, you can pay off any amount you want with no penalty at each renewal date.

Your final target, once all other debt has been eliminated, should be any tax-deductible loans you've incurred for business or investment purposes. The reason for leaving these until last is simple—once the tax advantages are taken into account, they're the cheapest form of borrowing available to most people.

Home Ownership

I have always been a strong believer in the financial benefits of home ownership, especially in retirement. There are three main advantages to having your own place—fully paid for, of course.

First, you'll eliminate a major cash drain on your retirement income. If you're a renter or paying down a mortgage now, take a moment to calculate how much of your income goes to meeting those costs every month. If you're like most Canadians, the percentage is significant. One of your primary goals should be to ensure you won't carry that particular cost burden into retirement with you. Of course, you'll still have to deal with all the other expenses associated with home ownership: property taxes, utilities, repairs and maintenance, and the like. But by knocking rent or mortgage costs off your retirement expense projections, you'll reduce your financial burden considerably.

The second benefit of home ownership is that it reduces the impact of inflation on your retirement budget. Housing is an important component of the Consumer Price Index. If you don't have to concern yourself with rising house prices or rents, even if the increases are modest, you're a step ahead.

Finally, home ownership provides a source of available capital that you can tap into if required. Home equity lines of credit and reverse mortgages allow you to use the capital in your home after retirement, while still living in it.

A Non-Registered Investment Portfolio

While making maximum use of registered plans is important, you must go further. The government has limited its tax assistance to allowing for contributions to registered plans that will generate about 70 percent of pre-retirement income when combined with other income support programs such as the Canada Pension Plan and Old Age Security. However, Ottawa's 70 percent target can be an illusion for many people. It requires 35 years of maximum contributions to achieve that level. And higher-income earners may find their payouts from registered plans, plus their CPP and OAS payments, fall well below the 70 percent mark because of a cap on the amount you can receive from employer pension plans.

All of this suggests you'll need income from other sources to achieve your retirement objectives. Unless you're planning to continue working part-time after you retire, that income will have to come from your non-registered investments: stocks, bonds, GICs, income trusts, mutual funds, rental properties, Canada Savings Bonds, and the like.

Building a non-registered investment portfolio should therefore form part of your retirement plan. However, it's important to keep your priorities straight. This should be the final item on your retirement list, to be undertaken only when the other objectives outlined in this chapter have been met. That doesn't mean building a non-registered portfolio isn't important. But you'll find it will be much easier once you've accomplished the other goals.

Net Worth Calculation

One of the most important pieces of information you need at the outset is an overview of your present financial condition. This is called a net worth statement. Most people have never done a net worth calculation but it's a worthwhile exercise because it allows you to see your total financial picture. This will give you a handle on how much you have put aside for retirement already and how much you have available to devote to future saving.

Your net worth is the total value of all your assets (or your family's assets) less any outstanding liabilities. To arrive at the number, list everything of value that you own and then subtract all your debts, such as mortgage principal, credit card balances, and consumer loans. The bottom line is your net worth. It's a good idea to review your net worth position annually to see where you stand and what changes have occurred. I've developed a net worth calculator that you can use to do this. It's available at no charge on my website in Excel format, so you'll need to have the appropriate software installed on your computer. You can download it by going to **www.buildingwealth.ca** and clicking on Your Net Worth on the home page.

7

How Much Will You Need?

In December 2004, *The Globe and Mail* carried an article written by Andrew Allentuck in which he described the case history of a British Columbia machinist who earned $90,000 a year. The man was 50 years old and wanted to retire at age 55. *The Globe* asked a financial planner named Derek Moran to review the situation, and he came to a conclusion that may surprise many people. Despite the machinist's high income, all projections indicated that if he wanted to maintain his standard of living he would have to work for an additional five years beyond his hoped-for retirement date. Otherwise, he could end up in financial difficulty down the road.

I cite this story because it emphasizes a critical point that most Canadians fail to grasp: early retirement is a pipe dream. The overwhelming majority of people will have to continue to work until at least age 60 and probably beyond for one simple reason: we're living longer and healthier lives. A longer life means your money must last for more years. A healthier life means you will probably want to spend more on such expensive luxuries as travel and a Sunbelt winter residence.

Of course, if you are prepared to live frugally in your retirement years you may be able to quit earlier. But that's not the dream of most people.

They want to live that period to the fullest, to shower gifts on their grandchildren, and to leave a reasonable estate for their heirs when it all comes to an end. If that sounds like you, then be prepared to stay in the workforce for a while.

There's another barrier to early retirement: inflation. Even though it has been tame in recent years, even a modest annual increase in the cost of living can have a surprising impact over time. A man who retires at age 55 can reasonably expect to live at least another 25 years. His $50,000 a year income may seem to be perfectly adequate when he stops work, but if inflation averages 2 percent annually his buying power will be reduced by about 40 percent by the time he is 80. At that point, he will need income in excess of $82,000 a year just to stay even. That's not impossible, considering that he will be able to draw on Old Age Security and the Canada Pension Plan when he gets older, but it will require meticulous planning and money management.

The following table shows the effect of early retirement on an RRSP assuming annual contributions of $5,000 and an average annual compound rate of return of 6 percent.

THE EFFECT OF EARLY RETIREMENT ON AN RRSP

Starting Age	Annual Contribution	Value at 55	Value at 65
25	$5,000	$419,008	$820,238
30	5,000	290,782	590,604
35	5,000	194,964	419,008
40	5,000	123,363	290,782
45	5,000	69,878	194,964

Even if you start young, the value of your RRSP at age 55 is only about half what it would be 10 years later. That may not seem logical considering that the extra 10 years only account for 25 percent of your total contributions but this is the way compounding works, and the higher your average annual return, the greater the difference. If you were able to coax 10 percent a year out of your portfolio starting at age 25, it would only be worth about a third as much at 55 as it would at 65.

So my advice is to forget about early retirement. It's marketing hype! If events conspire to make it feasible, fine. But don't count on it or you could be bitterly disappointed.

Step One: Deciding on a Lifestyle

A comprehensive retirement plan begins with a clear understanding of the kind of lifestyle to which you aspire once you stop work. Everything else, including the financial projections, flows from there. Simply saying that you want to live comfortably when you retire isn't enough. You must have an understanding of what that will mean in terms of your lifestyle and what it will cost to achieve and maintain it. Clearly, the younger you are, the more difficult it is to contemplate what your life might be like in 30 or 40 years from now. But we are not carving anything in stone at this stage. A retirement plan is a constantly evolving exercise that should be reviewed annually. As the years go by, it will be gradually transformed until by the time retirement comes you will know exactly where you are going and the resources that are available to you.

So to begin with, let your imagination roam. You know what you like and don't like. Your tastes and your dreams are probably not going to change a lot as you grow older but even if they do there is plenty of time to make adjustments.

To give you a personal example, from the time we were married, my wife and I knew we would one day like to live by the sea. That wasn't possible through most of my working career, but we never lost sight of that goal. We finally achieved it in 1997 with the purchase of a winter home in Florida that looks out on a bay teeming with dolphins, aquatic birds, fish, and even manatees. To us, it is paradise, the place where we want to spend a large portion of our remaining years together.

What do you want when you retire? Something similar? A ski chalet in Whistler? A cottage in Muskoka or the Laurentians? None of the above? This is not an exercise in idle dreaming. It is the first stage of a long-range plan that will enable you to decide how you would like to spend your later years and build the financial resources needed to achieve your goals.

To get you started, here is a Personal Lifestyle Planner. Set aside an evening with your spouse or partner to go through it. You may discover some hopes and desires you have in common that you never knew about before.

PERSONAL LIFESTYLE PLANNER

	Self		Spouse
Target retirement age	_____		_____
Number of working years remaining	_____		_____

Housing	Yes	No	Not Sure
Continue to live in present house	❏	❏	❏
Move to less expensive house	❏	❏	❏
Move to more expensive house	❏	❏	❏
Move to a condo	❏	❏	❏
Move in with children	❏	❏	❏
Own more than one residence and will continue to do so	❏	❏	❏
Will acquire a second residence or RV	❏	❏	❏
Will acquire more than one additional residence	❏	❏	❏

Lifestyle Goals	Yes	No	Not Sure
Spend more time with family	❏	❏	❏
Travel frequently	❏	❏	❏
Spend winters in the Sunbelt	❏	❏	❏
Be more active in sports (e.g., golf, tennis, fishing)	❏	❏	❏
Spend more time gardening	❏	❏	❏
Devote time to reading, TV watching	❏	❏	❏
Take educational courses	❏	❏	❏
Spend time with computers, the internet	❏	❏	❏
Devote time to hobbies	❏	❏	❏
Begin a second career, consulting, part-time work	❏	❏	❏
Have a more active social life (e.g., dinners, parties)	❏	❏	❏

	Yes	No	Not Sure
Join a club	❏	❏	❏
Play bridge, canasta, or similar	❏	❏	❏
Take up (or do more) boating	❏	❏	❏
Do volunteer work	❏	❏	❏

Other (fill in your own priorities) _____

_____

_____

Material Goals	Yes	No	Not Sure
Buy a new car at least every three years	❏	❏	❏
Renovate the house	❏	❏	❏
Dine out frequently	❏	❏	❏
Buy the latest high-tech equipment (e.g., TV sets)	❏	❏	❏
Provide for grandchildren's education	❏	❏	❏
Help children or other relatives financially	❏	❏	❏
Give large amounts to charities	❏	❏	❏
Leave a large estate for heirs	❏	❏	❏

Other (fill in your own priorities) _____

_____

_____

Finally, you and your spouse/partner should decide which of the following statements best describes how you hope to live in retirement.

(a) We want to maintain our current standard of living.

(b) We want to have a higher standard of living with enough money to spend on luxuries.

(c) We have modest needs and will not need much income to be comfortable in retirement.

Step Two: Estimating Your Expenditures

Once you have decided on your initial goals, you need to put a price tag on them. That will require some work but it will be time well spent.

Giving up a few hours of television now may change your entire way of living in future years.

There are two ways to estimate your retirement income needs. One is the quick method. This simply involves using your current family after-tax income as a base and multiplying by a target percentage. What percentage should that be? This is where your response to the final question in Step One comes into play. If you chose option (a) you will probably need about 80 percent of your pre-retirement income to live comfortably. In this case, the quick formula would be:

This year's family gross income x 80% = Retirement spending needs

So if your family income this year is $50,000, after retirement you'd need $40,000 in today's purchasing power to maintain your standard of living.

Option (b) will cost more so you need to set your sights higher—say, 100 percent of pre-retirement income. If you will be content with a very modest retirement lifestyle and selected option (c), you should be able to get by on around 60 percent of your working income. If you selected (b) or (c), substitute the appropriate percentage in the above formula.

If you want more precise figures, you'll have to do some additional work. The Expense Estimator on pages 65–67 will help you prepare a more accurate projection of your anticipated costs when you stop work. You may wish to make photocopies before filling it out so you'll have extra sheets for future updates.

Before you begin, you'll need to know approximately how much your family is spending annually now in each category. If you don't have a current budget, this is a good time to create one. You can download a free family budget spreadsheet in Excel format at **www.buildingwealth.ca**.

Use today's dollars when completing the Expense Estimator. I'll explain how to take inflation into account later. Also, leave taxes aside for the present, except for Canada Pension Plan and Employment Insurance premiums.

Here are some other considerations to keep in mind.

Housing. You may still be paying off a mortgage, but look into the future. Based on the current amortization schedule, or on any mortgage pay-down plans you may have, will it be fully discharged by the time you stop work? If so, the mortgage component can be eliminated from your retirement spending estimates. Under utilities, include the cost of heating, hydro, water, cable TV, telephone (including long distance), internet service provider, and any special costs you may have, such as a water softener, water filter, or security system. The improvements and replacements line is for the cost of renovations or new furniture and appliances. Don't underestimate these expenses: many people like to spend time after retirement fixing up their home or buying new furniture, drapes, and carpets. If your lifestyle plans call for you to move to a less (or more) expensive home after retirement, adjust your spending estimates accordingly. Do not include any allowance for the profit you may make on the sale of your present home—that will be dealt with later.

Recreational property. You may not own a cottage, Sunbelt condo, or vacation property now, but if you want one after you retire you'll have to build in the cost. Many retirees buy a place in the sun to spend the winter months. If this is part of your desired retirement lifestyle, start planning for it now. If you want a rough rule of thumb on the annual costs of carrying such a property, assuming it's mortgaged, use 15 to 20 percent of your estimated purchase price. A condo in the Sunbelt will usually cost at least as much to carry as a comparable residence in Canada—what you save in heating bills you'll pay out in higher costs for electricity, property taxes, insurance, and maintenance charges.

Food. Your current food costs may not be indicative of what you can expect to pay after retirement. Your children will probably have left home by the time you stop work. Many people also find they eat smaller portions as they age. Meals out may cost less, especially if you and your spouse both work and have lunches away from home five days a week. On the other hand, if your desired lifestyle calls for more socializing and entertaining, budget accordingly.

Clothing. If you and your spouse have to dress for work, whether it's in an office or on a construction site, those costs will be eliminated. You may have to build up your leisure wardrobe, but casual clothes usually cost less than business wear. If you have children living at home now, eliminate the cost of their clothing from the calculation unless you expect to have to support them after retirement. If you might have others living with you, such as an aged parent, factor that in.

Transportation. For most people, the family car is the largest single expense in this category. You'll almost certainly want to retain at least one car when you stop work, so you'd better plan for it. Remember to include all relevant costs: gas, oil, insurance, licence, and maintenance. I've also added a line for public transportation (remember many communities offer seniors' discounts) and one marked "reserve." This is for putting aside money to purchase a new car every five years or so.

Health care. This is a tough one to estimate. Your personal health costs will almost certainly be higher after you retire and you may not have ongoing group plan protection. Dental care and glasses may cost more and you may have to purchase a hearing aid. However, if you're currently paying large sums for health care—perhaps your daughter just got braces on her teeth—the increase may not be overly dramatic. Make inquiries about the cost of individual health insurance for older people and include this in your post-retirement projection. Note that some provinces subsidize prescription costs for older people. Ontario, for example, picks up most of the expense for qualified medical prescription drugs for all people over 65, regardless of income (although there has been talk of that benefit being cut back).

Personal care. Cosmetics, hair care, perfumes, and the like all cost money. Allow for it here. Also include any spending on tobacco and alcohol on this line.

Life/disability insurance. If you have a young family, your annual premiums may be quite high at present. However, you shouldn't need as much insurance after the kids have grown up, especially if you've built a solid retirement plan that will comfortably support both you and your spouse through the rest of your lives. Unless you want to use life insurance to leave a big estate to your children, plan to reduce your costs once you stop work. Disability insurance is valuable as long as you're working, but once you retire there is no point continuing it. Any money you're now spending on disability premiums can be directed elsewhere.

Family. Take a close look at what your dependants are costing you now. If you have children in university, for example, you're probably laying out thousands of dollars annually that won't be required in a few years. On the other side of the coin, consider your parents or other close family relatives. Are they in good financial shape, or are they likely to need help from you in later years? Also, don't lose sight of the grandchildren that may come along (or be here already). They can cost a lot of money in gifts and visits.

Travel. If you want to see the world, or at least the sunny south, after you retire, this is the time to start planning for it. If you don't spend a lot on holidays now, this may be the component of your budget that shows the largest percentage increase. Remember to factor in the cost of out-of-province travel insurance; the older you get, the more it will cost. A five-month winter stay for a couple over 70 could carry an insurance premium of several thousand dollars.

Recreation. You're probably going to want to be active in your spare time, so don't skimp here. If you're a golfer, you may want to join a club (if you don't belong already) or purchase new golf clubs. Hobbies can be costly—I happen to enjoy collecting fine wines and I don't intend to give it up when I stop work. Many retirees like gardening, which can be expensive. You may want to buy some compact discs or rent movies. How about some nights on the town? Will you be doing more reading? Do you plan to buy a boat? A state-of-the-art home entertainment system? A new computer? This is your chance to do all those things you've complained you never had time for, so make sure the money is available in your budget.

Pet care. Many retired people like the companionship of a dog, cat, or other pet. If that sounds like you, put some money in your budget at this line. Don't underestimate the cost. Vet fees can be expensive, and if your pet requires regular grooming the way our shaggy sheltie did, that will set you back $50 to $75 every month or two.

Debt repayment. You may be servicing a lot of debt right now: credit card balances, a car loan, investment loans, etc. Include the annual interest cost of everything except your mortgage in the Present Costs column. Your target should be to pay off all your debts before retirement to reduce that outlay to zero, thereby freeing up cash for other post-retirement needs.

Professional services. You may need the services of a lawyer, accountant, financial planner, and/or investment counsellor when you retire. Budget for those costs at this line.

Donations. If you give regularly to charitable organizations, you'll want to continue doing so when you retire. Include an appropriate amount here.

Canada Pension Plan/Employment Insurance. You're probably paying several hundred dollars each year in premiums, and the higher your income, the greater the amount deducted. This expense will disappear when you retire.

Retirement savings. You should be contributing several thousand dollars each year to retirement programs, such as pension plans and RRSPs. This is another outlay that will stop once you retire.

Other expenses. Most people find they spend at least 10 percent of their income on items for which they can't readily account. Make an appropriate allowance on this line. If you have any unusual expenses, such as alimony payments, also add them at this point.

EXPENSE ESTIMATOR

	This Year's Costs	Retirement Percentage	Retirement Cost
Principal Residence			
Mortgage/Rent	_____	_____	_____
Property taxes	_____	_____	_____
Maintenance/repairs	_____	_____	_____
Utilities	_____	_____	_____
Improvements/replacements	_____	_____	_____
Recreational Property			
Mortgage/rent	_____	_____	_____
Property taxes	_____	_____	_____

	This Year's Costs	Retirement Percentage	Retirement Cost
Maintenance/repairs	_____	_____	_____
Utilities	_____	_____	_____
Improvements/replacements	_____	_____	_____

Food

At home	_____	_____	_____
Meals out	_____	_____	_____

Clothing

You	_____	_____	_____
Spouse/partner	_____	_____	_____
Other person (e.g., parent)	_____	_____	_____
Laundry/cleaning	_____	_____	_____

Transportation

Car(s)	_____	_____	_____
Public	_____	_____	_____
Reserve	_____	_____	_____

Health Care

Insurance premiums	_____	_____	_____
Medical costs	_____	_____	_____
Prescriptions	_____	_____	_____
Dental care	_____	_____	_____
Eye care	_____	_____	_____
Hearing care	_____	_____	_____
Physiotherapy	_____	_____	_____
Other	_____	_____	_____

Personal Care
_____ _____ _____

Life Insurance
_____ _____ _____

Family

Children	_____	_____	_____
Other relatives	_____	_____	_____

	This Year's Costs	Retirement Percentage	Retirement Cost
Travel/Holidays	_____	_____	_____
Recreation			
Memberships/fees	_____	_____	_____
Equipment	_____	_____	_____
Hobbies	_____	_____	_____
Other	_____	_____	_____
Debt Repayment			
Credit cards	_____	_____	_____
Loans	_____	_____	_____
Professional Services	_____	_____	_____
Donations/Gifts	_____	_____	_____
CPP/EI Premiums	_____	_____	_____
Retirement Savings	_____	_____	_____
Other Expenses	_____	_____	_____
Total	_____	_____	_____

The total amount in the Retirement Cost column represents your estimated expenses *in today's dollars* once you stop work. But the purchasing power of those dollars will be eroded over time by inflation and you must take that into account in your planning.

Step Three: Adjusting for Inflation

The amount of money you'll need when you stop work will be directly affected by the increase in the cost of living between now and then. The more years that remain until retirement, the greater the inflationary impact will be. In recent years, inflation has been under control. The Bank of Canada has a target range of 1 to 3 percent for annual increases; if there is a danger that inflation will rise above that band, watch for the Bank to aggressively raise interest rates to control it. The mid-point of the official target range, 2 percent, is a reasonable factor to use now, although that could change going forward.

The table that follows enables you to convert today's dollars to a future purchasing power value, based on the number of years to retirement and the expected inflation rate. To use it, select a target rate of inflation to determine how much your current dollar expenses will increase over the time. For example, the inflation adjustor for 10 years at a 3 percent average annual inflation rate is 1.34. That means for every $10,000 in projected retirement expenses, you'll need $13,400 after a decade to maintain your standard of living.

THE INFLATION EFFECT

Years to Retirement	Inflation Adjustor at					
	1%	2%	3%	4%	5%	6%
1	1.01	1.02	1.03	1.04	1.05	1.06
2	1.02	1.04	1.06	1.08	1.10	1.12
3	1.03	1.06	1.09	1.13	1.16	1.19
4	1.01	1.08	1.13	1.17	1.22	1.26
5	1.05	1.10	1.16	1.22	1.28	1.34
6	1.06	1.13	1.19	1.27	1.34	1.42
7	1.07	1.15	1.23	1.32	1.41	1.50
8	1.08	1.17	1.27	1.37	1.48	1.58
9	1.09	1.20	1.31	1.42	1.55	1.69
10	1.11	1.22	1.34	1.48	1.63	1.79
11	1.12	1.24	1.39	1.54	1.71	1.90
12	1.13	1.27	1.43	1.60	1.80	2.01
13	1.14	1.29	1.47	1.67	1.89	2.13
14	1.15	1.32	1.51	1.73	1.98	2.26
15	1.16	1.35	1.56	1.80	2.08	2.40
16	1.17	1.37	1.61	1.87	2.19	2.54
17	1.18	1.40	1.65	1.95	2.29	2.69
18	1.20	1.43	1.70	2.03	2.41	2.85
19	1.21	1.46	1.75	2.11	2.53	3.03
20	1.22	1.49	1.81	2.19	2.65	3.21

Years to Retirement	Inflation Adjustor at					
	1%	2%	3%	4%	5%	6%
21	1.23	1.52	1.86	2.28	2.79	3.40
22	1.25	1.55	1.92	2.37	2.93	3.60
23	1.26	1.58	1.97	2.47	3.07	3.82
24	1.27	1.61	2.03	2.56	3.23	4.05
25	1.28	1.64	2.09	2.67	3.39	4.29
26	1.29	1.66	2.16	2.77	3.56	4.55
27	1.31	1.67	2.22	2.88	3.73	4.82
28	1.32	1.69	2.29	3.00	3.92	5.11
29	1.33	1.71	2.36	3.12	4.12	5.42
30	1.35	1.72	2.43	3.24	4.32	5.74
31	1.36	1.85	2.50	3.37	4.54	6.09
32	1.38	1.89	2.58	3.51	4.77	6.45
33	1.39	1.92	2.65	3.65	5.00	6.84
34	1.40	1.96	2.73	3.79	5.25	7.25
35	1.42	2.00	2.81	3.95	5.52	7.69
36	1.43	2.04	2.90	4.10	5.79	8.15
37	1.45	2.08	2.99	4.27	6.08	8.64
38	1.46	2.12	3.08	4.44	6.39	9.15
39	1.47	2.17	3.17	4.62	6.71	9.70
40	1.49	2.21	3.26	4.80	7.04	10.29

For example, if you have 30 years remaining until retirement, you must increase your cost projection by more than one-third to maintain the purchasing power in today's dollars if inflation averages only 1 percent annually over that time. At a 2 percent average inflation rate, you will need to increase your estimate by 72 percent. So if the Retirement Cost total is $50,000, you would need to adjust that to $86,000 after 30 years and use that number as your target.

So how do you cope with this situation, especially since we don't know what will happen to the inflation level in the years to come? Here are some ways to deal with the problem.

1. Assume a higher rate of inflation than you actually expect. Let's go back to Ottawa's 1 to 3 percent range. In effect, the federal government is telling us that it won't switch back into a strong anti-inflation mode until the CPI starts to move toward the upper end of that band. So the 2 percent figure looks like a decent average to work with, at least under present conditions. But the prudent planner will want to build in something of a cushion. So I recommend you use 3 percent as your average annual inflation target. If inflation comes in below that, it will simply mean that you have some extra spending money available.

2. Determine how much of your anticipated retirement income will be inflation protected. All of the main government support programs (CPP, OAS, and GIS) have built-in inflation adjustors. If that policy is maintained, that part of your income will be secure in purchasing power terms. Some pension plans also offer inflation protection, especially for those working in the public sector. If you are a pension plan member, find out the policy in this regard. If your plan does not have inflation protection now, it's unlikely to be added in the future because of the high cost involved. RRSPs may also come with some inflation protection, although you have to set up your income programs to make it work out that way. If you design a RRIF or LIF (life income fund) to make payments under the government's minimum withdrawal formula, the amount you receive will increase each year, as long as the capital base isn't eroded (more on this in a later chapter). However, if inflation returns to higher levels, the annual payment increases may not be enough to compensate. There are also inflation-indexed annuities available, although they are expensive.

Once you are able to estimate how much of your retirement income will have built-in inflation protection, you will have an idea of what percentage is fixed and therefore vulnerable to rising prices.

3. Develop plans to ensure your income will rise according to your needs. There are several possible ways to increase retirement income. They include:
- *Postpone CPP payments.* Although you become eligible for full payments at 65, you don't have to start collecting Canada Pension Plan

benefits until age 70. Every year that you wait increases the amount of your pension by 6 percent. So if you don't need your CPP immediately to make ends meet, put it off. When you do start to draw it, the extra income should more than compensate for inflation in the intervening years. In the case of a couple who both qualify for CPP, you may want to start drawing one pension first and keep the other in reserve as long as possible.

- *Postpone converting RRSPs.* You don't have to close your RRSP until the last day of the year in which you turn 69. If you don't need the money in your plan immediately, leave it alone. The longer the assets in your RRSP continue to grow tax-sheltered, the more capital you will have to draw on when it's needed. If you need only some of the RRSP income now, arrange for a partial withdrawal. That is now permitted under the law. You'll obtain immediate cash flow while the balance can continue to grow.

- *Manage your RRSP/RRIF for continued growth.* Just because you've retired doesn't mean your RRSP savings need to stagnate. Although you should put a greater emphasis on safety at this stage, don't go overboard. Retain a significant growth component in your RRSP, and in your RRIF when you move on to that stage, so that your capital base can increase. We'll look at ways to do that in subsequent chapters.

- *If possible, continue investing.* You may find yourself in the fortunate position of having more income than you really need in your early retirement years. Believe it or not, it does happen. Take advantage of this by investing the surplus. You probably won't be able to contribute any more to RRSPs, but this is a good opportunity to continue to build your non-registered investment portfolio. This will increase the capital available for income generation later.

- *Look for new sources of income.* You'd be amazed at the imaginative ways people can generate additional retirement income. You'll find all sorts of ideas later in this book, in Chapter 22.

So there are many ways to beat the inflation problem. It's simply a matter of planning.

8

Sources of Income

After completing the forms in the last chapter, you now have an idea of what your cost of living will be in retirement, both in current dollars and in inflation-adjusted dollars. Now it's time to match that against your projected retirement income so you can see where you stand and what needs to be done. There are several potential income sources to consider, so we'll look at each of them in detail.

Government Programs

Many people may not realize it but Canadians are very lucky when it comes to government-sponsored retirement support programs. While the battle rages in the U.S. over the future of Social Security, Canadians can sit back comfortably, secure in the latest assurances that our government programs are in great financial shape. In the latest mandatory three-year actuarial report, covering the period to the end of 2003, the number crunchers who work for the Superintendent of Financial Institutions concluded that the Canada Pension Plan will continue to increase its assets until about 2050. At that time, the CPP, which had $68 billion at the end of 2003, is projected to grow to almost $1.6 trillion! And that's with no change in the present contribution rate.

Finance Minister Ralph Goodale was ecstatic when he tabled the report in the House of Commons in December 2004. "Canada is one of the few countries in the world with a rock-solid public pension system," he said in a statement. "Canadians can therefore continue to have confidence in the Canada Pension Plan and can count on it as an important part of their retirement savings."

Some Canadians are still not convinced, according to pollsters, but the actuaries who studied the plan seemed to be brimming with confidence. The executive summary released with the report contained a long list of reassuring numbers. Among them:

- At the current contribution rate of 9.9 percent of eligible earnings, the CPP's ratio of total assets to the following year's expenditures will increase from 3.1 in 2004 to 5.6 by 2021.
- The plan is actuarially sustainable at a contribution rate of 9.8 percent, a tenth of a point less than the present level.
- By the end of 2010, the CPP will have $147 billion in assets.
- Contributions will be more than enough to pay benefits to retirees until 2021. After that, a portion of investment earnings from the plan will be needed to maintain the benefits level. The report estimates that by 2050, the amount of investment earnings needed for this purpose will be 29 percent. Put another way, at that time less than a third of the income earned by the CPP's investments will have to be spent; the rest will be added to the fund, which will continue to grow.
- The CPP will continue to add to its asset base despite the fact that the ratio of working Canadians to those age 65 and older will fall from 4.9 in 2004 to 2.3 in 2050. So even when we reach the stage where almost a third of Canadians are drawing CPP benefits the fund will not only remain solvent but will continue to grow.

This is encouraging news indeed, but it wasn't always thus. Canadians can thank the governments of Brian Mulroney and Jean Chrétien for taking the tough decisions that Americans are currently resisting, thereby putting the CPP on a sustainable footing for the foreseeable future. In fact, it wasn't until a federal–provincial conference in 1997, more than 30 years after the plan came into being, that a contributions/benefits schedule was put into place that ensured the CPP's long-term viability.

A subsequent decision to allow a portion of the portfolio to be invested in stocks, real estate, income trusts, and other securities enhanced the return potential. After a slow start because of the bear market of 2000–2002, the Canada Pension Plan Investment Board (CPPIB) announced a gain of 17.5 percent in fiscal 2003–2004 that included a $7.2 billion profit from equities and real estate. However, the CPPIB doesn't need to average 17.5 percent a year or anything like it to meet the latest projections. The actuarial forecasts are based on the assumption of a 4 percent annual rate of return. The CPPIB itself uses a 4.5 percent target.

So as things stand right now, the future looks rosy for the CPP, and its solvency should not be on your list of retirement concerns. But don't let that make you overconfident. You can't build a retirement plan on the CPP alone. Rather, it should be considered a supplement that will top up your other income. Assume that it will contribute about one-quarter of your retirement income needs. The rest will have to come from other sources.

What to Expect from CPP/QPP

Many Canadians consider the CPP and the Quebec Pension Plan (QPP) as one of the cornerstones of their retirement income without having a clue what to expect from these programs. A survey by Decima Research published in early 2005 revealed that almost half the respondents would not even hazard a guess as to how much they would receive from the CPP when they stopped work. Particularly worrisome was the fact that among interviewees over 55, the folks who should be most concerned about this, 39 percent wouldn't offer a guess.

Among those who did offer a figure, the majority expected that the government plans would pay them a lot more than they'll actually receive. The average guess was $13,200 a year, more than 30 percent over what retirees will receive at age 65. Younger Canadians expected the CPP to be even more generous. Respondents between the ages of 18 and 24 predicted a retirement benefit of $25,600, more than two and a half times the correct amount. Only people who were already retired and presumably drawing CPP benefits came close to estimating the amount of the annual payments.

If those results are anywhere near accurate, they are both surprising and worrisome. They suggest that not only are people almost completely uninformed about the CPP but they expect the government will provide them with far more income in retirement than is the case. This attitude may explain why Canadians seem to be chronically unwilling to make RRSP contributions, leaving billions of dollars in tax deductions on the table every year.

Let's set the record straight right now. The maximum monthly retirement benefit in 2005 was $828.75 for both the CPP and the QPP, or just under $10,000 a year. CPP/QPP payments are fully indexed for inflation. If that policy is maintained (and right now there is no suggestion that it won't be), you'll receive a pension from this source that is equivalent to $10,000 a year in today's purchasing power when you retire. If your spouse/partner is also eligible for full retirement benefits, the CPP/QPP will be worth almost $20,000 a year to your family.

However, don't take for granted that this is the actual amount you will receive. There are several ways in which the CPP/QPP benefit can be reduced, some of which may come as a surprise to the newly retired. They include early retirement, which reduces your contributory years, and early application for benefits (if you start to draw before age 65, your payments are reduced).

Getting Your Fair Share of the CPP

The Canada Pension Plan offers a range of benefits that can sometimes be confusing. One of the country's most prominent tax experts, author and speaker Evelyn Jacks, has been highly critical of what she calls "trick questions" and complicated jargon that she says have short-changed beneficiaries to the tune of $1 billion. "It is unacceptable to have a 15 percent error factor on the completion of benefit entitlement forms resulting in an average retroactive payment of $2,800," Ms. Jacks said in commenting on a study released by the Retirement Planning Institute for Canada's Association for the Fifty-Plus. "No one should miss out so significantly on benefits from government plans they have been required to pay into all their working lives."

To help you through the CPP maze, here is a summary of the benefits that are offered.

Retirement benefits. Obviously, retirement benefits are the basic reason for the plan's existence. But contrary to what many people believe, the money doesn't flow automatically when you stop work. You have to make it happen by completing an application. Your pension begins the month after you apply and cannot be made retroactive unless you're over 70. So if you want to collect, don't put it off.

Your CPP retirement benefit is calculated on the basis of 25 percent of your qualifying career average earnings, with the lowest 15 percent of your qualifying years dropped off. So if you retire having contributed to the CPP for 35 years, the lowest five years of your earnings would be dropped from the calculation of your pension income. Mothers get a special break for periods when they stopped work or had reduced income because they were raising children under age seven. Special provisions are also made for people over 65 who are still working and for periods of disability.

Canadians with several years of low earned income who don't come under the exceptions will see their CPP benefits reduced, even if they reached the maximum pensionable level years ago. For example, anyone who retires early may have a number of years with no pensionable earnings for CPP purposes (employer pension and investment income don't count). Those zeros on a record will reduce the allowable benefit. This is one reason why many people start collecting CPP as soon as they become eligible. They don't want to accumulate zero income years after age 60, thereby reducing their pension benefits.

Even if you qualify for the maximum pension, your CPP payments will not exceed 25 percent of your pre-retirement income. If your income is higher than the maximum pensionable earnings ($41,100 in 2005), the percentage of your income replaced by the CPP at retirement will be even lower.

If you're over 40, you should be receiving a periodic Statement of Contributions from Social Development Canada. It spells out in detail the

CPP contributions you've made to date and your pension entitlement if you were eligible to make a claim now. If you are receiving these reports, consult the latest one to see what your CPP benefit would be. If not, check with a local office for your current status (be sure to have your Social Insurance Number ready when you call).

To receive a full pension, the rules state you must contribute for at least 85 percent of the years from the time you start work (or from the beginning of 1966, when the plan was launched) until you retire.

Survivor benefits. Besides providing pensions, the CPP offers three types of survivor benefits. The first is a lump-sum payment to a maximum amount of $2,500, which will be paid, in order of priority, to the estate, the person responsible for funeral costs, the surviving spouse or common-law partner, or next of kin. (Note that under the CPP definition, common-law partners include same-sex couples living in a conjugal relationship.)

Next, your spouse (including a common-law spouse or partner) is entitled to a regular income, even if you die before retirement. A number of factors are taken into account in calculating how much this will be, including the amount the pensioner was receiving (or would have received at the time of death), the age of the surviving spouse, the amount of time the contributor paid into the CPP, and whether the survivor is disabled. The maximum survivor's benefit payable under the CPP to a spouse under 65 was $462.42 a month in 2005. At 65 and older, the maximum is equal to 60 percent of the retirement pension, which worked out to $497.25 a month in 2005.

Finally, dependent children may receive a special orphan's benefit. This was $195.96 a month in 2005. All children under age 18 qualify, as do older children who are attending school full-time.

To obtain CPP survivor benefits, you must apply to Social Development Canada. You'll need to provide a number of documents; check with a local office for details. You should apply as soon as possible after the contributor's death. Don't delay or you may lose benefits, since the CPP will only make back payments for up to 12 months.

Disability benefits. CPP contributors who become disabled have their own benefits program. However, the criteria for eligibility are quite strict.

You must be certified by a physician as having a physical or mental disability that is "severe and prolonged," which does not allow you to work. You must also have contributed to the CPP for at least four of the last six years.

Disability benefits provide income until age 65, when they are replaced by regular CPP payments (you can't collect both at the same time). Payments are also provided for dependent children. The maximum CPP disability payment in 2005 was $1,010.23 a month, plus an additional $195.96 per child.

To get a disability pension, you have to apply in writing. You can get an application kit by calling 1-800-277-9914 or you can download it from the website of Social Development Canada at **www.sdc.gc.ca**.

When to Apply for CPP

Full CPP benefits are payable at age 65. However, you can begin collecting as early as age 60, as long as you are "substantially retired." That means you've either completely stopped working or any employment income you receive during the month before your pension begins and the month it starts does not exceed the maximum CPP benefit available at that time ($828.75 a month in 2005). After that, employment income restrictions don't apply. Note that the rules for members of the Quebec Pension Plan may vary. For details check their website at **www.rrq.gouv.qc.ca/an/rente/11.htm**.

If you choose to start collecting benefits early, your pension entitlement will be reduced by half a percent for each month you collect before your 65th birthday (6 percent a year). So if you start drawing CPP payments as soon as you turn 60, your payments will be 70 percent of your entitlement at age 65. Remember, however, that your pension entitlement may also be reduced if you postpone applying as this will add several years with no pensionable earnings to your career total. In 2005, the maximum CPP benefit was $828.75 a month, or slightly less than $10,000 a year. Therefore, if you started collecting at age 60, the most you could receive would be $580.13 a month ($828.75 x 70 percent), or $6,962 a year.

Alternatively, you can wait until as late as age 70 to start collecting your payments. For every month you wait after your 65th birthday your pension will increase by half a percent. So if you put off drawing your CPP retirement benefit until the last possible moment, you'll be allowed

130 percent of your normal entitlement. Based on the 2005 maximum payment, the most you could draw from the CPP if you waited until age 70 to start would be $1,077.38 a month, or $12,929 a year.

So which is the better course—to start drawing as soon as possible, even though the payments will be less, or to wait until you're 70? For most people, starting as soon as they're eligible is the best choice. You begin receiving money immediately and you protect your pension against being eroded by several years of non-pensionable earnings (once you apply, the book is closed on your career earnings).

The other side of this coin is that the longer you live, the greater the advantage in waiting to draw your CPP. The problem, of course, is that we can't predict our own lifespan. The average 65-year-old woman can expect to live another 20.6 years according to 2002 figures from Statistics Canada, the latest available at the time of writing. Men the same age have a life expectancy of 17.2 years. However, specialized studies done by pension consultants have found that people who buy annuities tend to live longer than the general population.

If general life expectancy were the sole criterion in deciding when to start drawing CPP, it would suggest that men should probably start no later than age 65, while women would do better waiting until 70. However, for most people, other considerations will come into play. These include:

- *Income needs.* Clearly, if you're short of money and need CPP payments to make ends meet, it makes no sense to delay your application. Start drawing your pension as soon as possible.

- *Pensionable earnings.* As I've already explained, if you have no pensionable earnings while you're waiting, you may reduce the ultimate benefit you receive. Do your calculations (or ask Social Development Canada to help you do them) before making a decision.

- *Inflation protection.* If you don't need your CPP money to live comfortably, you could hold it in reserve for a few years, especially if you feel you may have some difficulty keeping up with inflation down the road. The CPP will give your buying power a boost when you do start to collect it, and the longer you delay before age 70, the higher your pension will be.

- *Lifestyle priorities.* Some retirees want more money in the early years of their retirement, while they're still healthy and relatively young, so they can travel or fulfill other lifelong objectives. Your CPP payments may be enough to give you the extra spending power to achieve those dreams.

- *Taxes.* CPP payments are taxed at your full marginal rate. If you expect your tax bracket to be lower in the future, you may wish to postpone applying until that time, to give you a greater after-tax return.

Splitting CPP Payments

When you've made up your mind when to start collecting CPP, there's another decision to make—whether or not to split your payments with your spouse or common-law partner. If you're both age 60 or older, CPP payments can be divided between spouses on the basis of a set formula. If both spouses are eligible for CPP payments, both must apply for benefits and the income from both pensions must be divided between them. The division is based on the years they have been married or cohabitating compared to the total number of contributory years.

Social Development Canada offers this example of how CPP splitting works. If a couple lives together for 20 years during which both are contributing to the plan, they would add the pension earned by each during the 20-year period. That amount will then be divided equally between them. Each spouse or partner keeps the rest of any pension entitlement earned outside the time they lived together. The combined total amount of the two pensions stays the same.

CPP splitting works best if one spouse had a much lower pension than the other. In that case, it could be advantageous from a tax perspective. For example, suppose a husband qualifies for the maximum CPP benefit and has an employer pension that pays $50,000 a year. He'll be required to pay tax on his CPP payments at his top marginal rate, which would be in the 30 to 35 percent range depending on his province of residence. If his annual payment in 2005 was $9,500, he'd have to fork over about $3,000 of that in taxes. Suppose his wife had no employer pension plan and the only income she expects to receive in retirement is Old Age Security and a modest CPP benefit. By splitting their CPP, he could direct a portion of his payment to her and, in effect, shelter most or all of it from tax.

CPP splitting may also be useful as a strategy to reduce the impact of the Old Age Security clawback, which we'll look at in more detail later in this chapter.

If you want to apply for pension splitting, be prepared to gather up a lot of information for the government. They'll want to see an original birth certificate or a certified true copy for both of you and your original marriage certificate or a certified true copy or proof of your common-law relationship.

Retiring Abroad

One major advantage of the Canada Pension Plan is that you never lose the right to collect it, no matter where you live after you retire. Your entitlement is based on the contributions you made to the plan over many years, not on your country of residence. In fact, if you retire to the States, Social Development Canada will even arrange to have your cheques deposited directly into your account at a U.S. bank. Now that's service!

So if you're considering retiring abroad, perhaps to the Sunbelt, don't forget to apply for your CPP anyway. After all, you and your employers have paid enough into it so you might as well get the benefits.

Old Age Security

The other cornerstone of Canada's income support program for retirees is Old Age Security (OAS). This plan, which has been a part of the country's social welfare fabric since 1952, differs from the CPP in four significant ways.

1. It is not a contributory plan. No payroll deductions are made to finance it. The benefits are paid out of general revenues.
2. All eligible Canadians are entitled to receive it at age 65.
3. The amount of the payment is fixed. It does not vary because of income levels during a person's working years.

4. Higher-income retirees have part or all of their OAS benefits clawed back by a special tax, known as the social benefits repayment tax. More on this later in the chapter.

OAS payments are made to all Canadians age 65 and older. During the third quarter of 2005, the maximum amount was $476.97 a month, or just over $5,700 a year. So a couple would receive about $11,400 a year from this source. Again, these benefits are fully indexed so if there is no change in policy the current purchasing power will still be there when you retire.

Whether you get to keep the full amount of your OAS cheque is another matter. Retired people in high income brackets are hit with what the federal government euphemistically calls a "social benefits repayment tax," more popularly (or unpopularly) known as "the clawback."

OAS Rules

Here are the basic rules governing Old Age Security.

Eligibility. Anyone age 65 or older who is a Canadian citizen or legal resident of Canada is eligible for OAS. If you're a resident, you must have lived here for at least 10 years after age 18. Non-residents are also eligible if they lived in Canada at least 20 years after age 18. The amount of the benefit will be affected by the number of years the applicant has been a Canadian resident. Full benefits are paid to those who lived in Canada at least 40 years after age 18.

When to apply. Submit an application at least six months before you're eligible to draw benefits. You can apply up to a year in advance.

How to apply. You can get an application kit from any Social Development Canada office—check the blue pages in your phone book for an address or call 1-800-277-9114 to have one sent. The forms can also be downloaded from the departmental website, **www100.hrdc.gc.ca/indisp3000e.shtml**.

Required documentation. You'll be required to provide proof of age, in the form of a birth or baptismal certificate. If you were born outside of Canada, you'll also need to supply citizenship or immigration documents.

When you'll collect. Payments start the month after your 65th birthday.

Payment frequency. Payments are distributed at the end of each month.

Payment options. You can have a cheque sent by mail, but the most convenient way is to arrange direct deposit to your bank account, either in Canada or the United States.

Indexing. OAS payments are fully indexed to inflation with adjustments made every quarter.

Taxation. If you are not subject to the clawback, your OAS payments will be taxed as regular income.

The OAS Clawback

The clawback provision was introduced in 1989 by the Progressive Conservative government of the day and applied to all OAS recipients with net income in excess of $50,000. It was a controversial move at the time, especially because the income threshold at which the special tax became effective was not indexed to inflation, which meant that an ever-growing number of older people would be subject to the clawback each year. Fortunately, Paul Martin changed that in the 2002 budget, when he was finance minister, by introducing full indexing for the threshold. By the 2005 tax year, the threshold had increased to $60,806.

While Martin's move was a huge step in the direction of fairness, there is another issue that still needs to be addressed in the name of equity: the use of net income to determine whether a person will be subject to the clawback. Net income covers revenue from all sources, including employment, private and government pension payments, interest, rental income, taxable capital gains, the taxable amount of dividend income, business and professional income, etc. From this, certain deductions are allowed, including pension and RRSP contributions, child care expenses, support payments, moving expenses, carrying charges, and the like.

The decision to use net income as the threshold figure creates a serious inequity for OAS recipients who rely on investments for part of their income. This problem involves dividend payments and the gross-up provision, which provides that the actual amount of dividends received be increased by 25 percent for tax purposes. This is the figure used in the net income calculation. Later in the tax form you receive an offsetting benefit called the dividend tax credit but it comes too late in the calculation to affect the clawback formula. Because net income includes grossed-up dividends, some people are in the position of having their OAS benefits clawed back on the basis of income they never receive.

This system penalizes OAS beneficiaries with high dividend income. For example, suppose Shirley Green has income of $60,000, half of which comes from interest earned on GICs. She would not be subject to the clawback. Carolyn Jones also has an income of $60,000, half of which also comes from investments. But in her case, the investment income is received in the form of dividends paid on preferred shares she owns. For tax purposes, this portion of her income is grossed up, adding $7,500 to her net income and pushing her over the clawback threshold. As a result, she'll have to repay several hundred dollars of her OAS benefit. Her real income is exactly the same as that of Shirley Green, but she's worse off in after-tax terms because of the way in which the clawback is applied.

Circumventing the Clawback

If one spouse is likely to have a relatively high income in retirement while that of the other spouse will be low, steps should be taken to reduce the impact of the social benefits repayment tax on the higher-income person. Ideally, the goal is to bring down the net income of that spouse or partner to below the threshold line but even if that cannot be achieved income-splitting can save significant tax dollars. Here are some strategies to consider.

- *Contribute to spousal RRSPs.* The higher-income spouse (let's assume in this case it's a wife) should direct all RRSP contributions to the plan of her husband. This will build his retirement income, while reducing hers.
- *Split CPP benefits.* Take advantage of the CPP pension-splitting provisions described earlier in this chapter to reduce the net income of the wife.
- *Plan investments carefully.* Invest any income earned by the husband with a view to increasing his interest or dividend payments after retirement. Use the wife's income to live on.

Here's an example of how these strategies may help circumvent the clawback. Suppose the wife in this example were to turn 65 this year and her net income is $65,000 including Old Age Security of about $5,700 a year. The husband is also turning 65 and has a net income of $20,000 a year, also including OAS.

The husband will be taxed on his OAS payment at his marginal rate, which will be quite low given his income (about 22 percent depending on the province of residence). But the wife will see a large chunk of her OAS benefit disappear in the form of taxes. To begin with, her marginal tax rate will be much higher, somewhere in the vicinity of 33 percent. On top of that, she'll be hit by the clawback, which adds an additional 15 percent tax on her income above the threshold, which was $60,806 in 2005. The result in this case would be extra tax totalling about $630. So her total tax payable on the $5,700 OAS benefit is around $1,900. (Note that once the entire OAS benefit has been taxed away the clawback mechanism no longer applies. In 2005, that happened when a person's net income exceeded $98,547.)

Let's assume that by using some of the strategies outlined above, the couple managed to switch $5,000 a year in income from the wife to the husband. She would then have a net income of $60,000 while the husband receives $25,000. There is no difference in the total income—in both examples it comes to $85,000. But in this situation, no clawback will apply. The wife will pay only her marginal tax rate of 33 percent on the benefit. The $5,000 that was switched to the husband will be taxed at his marginal rate of 22 percent. By careful planning, this couple just saved $630 in clawback tax plus $550 in regular tax because of the shift of $5,000 to the husband. That's almost $1,200 more in their pockets!

One word of caution: before you embark on any of these strategies, do some careful post-retirement income projections. It may be that even by using these techniques you won't be able to change the end result as far as the clawback is concerned. Even worse, you could put more income into your spouse's hands while not reducing your own by enough to make a difference (this is a particular danger in the case of higher-income couples). The result could be that both of you lose part or all of the OAS benefit.

Even if the entire OAS payment will be clawed back, you'd still be well advised to apply for it. You won't see any money because it will all be taxed back at source, but if your financial situation changes the cheques will begin to arrive in the next tax year because all the paperwork has been done.

Guaranteed Income Supplement (GIS)

You don't want to get this one and it should not be included on your Sources of Income list. These are support payments provided by the federal government to low-income individuals. Only those eligible for OAS can apply for the GIS and you will have to pass an income test. For a single person, the GIS is available only if income is less than $13,608 (2005 third-quarter figure), not including OAS. For a couple, the minimum is $17,760.

The maximum payment in the third quarter of 2005 was $566.87 a month for a single person or for someone married to a non-pensioner. For someone married to a pensioner, it was $369.24.

There is also an Allowance program for low-income people age 60 to 64 or their surviving spouses/partners. In the third quarter of 2005, this program was paying up to $846.21 a month to qualified recipients and up to $934.24 to surviving spouses. It terminates at age 65 when OAS and GIS cut in.

For more information about the GIS and the Allowance, contact a Social Development Canada Office or visit their website.

Employer Pension Plans

If you are fortunate enough to have an employer pension plan, it will likely be one of your main sources of retirement income. But don't let this lull you into a sense of false security. Many people have found to their dismay that what they thought would be a generous pension benefit turned out to be a mere pittance in relation to their total retirement income needs. As with the CPP, we tend to overestimate the benefits and only discover our mistake when it's too late to do anything about it.

If you have a defined benefits plan, obtain an estimate of the income you can expect from it as soon as possible. Obviously, the closer you are to retirement the more accurate the estimate will be. Your employer should provide you with an annual benefits report that shows your current status. However, any pension projections will be based on your current level of compensation. Few benefits reports attempt to project your income at retirement because of the many variables involved. If you want to get a better fix on what you can expect at retirement, ask the plan administrator to do a projection based on your current income and assuming that you will remain in the plan until you retire. This will provide a good estimate of the percentage of your current income that you can expect to receive as a pension.

If your plan is of the defined contribution type or is a group RRSP, the estimate becomes more difficult. Your pension benefit won't relate to your salary or years of service at all; rather it will be a function of how much you and your employer contribute to the plan over the years and how well the invested money performs. However, you can't build your retirement income projection without some idea of how much you might draw from a program of this type so ask your plan administrator to give it a shot using current contribution levels and a conservative average annual rate of return (say, 6 percent).

Of course, if you have no pension plan, which is the case with the majority of working Canadians, your retirement income from this source will be zero.

RRSPs

If you don't have an employer pension plan, an RRSP (or a combination of them) is likely to be the single most important source of your retirement income. Even if you expect to receive a pension, RRSP income can form a significant part of your cash flow after retirement.

The first step in assessing the income potential of your RRSPs (I use the plural because many people have more than one) is to calculate how much your current RRSP assets will be worth at retirement. The value of these assets will depend on how well you manage them and what kind of return you can generate. The following table shows how much each dollar now in your RRSP will be worth when you retire, assuming various average annual rates of growth. To be conservative, I suggest you use the 6 percent column for your estimates. If your investments do better, it will be a bonus.

HOW YOUR PRESENT RRSP WILL GROW

Years before Retirement	Future Value of $1 at Growth Rate of		
	6%	8%	10%
1	1.06	1.08	1.10
2	1.12	1.17	1.21
3	1.19	1.26	1.33
4	1.26	1.36	1.46
5	1.34	1.47	1.61
6	1.42	1.59	1.77
7	1.50	1.71	1.95
8	1.59	1.85	2.14
9	1.69	2.00	2.36
10	1.79	2.16	2.59
11	1.90	2.33	2.85
12	2.01	2.52	3.14
13	2.13	2.72	3.45
14	2.26	2.94	3.80
15	2.40	3.17	4.18
16	2.54	3.43	4.59
17	2.69	3.70	5.05
18	2.85	4.00	5.56
19	3.03	4.32	6.12
20	3.21	4.66	6.73
21	3.40	5.03	7.40
22	3.60	5.44	8.14
23	3.82	5.87	8.95
24	4.05	6.34	9.85
25	4.29	6.85	10.83
26	4.55	7.40	11.92

Years before Retirement	Future Value of $1 at Growth Rate of		
	6%	8%	10%
27	4.82	7.99	13.11
28	5.11	8.63	14.42
29	5.42	9.32	15.86
30	5.74	10.06	17.45
31	6.09	10.87	19.19
32	6.45	11.74	21.11
33	6.84	12.68	23.23
34	7.25	13.69	25.55
35	7.69	14.79	28.10
36	8.15	15.97	30.91
37	8.64	17.25	34.00
38	9.15	18.63	37.40
39	9.70	20.12	41.14
40	10.29	21.72	45.26

To find the value of your current RRSP assets at retirement, use the following formula:

Present value of RRSP x Growth factor = Future value of RRSP

For example, suppose you have $25,000 in an RRSP today and 30 years remaining until you plan to retire. As you can see from the table, if your average annual growth rate is 6 percent, every dollar will grow to $5.74 at the end of 30 years. The value of your existing RRSP assets at that time will therefore be:

$25,000 x 5.74 = $143,500

The table also provides an illustration of how good money management can greatly enhance the final value of your RRSP. If you achieve an average annual compound rate of return of 8 percent in your plan, every dollar will be worth $10.06 at the end of 30 years. The value of your RRSP in that case would be:

$25,000 x 10.06 = $251,500

At an average annual growth rate of 10 percent, one dollar today becomes worth $17.45 in 30 years and the value of your plan is:

$$\$25,000 \times 17.45 = \$436,250$$

The numbers can become quite impressive when you use higher return projections, but as I said earlier, for planning purposes I strongly advise using the 6 percent figure. It is better to end up with more money than you anticipated rather than less.

But what about future contributions? The next table will enable you to work out the value of future RRSP contributions at retirement, assuming you keep adding to your RRSP every year at the same rate and that you make your new contribution at the start of each year.

VALUE OF FUTURE RRSP CONTRIBUTIONS

Years before Retirement	Future Value of $1 at Growth Rate of		
	6%	8%	10%
1	1.06	1.08	1.10
2	2.18	2.25	2.31
3	3.37	3.51	3.64
4	4.64	4.87	5.11
5	5.98	6.34	6.72
6	7.39	7.92	8.49
7	8.90	9.64	10.44
8	10.49	11.49	12.58
9	12.18	13.49	14.94
10	13.97	15.65	17.53
11	15.87	17.98	20.38
12	17.88	20.50	23.52
13	20.02	23.21	26.97
14	22.28	26.15	30.77
15	24.67	29.32	34.95
16	27.21	32.75	39.54
17	29.91	36.45	44.60
18	32.76	40.45	50.16

Years before Retirement	Future Value of $1 at Growth Rate of		
	6%	8%	10%
19	35.79	44.76	56.27
20	38.99	49.42	63.00
21	42.39	54.46	70.40
22	46.00	59.89	78.54
23	49.82	65.76	87.50
24	53.86	72.11	97.35
25	58.16	78.95	108.18
26	62.71	86.35	120.10
27	67.53	94.34	133.21
28	72.64	102.97	147.63
29	78.06	112.28	163.49
30	83.80	122.35	180.94
31	89.89	133.21	200.14
32	96.34	144.95	221.25
33	103.18	157.63	244.48
34	110.43	171.32	270.02
35	118.12	186.10	298.13
36	126.27	202.07	329.04
37	134.90	219.30	363.04
38	144.06	237.94	400.45
39	153.76	258.06	441.59
40	164.05	279.78	486.85

The formula for calculating the value of future RRSP contributions is:

Annual future contributions x Growth factor = Value at retirement

To illustrate, let's say you plan to contribute $3,000 a year to your RRSPs until your planned retirement in 30 years. To calculate the retirement value of these new contributions at an annual average growth rate of 6 percent, you would multiply that amount by the appropriate growth factor, which in this case is 83.80. Your new contributions would therefore be worth at retirement:

$$3,000 \times 83.80 = \$251,400$$

If you were to achieve an annual growth rate of 8 percent, your new contributions would be worth:

$$3,000 \times 122.35 = \$367,050$$

At 10 percent annual growth, the new contributions will grow to:

$$3,000 \times 180.94 = \$542,820$$

At this stage, you know how to calculate the future value of your current RRSP assets as well as how to project how much the contributions you make for the rest of your working life will be worth at retirement. Now let's put the two together to find the total projected value of your RRSPs.

To do this, add the final value of your planned future RRSP contributions to the estimated final value of the assets already in your plan. For the 6 percent illustrations I have used, assuming retirement in 30 years, the total final value in today's dollars will be:

$$143,500 + \$251,400 = \$394,900$$

With an average annual return of 8 percent, the end value of your RRSPs increases to:

$$251,500 + \$367,050 = \$618,550$$

At an annual average return of 10 percent, you'll end up with:

$$436,250 + \$542,820 = \$979,070$$

You can use the inflation table in Chapter 7 to convert your numbers into future dollars.

The amount of annual income your plan will generate will depend on how you withdraw the money. Let's assume that you move the assets into a registered retirement income fund (RRIF) when you retire at age 65 and decide to withdraw the minimum amount required by the government each year. You'll find more details about RRIFs in Chapter 19, but for now we'll assume you start receiving your payments in the year in which you turn 66. The formula for calculating the minimum amount you must withdraw that year is:

$$\frac{\text{Value of RRIF on January 1}}{90 - \text{Your age on January 1}}$$

(*Note:* This formula only applies until age 71, after which a specific withdrawal percentage is used.)

Unless your 66th birthday is on January first, your age at the start of the year will be 65. So your first year minimum withdrawal in today's dollars, using the total RRSP value based on a 6 percent annual average growth rate, would be:

$$\frac{\$394,900}{90 - 65} = \frac{\$394,900}{25} = \$15,796$$

Unless your investments take a big drop in value, this amount should increase each year, because the government requires you to withdraw a higher percentage of the plan as you age.

Using an 8 percent annual growth rate, the first year's income from the RRIF will be:

$$\frac{\$618,550}{90 - 65} = \frac{\$618,550}{25} = \$24,742$$

If your investments grew at the rate of 10 percent a year, your first year RRIF income would be:

$$\frac{\$979,070}{90 - 65} = \frac{\$979,070}{25} = \$39,162.80$$

Non-Registered Investments

You should supplement your retirement income with additional revenue from a non-registered investment portfolio. However, you should only start building such a portfolio after you have maximized your RRSP and pension plan contributions.

A non-registered portfolio can include any type of security or asset—stocks, bonds, mutual funds, real estate, income trusts, you name it.

However, if you want the portfolio to provide some income, you should choose your assets with care. An original Picasso may appreciate in value and look great on your wall, but it won't spin off any monthly cash flow.

The first step in estimating how large a non-registered portfolio you may have at retirement is to work through the net worth calculation, which you'll find on the **www.buildingwealth.ca** website. The key figure will be the total of your non-registered liquid assets. The future growth in the value of these assets will depend on a variety of factors, one of which will be taxes. Unlike your RRSPs, you will be taxed on the growth of your non-registered portfolio. But the rate of tax will vary, depending on whether the growth is achieved through compound interest, dividends, capital gains, return of capital, or rents. Also, you will pay no tax on capital gains until you actually sell the asset. So a stock or equity mutual fund could increase in value over many years with no capital gains taxes being assessed.

Since we are only preparing estimates at this point, let's assume that, with all factors taken into account, your non-registered portfolio is invested mainly in growth securities like equity funds, and that you achieve an average annual after-tax rate of return of 6 percent. You can refer back to the 6 percent column in the "How Your Present RRSP Will Grow" table to estimate what the value of your present non-registered portfolio will be when you retire.

So if, for example, your current non-registered liquid assets are $10,000 and there are 30 years to retirement, you multiply that amount by a factor of 5.74.

$$\$10,000 \times 5.74 = \$57,400$$

That represents the value of your non-registered portfolio at that time. However, remember that there may be taxes still to be paid on any portion of that amount that consists of unrealized capital gains.

Suppose you decide to put aside another $1,000 a year for your non-registered portfolio—money that you are investing after making your full RRSP contribution. You can use the 6 percent column from the table Value of Future RRSP Contributions to see approximately how much that will be worth when you stop work. In this case, the factor is 83.80.

$$\$1,000 \times 83.80 = \$83,800$$

So, to carry this illustration to conclusion, the value of your non-registered portfolio at retirement would be:

$$\$57,400 + \$83,800 = \$141,200$$

How much will that add to your retirement income? Let's say you decide to invest the proceeds in government bonds with a yield of 5 percent (there are better choices, but we'll keep things simple for now). You liquidate the portfolio for this purpose. Taxes incurred as a result total 15 percent of the assets, or $21,180, leaving you with $120,020 to invest in the bonds. Your annual income from this source would be:

$$\$120,020 \times 5\% = \$6,001$$

Note: If you plan to sell your home at retirement and move to a less expensive place, add your anticipated profit to your non-registered portfolio total. This money will be received tax free.

Other Income

If you expect to receive retirement income from other sources (e.g., a share in a business, consulting work, second career, reverse mortgage, etc.), that should be taken into account as well. Usually, the likelihood of revenue from such sources does not become apparent until you are approaching retirement age.

Adding It Up

You now have enough information to do a preliminary retirement income estimate. Complete the following Retirement Income Projection, using the results you have obtained to this point.

For the tax calculation, refer to your latest tax return plus that of your spouse/partner if you have one. Divide the tax payable by the total income to determine your effective rate of tax. Admittedly, this is a very rough estimate since it is impossible to know what the tax brackets will look like in 20 or 30 years. However, taxes as a percentage of your total income should decline after retirement, at least in theory. So using your current effective tax rate should produce a conservative result—your actual taxes due will likely be less than you will calculate here.

The end result may show that your projected income will be less than your projected expenses. Not to worry. One of the purposes of this book is to show you how to bridge the gap. Once you see how large that gap is, you'll have a much better idea of how much work still has to be done.

RETIREMENT INCOME PROJECTION

CPP/QPP annual payments (current figures)	_____	(1)
Old Age Security payments (current figures)	_____	(2)
Pension income	_____	(3)
RRIF income	_____	(4)
Non-registered income	_____	(5)
Other income	_____	(6)
Total before taxes (lines 1 to 6)	_____	(7)
Effective tax rate	_____	(8)
Taxes (line 7 x line 8)	_____	(9)
After-tax income (line 7 – line 9)	_____	(10)
Subtract estimated spending (from Chapter 7)	_____	(11)
Projected surplus (shortfall) (line 10 – line 11)	_____	(12)

Line 12 gives you a snapshot of where your retirement program stands at this moment in time. Obviously, it will change as the years pass but now you at least have a starting point. You know approximately how much it is going to cost in current dollars to maintain the lifestyle you have chosen for retirement and you have matched those expenses against your projected income. If you wish to do inflation-adjusted projections, the table in Chapter 6 allows you to do so.

You can never get to a destination unless you know where you're starting from. You now have that knowledge, so let's move forward.

9

Building an Investment Portfolio

This may be the single most important chapter in this book. If you read it carefully and follow the advice it contains, your chances of retiring in comfort will be improved ten times over. I say this because, to put it bluntly, most people don't have a clue about how to create an investment portfolio. They fumble and flounder and make mistakes galore that end up costing thousands of dollars and many lost years of investment growth.

It doesn't have to be that way. You don't need to be a financial genius to build a winning portfolio. What you do need is some knowledge and a lot of self-discipline. If you are not willing to take the time to learn the basics and to implement them, for heaven's sake do yourself a huge favour and go find a competent professional advisor to help you. Don't try to wing it. The odds are almost 100 percent against you.

The fundamental rules of portfolio building apply for both registered plans (e.g., RRSPs) and non-registered plans. However, there are a few nuances, which we will get to later.

Asset Allocation Is the Foundation

Every portfolio needs a foundation, and it all starts with asset allocation. This is the process whereby you decide how the securities are going to be distributed. Only when that is clearly established should you proceed to the next step of selecting specific securities. Nine times out of 10 (or maybe 99 times out of 100), people reverse the order. That's where the trouble begins.

Asset allocation is the single most important decision you can make in terms of structuring a portfolio. If you get it right the first time, the chances are that your investments will do just fine. There are four stages in the asset allocation process: asset class selection, geographic distribution, style diversification, and risk management. Let's consider each separately.

Asset Class Selection

Selecting assets by class is the most basic part of the process. Even if you never move on to the other three stages, you should at least implement an asset class selection before you begin to buy securities. There are four basic types of assets in every investment portfolio. They are:

- *Cash.* This consists of currency and highly liquid cash-equivalent securities such as Treasury bills, money market funds, and Canada Savings Bonds. In fact, any asset that can quickly be converted to cash for its full face value qualifies.
- *Fixed income.* These securities pay a specified (fixed) rate of return and have a maturity date, at which time your principal is returned. If they are sold or cashed in before that date, the result may be a loss or a penalty to the investor. Bonds, mortgages, fixed-rate preferred shares, and GICs fall into this asset class.
- *Variable income.* In years past, this was not considered to be a separate asset class, but times and markets change. A variable-income security offers cash flow on a predictable basis (usually monthly or quarterly) but the amount of the payment is not guaranteed and may vary considerably. These securities may or may not have a maturity date. Examples include floating-rate preferred shares and income trusts.

- *Growth*. Assets in the growth category add value mainly through capital gains. Stocks and equity mutual funds are the most common examples.

Now that you know the four asset classes, what you have to do is decide how much of each you want to hold in your portfolio. There are several factors to consider, including your age, your time horizon, your tax situation (if it is a non-registered portfolio), the economic climate, and your risk tolerance.

Generally, the higher the percentage of cash and fixed-income securities in your portfolio, the less risky it will be. However, the trade-off is that your profit potential will be reduced as well. The more variable-income and growth securities you have, the greater the chance that you will achieve above-average returns. But you will also expose yourself to greater losses during periods when the stock market is in decline or when interest rates are moving sharply higher. This is what makes the decision difficult. You have to weigh these considerations and decide where you want to place your portfolio on the scale. If you choose to be ultra-conservative, you need to reconcile yourself to the fact that it will probably take quite a bit longer to build a retirement portfolio with the value you require. If you decide in favour of growth, you must be ready to accept the ups and downs of volatile stock and income trusts markets.

I recommend that you start from the position that you will include all four asset classes in your portfolio. I have heard ultra-aggressive investors say: "To heck with that. Stocks are where the action is and I'm going to put all my money there." Interestingly, I have never heard anyone use that argument during a severe market slump, only when a bull market is in full flight, as it was in the late 1990s. When stocks drop dramatically, as they did in 2000–2002, the brave suddenly turn timid.

The real danger in choosing an all-growth portfolio at the outset is psychological. Suppose you had made a decision in late 1999 to load up with high-flying technology stocks or mutual funds? As we saw in Chapter 2, by the time the bear market came to an end in October 2002, the Nasdaq Composite Index had plunged 88 percent from its high point. There is not an investor in the world who could deal with that without a great deal of psychological trauma. Not only will it take a long time to recover from such a heavy loss, but you may well have been left with mental scars that will never heal. I once had a friend who, having lost heavily in the stock market collapse of the 1970s, never invested again in equities for the rest of his life. That's not a healthy, or a wise, approach.

So use all the asset classes. No zeros for any of the four. Rather, it's a matter of deciding how the distribution will be made.

Cash is normally allocated the smallest percentage in an investment portfolio because of the low return it generates. But there are two reasons for holding some. First, cash is the safest asset you can possess in difficult times. Second, a cash reserve allows you to take advantage of opportunities in the stock and bond markets that may appear. If you don't have any cash, you'll be forced to sell something else, which you may not want to do at that moment. The minimum cash holding in your portfolio should be 5 percent. The maximum should be 25 percent, and that would only be reached under very unusual circumstances, for example during a period when short-term interest rates are high and the stock and bond markets are slumping. These conditions do occur from time to time, the early 1990s being the most recent.

The percentage of fixed-income assets will be governed by two main considerations: your risk tolerance level and the outlook for interest rates. Under normal conditions, fixed-income securities carry much less risk than growth securities. So a portfolio that is weighted toward bonds and GICs will be less volatile than one that holds only a small percentage of such assets. In fact, certain types of fixed-income securities, particularly bonds, have the potential to generate above-average returns during periods when interest rates are falling so this can be another factor in your allocation decision. The range of fixed-income securities in a portfolio can vary from as low as 20 percent to as high as 50 percent, depending on the circumstances. Generally, an allocation in the 25 percent range is adequate.

Variable-income securities are trickier. These are most often used to generate cash flow after retirement but there is a place for them in a younger person's portfolio as well. The weighting should gradually increase as you grow older.

Growth securities should receive the largest allocation share when you're young, gradually diminishing as you approach retirement. The minimum allocation should be 25 percent, and you would be at that level only during full-blown bear markets or if you are approaching, or past, retirement. The maximum weighting for growth securities is 70 percent.

The following table shows model weightings for asset allocation based on age.

ASSET ALLOCATION BY AGE					
	20–25	26–49	50–59	60–65	66+
Cash	5%	5%	5%	5%	10%
Fixed income	30%	20%	30%	40%	40%
Variable income	10%	10%	15%	20%	25%
Growth	55%	65%	50%	35%	25%

For the 20 to 25 age group, you'll see that the income recommendation in the table is higher than for the 26 to 49 period, while the growth component is smaller. I believe younger people who are just starting out should take a balanced approach to investing until they have learned more about how securities perform and better understand the ins and outs of portfolio management. There is a danger—and I have seen it happen—that young people may tend to be somewhat aggressive with their initial investments. It's a risk I would advise you to avoid.

As a person becomes more comfortable with investing—and the ages shown here are only a broad guideline—the percentage of higher-risk variable income and growth securities in the plan can be increased. Someone in their late 20s, 30s, and even their 40s can take a long-term view of the markets and not be overly concerned by temporary setbacks. However, I recommend that a portion of all portfolios be kept in fixed-income securities, both to mitigate risk and to take advantage of those occasions when bonds outperform stocks.

As you approach your retirement years, you should gradually reduce the risk in your portfolio since the time left to ride out any severe stock market setback is running short. Build your cash and income components, which will be needed when the time comes to convert your savings to a revenue stream. However, I suggest you always retain a portion of your portfolio in growth securities as a protection against even modest rates of inflation. You don't want to outlive your money!

Geographic Distribution

Once you have decided on your initial asset distribution (which may change over time), the next step is to determine your geographic asset mix. There are two important factors to keep in mind in doing this: the overall risk/reward balance of your investment portfolio and the future outlook for the Canadian dollar.

There is a natural tendency to favour Canadian securities because they are familiar. However, it is easy to overdo this, to your detriment. Many studies have been conducted of what is known as the *efficient frontier*. This is a portfolio analysis technique that seeks to identify the point on a graph at which the blended domestic and foreign content attains maximum reward potential consistent with minimal risk. Although the numbers vary, the results almost always suggest that non-Canadian securities should comprise between 40 and 60 percent of your total mix. If that seems high, remember that Canada represents only 2 to 3 percent of the world's equity markets. We are a bit player on the international stage and we have relatively few multinational companies. Most of what we consider to be corporate giants, like the big banks, are pipsqueaks when measured against foreign competitors in the same field. As well, there are entire industries that are not represented in the Canadian stock market. We have no indigenous auto manufacturer, no retailer of Wal-Mart or Home Depot stature, no entertainment mega-company (Alliance Atlantis isn't in the same league as Disney or Time Warner), no software giant like Microsoft, no world-class pharmaceutical company like Pfizer, and on and on. If you want to participate in the growth of any of these businesses, you have to look beyond our borders.

You must also give some thought to the future course of the Canadian dollar. This does not mean you should involve yourself in currency speculation; that's a high-stakes poker game that can result in huge losses. But you need to think about whether your investment portfolio should have some protection against fluctuations in the value of the loonie, which has a record of high volatility. The following table, based on data obtained from the Bank of Canada website, shows the value of a U.S. dollar in Canadian dollar terms on December 31 of each year from 1995 to 2004.

CANADIAN DOLLARS NEEDED TO BUY ONE U.S. DOLLAR	
Year (Dec. 31)	U.S. $ Value in Canadian Currency
1995	1.3652
1996	1.3696
1997	1.4291
1998	1.5305
1999	1.4433
2000	1.5002
2001	1.5926
2002	1.5796
2003	1.2924
2004	1.2036

Source: Bank of Canada website: www.bankofcanada.com/en/rates/exchform.html; accessed October 19, 2005.

As you can see, between 1995 and 2001, the Canadian dollar was devalued by 16.7 percent against the U.S. greenback. It was a stealthy devaluation that was encouraged by the government of the day as being good for Canadian manufacturers and exporters, who were able to sell their products at a much more competitive price in international markets, particularly in the U.S., our largest trading partner by far. But the devaluation was bad news for consumers, who paid higher prices for imported goods, for travellers, for investors, and for retirees who hoped to spend some of their winters in the Sunbelt.

Then, in 2003, the loonie suddenly reversed course. In two years, it not only regained all the ground it had lost but had moved to valuations not seen since the early 1990s. The conventional thinking as this book is written is that the Canadian dollar will remain strong for the foreseeable future, but we cannot discount the possibility of a downward turn in the future, such as the one we saw in the 1990s. This suggests that wise investors should hedge their currency bets in structuring their portfolios through the process of geographic allocation. There are four main areas of the globe to consider.

- *Canada.* The majority of your securities should be in your home country and your home currency.
- *United States.* The number one economic power in the world should be strongly represented in all portfolios.
- *Europe.* The euro has been very strong in recent years so Europe should be included in your mix.
- *Pacific Rim.* China is rapidly emerging as one of the world's leading manufacturing countries while India is a growing hotbed for technology. Japan continues to be a potent economic force. The growth potential in this part of the world is huge, but the risks are also high.

Your first decision is what percentage of your assets to hold in Canada and how much will go to the rest of the world. That will depend on several factors, but as a general rule I recommend that you hold at least 40 percent and a maximum of 70 percent of your assets in Canadian securities. That means your foreign holdings will range from 30 percent to 60 percent of the total.

Next it's a matter of deciding how to distribute those foreign assets. Let's consider the options.

United States. The lion's share of your foreign content should be placed in the U.S. There are two reasons for this: the massive weight of the U.S. economy and currency hedging considerations. Most of us don't know or care how the loonie performs against the euro or the yen but we do know and care deeply about what happens vis-à-vis the U.S. dollar.

You can invest in the U.S. in many ways. Stocks and mutual funds are the most obvious but you can also buy a range of debt securities (bonds, GICs, etc.) denominated in U.S. dollars, or even just open a U.S. dollar account at your local bank. Your selection of U.S. securities should be guided by your basic asset distribution.

I recommend that at least 50 percent of your foreign assets be placed in the U.S., to a maximum of 70 percent. A point midway between those two numbers is the ideal figure.

Europe. The long-term economic prospects for a united Europe are bright. There have been bumps on the road to economic and monetary union and there will continue to be, but there is no doubt that European businesses as a whole are much stronger today than they were a decade ago. There are now many world-class companies based in Europe that should be represented in your portfolio.

The easiest way to invest in Europe is through equity mutual funds that specialize in that part of the world and foreign bond funds with strong euro positions. European holdings should represent between 15 and 25 percent of your total foreign content.

Pacific Rim. Because of the volatility inherent in this part of the world, committing a large portion of a portfolio to the region will add significant risk, but it will also increase growth potential, especially over the long term. Pacific Rim or Far East equity funds can be used. The recommended range for this area is 15 to 25 percent of the total foreign weighting.

If you prefer, you can obtain exposure to Europe and the Pacific Rim through international equity funds that do not invest in North America. These may also include stocks from some emerging markets in other areas, such as Mexico, Brazil, Chile, and South Africa.

Here is a summary of the overall recommendations for geographic distribution.

OVERALL GEOGRAPHIC DISTRIBUTION		
Region	Range	Ideal
Canada	40%–70%	50%
U.S.	15%–42%	25%
Europe	6%–18%	15%
Pacific Rim	6%–18%	10%

Style Diversification

Even if you stopped your asset allocation process at this point, you would be light-years ahead of most investors, including many experienced ones.

But if you want to fine-tune your plan even more, the next step in the process is to consider style diversification.

There are several distinctive styles used by professional money managers to select securities. For our purposes, let's keep things simple and focus on the two most basic ones.

Value. The value approach looks for securities that are relatively cheap by using such traditional measures as price-to-book value and price/earnings ratio. This is a tried-and-true formula for achieving long-term success, and many of the world's greatest investors, like Warren Buffett and Sir John Templeton, use these techniques. But its effectiveness is cyclical. Value investors tend to underperform in red-hot markets such as those of the late 1990s. They excel in protecting capital when markets are weak, such as in the bear market of 2000–2002. Some Canadian value managers like Irwin Michael, Francis Chou, Peter Cundill, and Kim Shannon actually made money for their clients during those difficult years.

Growth. In this case the emphasis is on finding stocks of companies that have the potential to grow more rapidly than their competitors. Strong increases in revenue and market share assume greater importance in the valuation process than price/earnings ratios.

You should ensure that both these basic management styles are well represented in the variable income and equity sections of your portfolio. You can achieve this through individual securities selection; however, that will require a fair amount of analysis on your part or on the part of your financial advisor. It may be simpler to select equity and variable-income mutual funds that adopt each approach.

To reduce the problem to its most basic, let's assume that the entire Canadian equity portion of your portfolio is to be held in just two mutual funds. To implement style diversification in this situation, you want to be sure that one fund is managed according to firm value principles, while the other is run on a growth-oriented basis.

Risk Management

The final piece in the asset allocation puzzle is risk management. This involves a series of decisions that will determine the overall risk/return profile of your portfolio. Many purists will argue that risk management is not a function of asset allocation at all, but I include it here because I believe it is a basic part of the foundation we are building in this section.

All securities have their own risk/return profile, even those within the same asset class. For example, a U.S. dollar money market fund has to be considered as being higher risk than a Canadian dollar money market fund because it introduces an additional variable: currency fluctuation. Of course, that also means that the reward potential of the U.S. dollar fund is higher since the assets in it will be worth more if the loonie declines.

Risk management involves allocating your assets in accordance with your safety versus profits priorities. You already went partway down this path when you decided on your initial asset class selection. Now you're fine-tuning it.

It is very difficult to make generalizations about the risk/reward profile of broad asset categories, because there will be many shadings and nuances within each—even some total exceptions to the rule. But this table will give you a general idea. The higher the number of stars in each column (out of five), the higher the asset ranks on the scale. So an asset that receives ***** for risk and * for return is very safe but offers low profit potential.

RISK/RETURN SCALE

Asset Type	Risk	Reward
Canada Savings/Premium Bonds	*****	*
Canadian money market funds, T-bills	*****	*
US$ money market funds	****	**
GICs	*****	**
Mortgage funds	****	*
Mortgage-backed securities	*****	*
Short-term bonds, short-term bond funds	****	**
Mid-term bonds, regular bond funds	***	***
Long-term bonds, long-term bond funds	**	****
Foreign bonds, foreign bond funds	**	***
Large-cap Canadian stocks, large-cap equity funds	***	****
Small-cap Canadian stocks, small-cap equity funds	**	*****

Asset Type	Risk	Reward
Diversified Canadian equity funds	***	****
Large-cap U.S. stocks	***	****
Small-cap U.S. stocks, small-cap equity funds	**	*****
Diversified U.S. equity funds	***	****
International equity funds	***	***
Sector equity funds	*	*****
Index funds	***	***
Balanced funds	***	***
Income trusts and funds	**	****

Remember, there will be wide variations within categories. For example, a sector equity fund that focuses on the financial services industry will normally be less risky but will offer lower profit potential than one that specializes in high tech. Similarly, a conservatively managed value equity fund will offer lower reward potential but the safety factor will be much higher than for an aggressively managed growth fund. So use this table for purposes of general guidelines only.

To apply this system to the asset allocation plan you have already worked out, simply take each separate element and use a risk management overlay. For example, suppose that the process so far has resulted in a portfolio foundation that looks like this table.

SAMPLE PORTFOLIO (BASIC)

Asset Class	Allocation	Geographic Distribution	Style
Cash	5%	50% Can., 50% U.S.	N/A
Fixed income	30%	60% Can., 40% U.S. & Int.	N/A
Variable income	15%	80% Can., 20% U.S.	N/A
Growth	50%	50% Can., 30% U.S., 20% Int.	50% Value, 50% Growth

You can now fine-tune the various asset classes on the basis of the risk/return profile you want to achieve. Let's say your goal is for a portfolio with decent profit potential but with limited risk. Here's where you might end up.

SAMPLE PORTFOLIO (DETAILED)	
Type of Security	Allocation
Canadian money market funds	2.5%
U.S. money market funds	2.5%
Short-term bonds	7.0%
Mid-term bonds	8.0%
Long-term bonds	3.0%
Foreign bond funds	12.0%
Income trusts	8.0%
Canadian preferred shares	4.0%
U.S. REITs	3.0%
Diversified Canadian equity funds (value)	12.5%
Diversified Canadian equity funds (growth)	12.5%
Diversified U.S. equity funds (value)	7.5%
Diversified U.S. equity funds (growth)	4.5%
Small-cap U.S. equity funds (growth)	3.0%
Diversified international equity funds (value)	5.0%
Diversified international equity funds (growth)	5.0%

For a more aggressive portfolio, you could add some sector funds, change the proportion of growth to value funds, add more long-term bonds, add some Canadian small-cap stocks or funds, etc.

Registered versus Non-Registered

As mentioned at the start of this chapter, there are some factors that need to be taken into account in your portfolio structure depending on whether it is a registered or a non-registered account.

Taxes

Registered accounts, such as RRSPs, are tax-sheltered. This means that all income or capital gains earned within the plan are not subject to tax. You won't be hit by the government until you withdraw money from the plan and then everything will be taxed as ordinary income, regardless of how it was originally received. Therefore, you do not need to take taxes into account when creating a registered plan.

A non-tax-sheltered account is another matter. Here you need to give careful thought to the tax treatment of the various securities that you buy. Remember that interest income is taxed at your top marginal rate, so if possible you should hold interest-bearing securities in a registered plan. Tax-friendly securities to consider for a non-registered account include stocks, equity funds, preferred shares, real estate investment trusts (REITs), and some income trusts and funds.

If you have both taxable and registered accounts, combine the two for asset allocation purposes with a view to achieving maximum tax efficiency. It is not a good idea to overlay the same asset mix on each account separately because you'll end up with a lot of interest-bearing securities that will be exposed to a high rate of tax.

Risk

Think of your registered portfolio as a personal pension plan, which it is in actual fact. Now think about how professional money managers handle pension accounts. They are very conservative, and with good reason. These men and women have been entrusted with the retirement savings of all the contributors to the plan, who are depending on them to ensure that the money will be there when it comes time to draw on it. So the last thing they can afford to do is to take big risks that might result in heavy losses.

Your registered portfolio should be handled the same way. Risk should be kept to a minimum and your securities should be chosen accordingly. Over the years, I have seen a tendency in people to throw caution to the winds in their RRSP accounts and suffer the consequences for their recklessness. I believe there are two reasons for this. One is the fact that retirement seems a long way off, especially to anyone under 40. As a result, the assets in an RRSP take on a sort of Monopoly money aura. So taking some chances doesn't seem like a big deal. If things don't work out there will be no impact on the person's lifestyle, so why not roll the dice?

The second factor is greed. A conservative portfolio will not grow as quickly as a more aggressive one when markets are booming. But the flip side of that coin is the important one for an RRSP—a conservative portfolio will protect your capital during periods when stock markets are in decline.

If you want to take more risk in the hopes of increasing your returns, do so in a non-registered account. At least if you suffer losses there you can claim them on your income tax. In a registered account, not only is the money gone but you can't at least partially offset the loss with tax relief.

Geography

If you have two accounts, increase the Canadian weighting in your registered plan and use the non-registered portfolio to obtain more international exposure. The removal of the foreign content rule in the 2005 budget gives you carte blanche to add all the U.S. and foreign securities you want to an RRSP, but it's not always the best idea.

The reason is currency risk. Unless you are planning to move abroad permanently when you stop work, the majority of your expenses will be in Canadian dollars. You want to protect the purchasing power of those dollars as best you can, which means minimizing the currency risk in your registered plan. There are ways to achieve that and still add foreign securities to the RRSP; for example, the two RBC O'Shaughnessy U.S. funds are hedged back into the loonie, thereby ensuring that any movements up or down in the exchange rate are cushioned.

Of course, if you will be spending part or all of your retirement years in another area of the world, you should adjust your registered plan accordingly. I have received emails from readers who have retired to places like France. If that's part of your future, increase the percentage of European equities and bonds in your plan to protect the value of the euros you will one day need. If the U.S. Sunbelt beckons, add more American securities. In short, your personal geographic distribution should be influenced by your ultimate retirement plans.

Only when you have made all these decisions should you begin the process of selecting specific securities. We'll discuss how to assess the choices in later chapters.

10

RRSPs for Everyone?

For decades, it was an article of faith that everyone—everyone!—should have a registered retirement savings plan (RRSP). I agreed. I have long said that an RRSP is one of the key elements in a comprehensive retirement savings program, without qualification.

Well, now it appears that some qualification is in order following the 2003 publication of a report from the C.D. Howe Institute that raised serious questions about the suitability of RRSPs for lower-income people under existing conditions. The background paper is titled "New Poverty Traps: Means-Testing and Modest-Income Seniors." The author, Richard Shillington, holds a doctoral degree in statistics and has been carrying out research into health, social, and economic policies for 30 years. So his credentials are of the highest order. His analysis raises serious issues relating to how lower-income seniors who have saved for their retirement are penalized by the way in which government support programs are administered.

Dr. Shillington did not mince words, charging that millions of people who are at or approaching retirement age "are victims of a fraud, however unintentional." These people "have fallen for the bad advice coming from governments and the financial community: that everyone should save in an RRSP," he wrote. "The primary beneficiary of this saving will be the federal and provincial governments because most of the income from it will be confiscated by income-tested programs and income taxes. To the extent that these households have been misled, they have been defrauded."

The report makes a clear distinction between the value of RRSP saving for higher-income Canadians, who will ultimately benefit from their plans, and for lower-income people, who will not. His message was that all those with less than $100,000 in retirement assets are "futile savers." "They are likely to be GIS (Guaranteed Income Supplement) recipients, and much, if not all, of the proceeds of their savings will be lost to taxes and the clawback of income-tested benefits," he writes. GIS benefits are reduced by 50 cents for every $1 in income received. RRSP or RRIF withdrawals are considered as income for this purpose.

> After the GIS clawback and income taxes, many of these individuals receive at most 29 percent of their retirement funds. Overall, lower-income Canadians who use RRSPs receive some tax saving when they make their deductible contributions, but it is totally inadequate compensation for the clawbacks and the loss of income-tested benefits they face during retirement.... One weeps for those Canadians who follow the undifferentiated advice to save in RRSPs. They have scrimped to save modest amounts in RRSPs; only tax experts and the bureaucrats know that the effort will be of almost no value to them.

Dr. Shillington called for action on three levels to deal with the problem.

- Government policy-makers were urged to take a close look at this situation and to introduce policies to deal with it as quickly as possible. Specifically, he advocated the creation of tax-prepaid savings plans (TPSPs), similar to those in Britain and the U.S., which would meet the retirement savings needs of lower-income Canadians more effectively. He also suggested that the calculation of the age tax credit be adjusted for GIS recipients to reduce some of the tax burden they face.

  (Finance Minister Ralph Goodale did make reference to TPSPs in his 2003 and 2004 budget speeches, saying they would be studied.

But his 2005 budget made no reference to them and a spokesperson for the Department of Finance said that after meeting with experts it had been decided to put the idea on the back burner and simply raise RRSP contribution limits. Of course, that did absolutely nothing for lower-income people!)

- The financial community was asked to take a much more active role in guiding people toward retirement savings plans that are suited to their income and needs. Dr. Shillington did not condemn RRSPs as such, but he expressed the view that financial advisors and institutions have a responsibility to make it very clear who should use them, and who should not. I have seen no evidence that this is happening to any great extent.

- The report urged the media to take a stronger voice in explaining the reality of retirement savings programs to the general public so that people can make better-informed decisions.

I first wrote about the Shillington Report in the August 2003 issue of *50Plus* magazine. The column prompted a flurry of letters from readers, many of them quite irate. One even went so far as to accuse me of advocating that retirees should "abdicate their social responsibility in order to steal from their neighbours" by encouraging people to live off government handouts rather than being self-supporting.

Wrote another: "Excuse me if I sound like Chicken Little but ever since we retired last year we seem to be finding that so many of the benefits we thought we would enjoy in retirement are either being taken away from us or are costing us money. The article by Gordon Pape was the final straw! For years we have been advised to put as much as possible into RRSPs. Now it turns out we are being punished for the tax deferrals we had during our working years. Is it any wonder that the sky seems to be falling on retired pensioners?"

The barrage of correspondence required me to write a follow-up column for the magazine, which began by stating what I would have thought would be obvious: I was *not* suggesting for a moment that Canadians shouldn't save for retirement. The point of Dr. Shillington's paper, and why I felt it was important to publicize it, was to criticize a system that he believes penalizes lower-income Canadians who *do* put money aside.

The main focus of the paper was on people who qualify to receive GIS. In the third quarter of 2005, that meant anyone whose annual income, not including Old Age Security (OAS), did not exceed $13,608. Dr. Shillington estimated at the time the paper was written that about 37 percent of seniors were in this group. These people are living close to or below the poverty line, and the fact the percentage is so high is shocking. But then the government penalizes them for trying to improve their situation by saving during their working years through a clawback mechanism that taxes away half of their benefit for every pension cheque, RRSP withdrawal, or RRIF payment they receive, from the very first dollar!

What makes matters even worse is that Canada Pension Plan benefits get exactly the same treatment as income from pension plans and RRSPs. So it is not only low-income RRSP savers who are affected by this structure. Your GIS payments will be reduced even if you did nothing more than make mandatory contributions to the CPP!

For example, someone who has no income other than OAS received a maximum of $566.87 a month from the GIS in the third quarter of 2005. Now let's suppose that same person qualified for a Canada Pension Plan retirement benefit of $400 a month ($4,800 a year). Using first-quarter 2005 Social Development Canada tables, we find that the monthly GIS payment is reduced by $200, to $366.87. Half your GIS benefit disappears because you get CPP! Now let's suppose that same person receives another $200 a month ($2,400 a year) from RRSP savings. The GIS monthly payment will drop to $266.87. In effect, the value of your RRSP income has been cut in half!

Clearly, something is amiss here. We need a system that does more to encourage people at the lower end of the income scale to prepare financially for retirement, not one that socks them in the wallet for doing so. The ultimate goal should be to create a means to give lower-income people a chance at a better retirement lifestyle and to lessen their dependence on government. Dr. Shillington puts it this way: "Only when more Canadians are aware of the perverse treatment of lower-income Canadians' savings will Ottawa be forced to develop savings mechanisms that reward, rather than punish, those savings efforts."

So until Ottawa deals with this issue, and at the time of writing there is no sign that it is anywhere on their radar screen, we have to conclude that RRSPs are *not* for everyone. By the same token, however, neither is the Canada Pension Plan but we aren't given the choice of opting out of it. (See Appendix II for more on this subject.)

If you believe that your income after retirement will be below the poverty line and that you will have to depend on the GIS to survive, then you should not be putting money into an RRSP. If you have already done so and are coming up to retirement (or are already there) with only a small amount saved, you'd be wise to consider collapsing the plan and taking a one-time tax hit. Put the after-tax proceeds into a savings account or money market fund and draw out money as needed. Those withdrawals are not income for purposes of tax or government benefits—you're simply spending some of your own capital and that does not figure into the GIS calculation.

If you're still working and have some extra income that would normally go into an RRSP, use it to pay down your mortgage if you are a home-owner. A mortgage-free home will reduce your expenses in retirement by a considerable amount.

But remember, this advice applies only to people at the lower end of the income scale. In reality, I believe that virtually no one who reads this book is thinking in those terms. After all, who wants to plan for poverty? So now that I have laid out the details of the problem, let's move forward on the assumption that you expect your retirement income to be at a high enough level that the GIS won't be a consideration. That means RRSPs should be an important part of your agenda.

RRSP Challenges

Saying that an RRSP should be part of your retirement plan and actually making it so are two different things. Canadians for the most part are full of good intentions but when it comes to translating them into action, we often fall short.

There are four major obstacles that must be overcome to reach the stage at which you can truly say that you have a sound and growing RRSP. Here they are.

Obstacle #1: Making the Contribution

If you don't put money into your plan, everything else becomes academic. The majority of Canadians don't bother. According to Statistics Canada, 5.95 million people made contributions for the 2003 tax year, less than half of those with contribution room available. The total number of contributors was actually down slightly from the previous year, hardly an encouraging trend. Moreover, most of them did not contribute the maximum allowable amount. StatsCan says that only 9 percent of available RRSP contribution room was actually used.

What's the problem? Actually, there are several, including lack of available cash as the post-Christmas credit card bills roll in; the desire to spend the money elsewhere, perhaps on a winter vacation in the south; or a "mañana" mentality—we'll do it next year. That kind of thinking can cost you tens of thousands of dollars by the time retirement comes around.

Solutions. The short-term way to deal with a cash shortage is to take out an RRSP loan. All the banks promote them and the terms are very advantageous. Interest rates are often at prime or even below. Your payoff is immediate—an Ontario resident with taxable income of $50,000 in 2004 received almost one-third of the contribution back in the form of a refund (31.15 percent to be exact). Someone in the highest bracket (taxable income of $113,805 and up) got a refund of 46.41 percent. Use the refund to reduce the loan principal and pay off the balance within a year. Do not make the mistake of stretching the loan repayment beyond that. I know of people who have gotten into deep financial do-do that way.

The long-term solution is to set up an automatic contribution program at your financial institution. Estimate how much you want to contribute to your plan for the current tax year and have one-twelfth of that amount deducted monthly. By this time next year, the money will already be in the RRSP and you won't have to worry about it.

Obstacle #2: Finding the Right Balance

Many people have RRSP portfolios that make no sense at all. They have allowed their plans to grow like Topsy over the years, investing each new contribution in whatever type of security that seemed like a good idea at the time. When I used to give financial seminars, I would frequently ask audiences how many of them knew the asset mix in their RRSP. Invariably, only a few hands went up.

As we saw in the previous chapter, all investment portfolios need to be carefully structured. This is especially true in RRSPs, where your twin goals are to protect the capital base while allowing for modest growth. I stress the word "modest"—many people have a tendency to overreach within their plans, taking on far more risk than is appropriate. I am especially concerned when I see younger people doing this. They are the ones who are most likely to become discouraged if they experience big losses early on and to stop contributing as a result. More seasoned investors can handle the ups and downs better—as long as the downs aren't too severe.

Solutions. Before you make any investment decisions, review your RRSP portfolio and do at least a basic asset analysis—the percentage of cash, income, and growth securities in the plan. Young RRSP contributors and those within 10 years of retirement should take a more conservative approach. I suggest that no more than half their plans should be invested in growth securities; the rest should be in lower-risk alternatives. Yes, this may result in lower returns. But that's preferable to significant loss exposure at those critical life stages. Experienced investors with more than 10 years remaining to retirement can have up to 70 percent of their assets in growth securities. I would never advise going beyond that.

Obstacle #3: Finding Something in Which to Invest

There is never an "ideal" security. The stock market may be in turmoil. Interest rates may be too low. Income trusts may be too expensive. Bonds may be in a correction phase. If you allow all the negatives to get inside your head, you'll sit on your hands and never achieve anything.

This is not to say that you should blissfully ignore what is happening in the world. But don't be spooked by the naysayers. Remember, you have a long investment horizon—you and your RRSP will be together for many years. If the financial markets are in flux, stick with conservative securities like short-term government bonds for the time being. There is always something worth buying.

Solutions. Begin with the sectors you identify as being underweight when you do your portfolio analysis. The first priority should be to add assets in those classes to bring them up to appropriate levels. Be selective in your choices. Remember that you don't have to invest all the money at once. If there is nothing you find immediately attractive, hold the contribution in a money market fund within the RRSP and wait until a buying opportunity emerges.

Always err on the side of conservatism. Never lose sight of the fact that one of the main goals of RRSP investing is to preserve capital. If Canada Premium Bonds look like the best way to do that at a given point, go with them. The return may be low but it's better than zero or a minus sign.

Obstacle #4: Tempering Your Expectations

The roaring bull market of the 1990s was about the worst thing that could have happened to RRSP investors. It raised expectations to completely unrealistic heights and prompted an unprecedented level of risk taking in retirement plans that came back to bite people in the backside during the crash of 2000–2002.

Never, ever forget one of the most basic principles of investing: the higher the potential return, the greater the potential risk. If I sound like a broken record on this point, too bad. I have seen too many cases of people forgetting that rule, to their ultimate sorrow.

Solutions. Be realistic. Over the long term, a well-planned RRSP with minimal risk should be expected to return only 6 to 8 percent a year. If you expect more, you'll probably end up adding more risk to the plan than is appropriate. Save the speculation for your non-registered portfolio where you can at least claim a capital loss if things turn sour.

Rules of the Game

Before we move on to the nitty-gritty of setting up and managing an RRSP, let's review the rules of the game. You may think you already know all this, but they keep evolving—the 2005 federal budget, for example, contained some very important changes. So take a moment to scan through this section.

Eligibility. Everyone age 69 or less may contribute to an RRSP, as long as they have earned income. There is no minimum age for setting up an RRSP. Even a child may have a plan, provided he or she has earned income.

Contribution limits. The basic rule is that you can contribute up to 18 percent of last year's earned income. The maximum allowable contribution continues to rise, with the latest increases announced in 2005. The following table shows the revised scale. The Income Required column shows how much earned income you would need to have to reach the maximum allowable contribution under the 18 percent formula. After 2010, the maximum contribution will be indexed.

RRSP CONTRIBUTION LIMITS (AS PER 2005 FEDERAL BUDGET)

Tax Year	Maximum Contribution	Income Required
2005	$16,500	$ 91,667
2006	18,000	100,000
2007	19,000	105,556
2008	20,000	111,111
2009	21,000	116,667
2010	22,000	122,222

One point that leaps out in looking at the figures is that the changes announced in the 2005 budget will benefit only higher-income people. Middle-income Canadians received no retirement savings break at all, a deficiency that some government in the future needs to address.

Note: Members of registered pension plans and deferred profit-sharing plans have to deduct their pension adjustment (PA) from the amount they're allowed to contribute to an RRSP. Your employer will supply that number.

Deadline. The last day for contributions for the previous tax year is 60 days from January 1 of the next year. That usually makes the deadline March 1, except in the case of a leap year or when that date falls on a Sunday.

Carry-forwards. If you don't make your full contribution, you can carry forward any unused portion to a future date. The Canada Revenue Agency will track this for you and update your current RRSP status each year when you receive your notice of assessment.

Eligible investments. You can invest your RRSP money in almost anything you can think of, including guaranteed investment certificates (GICs), term deposits, Treasury bills, Canada Savings Bonds, savings certificates, most types of bonds, Canadian stocks listed on recognized exchanges, shares of foreign companies listed on recognized exchanges (within limits), over-the-counter stocks traded on Nasdaq and the Canadian Dealing Network (CDN), some limited partnership units, units in labour-sponsored venture capital funds, shares of small businesses, mutual funds, mortgages, including your own, call options, warrants and rights issued by companies listed on Canadian exchanges, bankers' acceptances, and Canadian cash. As a result of the 2005 federal budget, gold and silver bullion were added to the eligibles list. Major exclusions from RRSPs include foreign currency, real property, and collectibles.

Foreign property. The 2005 federal budget included a blockbuster announcement that surprised even the mutual fund industry, which had been lobbying for it for many years. The foreign content limit, which had been an integral part of RRSP planning ever since the concept was first introduced in the 1950s, was scrapped. This means you can now have as much of your RRSP invested in U.S. and overseas securities as you want. For how much is appropriate, see the previous chapter.

Number of plans. You can open as many separate RRSPs as you like, in any number of financial institutions. This allows maximum flexibility, but it can also create problems. Too many plans may be difficult to track. Also, they can be expensive, depending on what type of RRSPs you set up. So even though there's no official limit on the number of RRSPs you can have, use some common sense.

Claiming deductions. You must file an official receipt with your tax return to claim an RRSP deduction. If you've lost it, ask the financial institution to issue a duplicate.

Spousal plans. You may set up an RRSP for your spouse and contribute to it as long as he or she is within the RRSP age limit. The total contributions you make to your own plan plus the spousal plan may not exceed your personal limit. Common-law couples are also allowed to use spousal plans.

Transfers. You may transfer funds from one RRSP to another without penalty. Simply complete form T2033, which you can obtain from the Canada Revenue Agency or the financial institution to which you're transferring the money.

Withdrawals. Any withdrawals from an RRSP are taxable at your marginal rate, unless they are made under the Home Buyers' Plan or the Lifelong Learning Plan. You are allowed to withdraw part of the assets from a plan without having the whole plan deregistered. A withholding tax will apply for each withdrawal.

Creditor protection. Many people are concerned that the assets of their retirement plan can be seized by creditors if they run into financial difficulty. While there is no hard-and-fast guarantee this won't happen, case law seems to be evolving toward protecting RRSPs against this possibility in specific situations. For example, in 2004, an Ontario court ruled that if an RRSP has a designated beneficiary (not the estate), the assets of the plan cannot be seized by creditors from the estate of a deceased person. However, the ruling could be challenged on appeal and does not apply to other provinces. Also, it doesn't protect the plans of living people.

Laws, regulations, and judicial interpretations relating to the creditor protection issue are constantly evolving and there have been conflicting court rulings over the years, so take nothing for granted. If this is an important matter for you, seek legal advice.

Choose the Right Plan

The type of RRSP you choose can make a huge difference in the amount of money that will be available to you at retirement. Many people don't realize that an RRSP is not an investment in itself. They talk about "buying" an RRSP, when in fact all they are really doing is opening a shell that can be used to hold any type of qualified investment.

There are five basic types of RRSPs. They are:

- *Savings plans.* These are simply savings accounts dressed in RRSP garb to shelter the interest from taxes. They used to be quite common; today they're rare. The low interest rate environment that has prevailed for many years made such plans virtually obsolete. About the best you can say for them is that they're simple and protected by deposit insurance up to $100,000 (the limit was increased in the 2005 budget). But the returns will be very low unless interest rates move up sharply.

- *GIC plans.* This is the type of plan that you're likely to get if you walk into a financial institution, plunk your money on the counter, and ask to open an RRSP. Your money will be invested in a term deposit/guaranteed investment certificate for the period you select (usually one to five years) and automatically rolled over when it matures unless you give other instructions. Until interest rates really hit the skids after the recession of the early 1990s, most RRSPs were of this type. They're still popular, although not to the same degree. Various marketing techniques have been used to attempt to revitalize interest in these plans, such as linking GIC returns to stock market performance. However, these are simply gimmicks and should be ignored. If you are going to opt for GICs, stay with the basic type that guarantees a return and protects your capital.

- *Mutual fund plans.* These RRSPs invest your contributions in mutual funds of your choice. They can range from ultra-conservative money market and mortgage funds to higher-risk stock funds, or any mix thereof.

- *The Canada RSP.* Several years ago, the federal government decided it should more aggressively pursue some of the RRSP business that was flowing to the private sector. The result was the creation of a no-fee government RRSP, called The Canada RSP. The price is right but it is very restrictive: you can only hold Canada Savings Bonds and Canada Premium Bonds in this account.

- *Self-directed plans.* These RRSP plans allow you to invest in anything you want, as long as it's considered an "eligible investment." A self-directed plan can be as conservatively or aggressively managed as you wish; you're in full control. The rate of return will vary depending on what you put into your plan, as will the risk level.

So what's the right type of RRSP for you? I recommend starting with a mutual fund plan with a company you have confidence in. You can begin with a single Canadian balanced fund and build from there. As your RRSP grows and you gain more investing confidence, you can move to a self-directed plan.

The Carry-Forward

If you fail to make your full RRSP contribution in any given year, you don't lose the entitlement. It carries forward indefinitely, so as long as you have an RRSP you can always play catch-up. Your maximum allowable contribution will increase each year as the carry-forwards accumulate. The annual notice of assessment from the Canada Revenue Agency will show you exactly where you stand.

For example, suppose you were allowed to contribute $5,000 to an RRSP last year but only put $3,000 into the plan. You have a carry-forward credit of $2,000, which is added to your regular entitlement for the current year. You can use it now, or carry it forward to next year or beyond.

The carry-forward rule can be useful in certain situations. People who have difficulty scraping together the money for a full RRSP contribution will at least be able to make it up in later years, instead of losing their entitlement completely, as was the case before this reform was introduced in 1991.

But the carry-forward concept can be dangerous to your financial health if not managed properly. It could cost your RRSP many thousands of dollars if you allow it to. There are three basic problems to consider.

The first problem is psychological. When given an excuse to spend rather than save, people often grab it. The carry-forward rule provides just such an excuse. You might think of it as legitimized procrastination. After all, it's much more fun to use the money you've earmarked for your RRSP to take a winter holiday in Florida. You'll just make it up next year, you promise yourself. When next year rolls around, you find that your RRSP contribution limit has doubled, because of the carry-forward. Instead of being able to contribute, say, $6,000, you're allowed $12,000. How likely is it that you'll have that kind of money available? And what's going to happen after five or six years, when your carry-forward entitlement increases to $30,000 or $40,000? Chances are you'll never catch up. Even though you technically have the carry-forward contribution room available, you may never use it.

The second disadvantage of the carry-forward is that you lose your tax deduction for the current year. I'm a firm believer in taking advantage of tax benefits while you can; you never know what a future government is going to do.

My third warning about the carry-forward is the loss of years of compounding. Suppose you're 40 years old and you're entitled to make an RRSP contribution of $10,000 this year. You want to retire at 65. At 6 percent a year, your $10,000 will grow to about $43,000 over that time. But you don't make the contribution right away. Instead, you carry it forward for five years and finally get around to it when you're 45. You still want to retire at 65. What happens? Your contribution will now be worth only about $32,000 when you retire. By delaying five years and using the carry-forward, you've reduced the end value of your plan by about $11,000! This is obviously better than never making the contribution at all. So if it would have been absolutely impossible for you to make the contribution any sooner, the carry-forward has been of value. But if you've simply used it as an excuse for putting off contributing, it has cost you a lot of money. Think about that before using the carry-forward rule.

The table below illustrates how much the end value of an RRSP will be reduced for each dollar of contribution room you carry forward. I have assumed retirement age to be 65 and annual compound growth to be 6 percent.

Current Age	Cost per Dollar of a Delay of		
	1 Year	3 Years	5 Years
20	$0.77	$2.20	$3.47
25	0.69	1.65	2.60
30	0.44	1.24	1.95
35	0.32	0.92	1.45
40	0.24	0.69	1.08
45	0.18	0.52	0.81
50	0.14	0.39	0.61
55	0.10	0.29	0.45
60	0.08	0.22	0.34

As you can see, the younger you are and the longer the delay, the greater the impact on the final value of your RRSP. For example, if you are 25 years old and carry forward $2,000 for three years, the loss to the end value of your plan will be $3,300 ($2,000 x $1.65). If you are 45 years old and carry forward $12,000 for five years, the end value of your RRSP will be reduced by $9,720 ($12,000 x $0.81).

The greater the average annual return you expect to earn in your RRSP, the higher the loss to the end value will be. For example, if our 25-year-old were to manage his money so as to earn 10 percent a year instead of 6 percent, the cost of a three-year delay to the end value of his plan would balloon to more than $22,000! The cost of a five-year delay for the 45-year-old would be more than $30,000!

If you have a choice between carrying forward or not, calculate how much it will cost over the years before making a final decision. It may persuade you to postpone the Florida trip rather than the RRSP contribution.

Choosing Securities

Many people treat their RRSP money carelessly. They give less thought to their investments than they do to buying a new TV set, even though the performance of their tax-sheltered securities will have a profound impact on the way they live for the final 20 or 30 years of their lives.

It's essential that you choose the investments for your RRSP with care. There are many choices available—so many, in fact, that the whole process can at times seem incredibly confusing. Here's a rundown of the types of investments I feel are most suitable for an RRSP. Some of these can only be held in self-directed plans.

Cash-Type Securities

As discussed in Chapter 9, this group consists of cash in chequing or savings accounts as well as securities that can be easily converted to cash at full face value within a short period of time.

Money market mutual funds. These are the core cash holding for most RRSP investors. They may own Treasury bills, short-term corporate notes, and bankers' acceptances. They are conservatively managed and the net asset value (NAV) is fixed, usually at $10. However, when interest rates are down, as they were in the opening years of this century, returns are very low.

Treasury bills. These are short-term debt securities issued by the federal and provincial governments, usually in maturities of three months, six months, and one year. They're as safe an investment as you'll find and an excellent place to park cash in a self-directed plan if you're unsure where to invest or in the event short-term interest rates move up. You can buy Treasury bills through a stockbroker; however, you will find that the maturities they offer will seem somewhat unusual—52 days, or 4.5 months, or some other odd time frame. That's because brokerage firms buy T-bills from governments and hold them in inventory for later resale to retail clients. You'll also find that the rate they quote you is a bit lower than the rates printed in the business pages; the difference is the firm's profit margin.

Remember that T-bills are short-term investments that have to be rolled over at maturity, so the rate you receive is only guaranteed for a minimal time. During periods when interest rates are declining, this means you will get a lower return on your money every time a T-bill matures and your money must be reinvested. When rates are on the rise, on the other hand, the shorter term works in your favour since you can take advantage of upward movements in yields every few months.

Short-term deposits. Offered by financial institutions, these deposits are guaranteed and usually pay a higher return than you will receive from T-bills.

Canada Savings Bonds. Technically, they're misnamed. These aren't real bonds at all, but short-term savings certificates issued by the federal government. The interest rate reflects current short-term rates, and CSBs can be cashed any time for full face value.

Income Securities

The grinding bear market that opened this century prompted many investors to take a fresh look at the income side of their RRSP portfolio. In many cases, they discovered that they were woefully underweighted in bonds, GICs, and other types of income securities. Often, this was a direct result of the stock market exuberance of the late 1990s when greed overtook prudence as the dominant force in investment selection. In some cases, people used their own judgment in deciding to de-emphasize income securities; in others they were nudged (or pushed) in that direction by overly enthusiastic advisors who thought the bull would rage on for a decade. Whatever the reason, the end result was the same: high-risk exposure that led to big losses when stock markets dropped.

Building the income component of an RRSP is no longer a simple matter of deciding to add a few bonds or GICs. The range and variety of income products has grown exponentially over the past 15 years, as has the need to carefully assess which are the most appropriate for current conditions.

In times of low interest rates, yields on conventional securities like GICs and government bonds are depressed, so higher-yield alternatives like income trusts become more attractive. When rates are on the rise, you need to take steps to minimize the risk exposure of the income side of your portfolio. In all circumstances you must give careful thought to what type of income securities you want to hold, the level of risk you are prepared to accept, and your anticipated return. All RRSPs should have some assets in income securities. This requires a new approach to selecting them, so I've abandoned the traditional method of lumping all income securities into a single grouping. I now divide them into two categories: fixed income and variable income.

Variable-income securities have become extremely popular among older Canadians and they form a significant portion of many RRIF and non-registered income portfolios. But they also can play a valuable role in RRSPs and in non-registered retirement savings accounts when used correctly.

Remember that as a general rule interest-sensitive securities will see an increase in their market price and a decline in their yields when interest rates are falling. When rates are rising the opposite is true: market valuations will fall while yields will rise. However, that is a *general* rule only. Some types of income securities are less likely to be affected by interest rate movements than others. So you need to actively manage the income section of your RRSP to ensure you are holding the right type of assets at the right time.

Fixed-Income Securities

This type of security guarantees to make payments (interest or dividends) at a set rate on specific dates.

Guaranteed investment certificates (GICs). For many Canadians, these were the backbone of their RRSPs for many years. The classic GIC has a term of one to five years, during which time you are guaranteed a specific rate of return. Your principal is locked in for that period. There are also index-linked GICs available but I do not recommend them for registered plans.

Mortgage-backed securities. These are a useful investment for those who are looking for steady income with very little risk. They are actually much better suited for retirees in RRIF accounts, but you should be aware of them because they provide a conservative RRSP option.

Mortgage mutual funds. These funds invest in residential first mortgages and mortgage-backed securities, and their safety record is first-rate. Even in recessionary times, Canadians are very conscientious about their mortgage payments, which means that defaults are minimal. These funds hardly ever lose money over a calendar year. The one exception was 1994, when some funds suffered small losses when interest rates took a temporary jump. There will be some movement in unit price as interest rates rise and fall. But it won't be as dramatic as with a bond fund, because the average term to maturity of the holdings in a mortgage fund is less (typically around three years). You can ignore these shifts, or take advantage of them to add more units at a reduced price.

Don't go into mortgage funds looking for big gains. When interest rates are low, so are the returns. But you'll usually earn somewhat more than from a money market fund, with only slightly higher risk.

Short-term bonds. If rates are on the rise, short-term bonds are the safest type of fixed-income security to own. The term to maturity is no longer than five years, which means the market price of these bonds, and funds that invest in them, will be more stable. That doesn't mean they can't lose value, but any decline will be small compared to medium- and long-term bonds. Unless you have a large portfolio, you may not be in a position to invest in individual bonds. The cheapest alternative is an exchange-traded fund (ETF) that acts as a proxy for short-term bonds. One of the most popular is the iUnits Government of Canada Five-Year Bond, which trades on the Toronto Stock Exchange under the symbol XGV. It has a management expense ratio (MER) of only 25 basis points (0.25 percent); however, you will have to pay a sales commission to buy or sell your units. Short-term bond mutual funds are another option, and there are several no-load choices available from the major banks.

Mid-term bonds/long-term bonds. There are three efficient ways to add a mixture of medium- and long-term bonds to your portfolio. If you have enough assets to buy bonds individually, ask your advisor to create a "bond ladder" for you. This is a simple method for spreading your bond maturities over a range of dates. Alternatively, you can invest in a bond mutual fund, but be careful. Some of them have MERs that are far too high, especially during low interest rate periods. To keep your costs low and maximize returns, check the MERs carefully. The "e" units of the TD Canadian Bond Index Fund had a 0.48 percent MER at the time of writing and are an excellent choice.

There is also an iUnits exchange-traded fund that you can use. It's called the iUnits Canadian Market Broad Market Index Fund and it trades on the Toronto Stock Exchange under the symbol XBB. The fund is designed to replicate the return of the Scotia Capital Universe Bond Index. To achieve this objective, the fund invests in a regularly rebalanced sample portfolio of bonds that closely matches the characteristics of the Universe Bond Index, including yield, term to maturity, credit quality, and duration. The MER is capped at 30 basis points (0.3 percent).

High-yield bonds. Government issues and top-quality corporate bonds are the most sensitive to interest rate movements (this is true for bonds of all maturities). Lower-quality corporate bonds (the so-called junk bonds) are less vulnerable because their market price is driven by other factors apart from rates, such as credit risk. Therefore, when interest rates are on the rise you should consider investing part of your mid-term/long-term bond allocation in high-yield bond mutual funds. This will reduce the interest rate risk in your fixed-income segment. Unfortunately, it is hard to find a low-MER fund of this type. The only one that comes in below 1 percent is the Phillips, Hager & North High Yield Bond Fund, and it has a great record. However, you'll need $25,000 to take a position. If that won't work for you, the Renaissance Canadian High Yield Bond Fund is a good alternative, although the MER is a full percentage point higher.

These funds can pay off in a big way if conditions are right, but should only be used in RRSPs in very specific circumstances.

Foreign bonds. These perform best when two conditions prevail: world interest rates are falling and the Canadian dollar is weak. That combination occurred in 1998 and many of these funds turned in double-digit returns as a result. But when the Canadian dollar is rising, as it did in 2003–2004, foreign bond funds tend to be relatively weak performers.

This area can be a little tricky and it needs to be carefully thought through. Our sample portfolio in Chapter 8 showed a 12 percent weighting in foreign bond funds. This can be achieved by simply putting your money into a mutual fund that specializes in this field. However, MERs tend to be on the high side, in some cases exceeding 2 percent, which is very expensive for a bond investment. The CIBC Bond Index

Fund has an acceptable MER of 0.96 percent but its performance record is below average. The Friedberg Foreign Bond Fund has a low MER at 0.93 percent and a strong track record, but the minimum initial investment is $5,000 and at the time of writing a large percentage of the assets were in Government of Canada real return bonds, which certainly don't qualify as "foreign."

An alternative worth considering for U.S. dollar securities are bond iShares. These are exchange-traded funds (ETFs) that are administered by the U.S. branch of Barclays Global Investors and trade on the American Stock Exchange. There are several choices available, including a corporate bond fund that tracks the Goldman Sachs InvesTop Index, which focuses on highly rated issues, and several Treasury bond funds of varying maturities. The expense ratios in all cases are very low at 0.15 percent. You can find out more about these ETFs at **www.iShares.com**.

Stripped bonds. Some investors use stripped bonds as the backbone of their self-directed RRSPs. "Strips," as they're called in the investment community, have been available in Canada since the mid-1980s. The concept was imported from the U.S., where "zero coupon bonds," as they're known in that country, had been popular for many years. With strips, there are no surprises. If you're planning to retire in 15 years, you simply buy 15-year strips when interest rates are high, tuck them away in your RRSP, and forget them. The money will be there when you need it. And since financial dealers normally select only the highest-quality bonds to strip, the chance of the issuer defaulting is very low. Since strips are not covered by deposit insurance, this is an important consideration.

However, strips are much more volatile than regular bonds. They can experience some significant price swings as interest rates move up or down. If you intend to hold them for the long term, that's not a problem. But if you think you might sell before maturity, it's something to consider.

Real return bonds. Rising interest rates are usually a sign that inflation is also increasing, or is likely to do so. When that happens, another way to reduce the negative impact on your income securities is to use real return bonds. These are bonds that offer protection against increases in the consumer price index for both interest and principal. Several mutual fund companies now offer real return bond funds. For many years, there was only one fund available, TD Real Return Bond Fund, and it continues to be a first-rate choice with a low MER. But other companies that have launched real return bond funds recently include Dynamic, Investors Group, Mackenzie Financial, Renaissance, and SEI. So there are now plenty of choices available.

Fixed-rate preferred shares. There are two types of preferred shares. The fixed-rate type pays a set dividend that never varies, so we include it with the fixed-income securities. Floating-rate preferred shares are quite different, and we cover those in the variable-income section. A preferred share is a type of debt security issued by a corporation. Investors receive dividends and the shares are usually redeemable after a certain time or at stated intervals. Preferred shares rank behind bonds in terms of priority in the event a company runs into trouble, so they could be higher risk. Also, one of their main attractions is the eligibility of their payments for the dividend tax credit. That benefit is lost inside an RRSP, so keep that in mind in making your decision.

Variable-Income Securities

Variable-income securities differ from fixed-income securities in that the payment is not guaranteed and may vary according to a number of conditions. For example, in some cases the payment will rise or fall in line with changes in the Bank of Canada's key lending rate.

Corporate loan funds. This type of security has been available in the United States for many years but it has only recently been introduced into Canada. These funds invest in corporate debt paper. We aren't talking bonds or debentures here but rather corporate notes with varied maturity dates.

An example of this type of fund is the Van Kampen Senior Income Trust, which trades on the New York Stock Exchange under the symbol VVR. Van Kampen Investments is a Chicago-based money management company that traces its history back to 1927. Although the words "income trust" appear in the name, don't be misled. This fund actually invests in a portfolio of senior collateralized loans from corporations with low credit ratings (or in some cases with no credit rating at all), usually with maturities of less than five years. The portfolio is broadly diversified (about 300 positions at any given time) so that default risk is minimized. Since most of the loans held in the fund are variable or floating rate, it offers protection in times of rising rates and therefore qualifies for our variable-income category. If U.S. interest rates rise, the yields on the loans held by the fund will follow suit.

In early 2005, AIM-Trimark introduced the first Canadian mutual fund to specialize in corporate loans. It's called the Trimark Floating Rate Income Fund and it invests predominantly in corporate bank loans. These loans are senior to debt issues and tend to have better recovery rates than sub-investment-grade bonds, but are still considered below investment grade. While the fund has no mandated geographic allocation, the managers focus on U.S.-dollar denominated loans. In August 2005, GGOF launched a similar fund.

Floating-rate preferred shares. This type of preferred share offers protection against rising interest rates. The dividend is adjusted periodically according to a specific formula, which is usually tied to the prime rate. Otherwise, floating-rate preferreds have the same characteristics as straight preferreds. Preferred shares can be purchased on the Toronto Stock Exchange and the floating rate variety offer interest rate protection. They can add stability and cash flow to a retirement plan, although one of their main advantages, the dividend tax credit, is lost if you hold them inside an RRSP. If you decide to invest in them, be very careful. This is a minefield because preferred shares come with all sorts of unusual conditions. You need to know exactly what you are buying.

To begin with, determine whether you're looking at a fixed-rate or floating-rate preferred. Fixed-rate preferreds offer good capital gains potential when interest rates are falling but you can lose money if you buy when rates are on the rise. They should be counted among your fixed-income assets.

Second, see when the preferred is callable. This means the issuer has an option to redeem all the shares at a predetermined price, typically $25. You may come across a preferred share with an attractive yield that is trading for, say, $28.50. Be suspicious. The high yield may be an indication that there is significant danger the shares will be called before long, leaving you with a capital loss.

Finally, check out the credit rating on the issue. You can find this information at Standard & Poor's Canada and Dominion Bond Rating Service.

One of the best sources for information about individual preferred share issues is *FP Equities: Preferreds and Derivatives,* which is published annually by the *Financial Post.* It's expensive so check your local library for a copy.

If you would rather let someone else choose your preferred shares, consider the Diversified Preferred Share Trust, a closed-end fund that trades on the Toronto Stock Exchange under the symbol DPS.UN. As the name suggests, it invests in a portfolio of preferred shares and pays quarterly dividends.

Income trusts. Trusts are mostly used by older investors seeking income. But they have a role to play in the income section of an RRSP because the best of them can offer a combination of steady cash flow and modest growth potential. Selection can be difficult, however.

The first rule to keep in mind is that the higher the yield, the less suitable the trust is likely to be for a retirement savings account. The reason is simple: yield equates with risk. Nobody gives away something for nothing in the investment world, so if an income trust is offering a big payout, there's a reason. Since one of the priorities of RRSP management is to keep risk within reasonable limits, my advice is to focus on income trusts that are at the lower end of the yield range.

Second, avoid highly volatile sectors. Many oil and gas trusts posted big gains from 2001 to 2005, driven in part by investors seeking higher yields and in part by record prices for natural gas and crude oil. But the energy sector is notoriously cyclical. A worldwide recession would knock back oil prices and the market value of these trusts would suffer accordingly. A retirement plan is not the right environment for that kind of risk.

Finally, focus on trusts that have clearly defined business models that are suitable for retirement plans. It should be no surprise that one of the most widely held income trusts among pension plans is Yellow Pages

Income Fund, which trades under the symbol YLO.UN. Yellow Pages holds a virtual monopoly on telephone directory advertising in Canada as a result of its purchase of western-based SuperPages in March 2005. The trust's income is steady and predictable and there is some growth potential over time. That combination makes it a good choice for a long-term retirement investment.

Income trusts mutual funds. The rapid growth in the income trusts sector has, predictably, spawned the emergence of a whole new category of mutual funds, known as Canadian income trusts funds. These funds invest in a portfolio of trusts and generate significant cash flow for investors. If you don't want to select trusts yourself, this is an alternative to consider.

Income trust closed-end funds and ETFs. You can also invest in the sector through funds that trade on the Toronto Stock Exchange. There are two types. The closed-end funds are actively managed, in the same way as a mutual fund. A manager chooses the securities and makes the buy-and-sell calls. The Citadel organization is one of the leaders in this area, with several funds available, each with a slightly different investment perspective. ETFs track an index that monitors the performance of the income trusts sector, such as the S&P/TSX Capped Income Trusts Index. Barclays Global Investors offers two ETFs of this type, and there are others available.

Income funds. Another type of mutual fund that specializes in generating cash flow is the income fund. These invest in a portfolio that includes a mix of income trusts, preferred shares, bonds, and high-yielding common stocks. Most of the big banks offer one or more of these funds, as do many of the load-fund companies.

Dividend funds. There are two types of dividend funds. Only one fits into the variable-income category and there are just a few of them available. You can recognize them by looking at their portfolios. If they hold a large number of preferred shares, they belong here. If they don't, think of them as blue-chip stock funds and slot them in with your growth securities. True dividend funds usually pay monthly or quarterly distributions.

A classic example is the Signature Dividend Fund offered by the CI group. At the time of writing, it was paying monthly distributions of $0.04 a unit, plus a larger year-end capital gains distribution. About half of the portfolio was in preferred shares.

U.S. REITs. There is no American equivalent to the booming Canadian income trusts market, except for real estate investment trusts. There are lots of these and they trade on the big U.S. exchanges, but most Canadians are not familiar with them and they receive little attention in this country. However, they can be useful for adding U.S.-dollar income securities to an RRSP portfolio. A simple way to obtain some exposure here is to buy units of the iShares Cohen & Steers Realty Majors Index Fund. Its mandate is to produce returns that correspond to the performance of large, actively traded U.S. real estate investment trusts. The units trade on the American Stock Exchange under the symbol ICF.

I've discussed a number of investment options in this section that you may not have previously considered in terms of income securities for your RRSP. That's why I contend that a whole new approach is needed for this sector. If you go about it properly, you can add significant diversification, increase profit potential, and reduce overall portfolio risk by careful selection of your income investments. But it requires a complete rethink. The old methodology no longer works.

Growth Securities

Growth assets add value to a portfolio mainly through capital gains.

Stocks. These are the classic growth securities. If you have a self-directed RRSP, you may invest directly in the stock markets, either Canadian, U.S., or international. This can be good or bad, depending on your stock-picking skills and your timing. Generally, I suggest that only seasoned investors go this route with their RRSP. We'll get into stocks in more detail in a later chapter.

Canadian equity funds. For most people, equity (stock) mutual funds are the entry point to growth securities. That's because they're readily available, affordable, and offer professional money management. Canadian equity funds are the most common type sold in this country, partly because they are the most familiar and partly because RRSP investors were forced into them for years by the foreign content limit. However, the Canadian stock market has historically not performed as well as that of the United States, so you may wish to consider other options for your RRSP now that there are no restrictions on where you can invest.

International equity funds. These cover a huge range, from U.S. stock funds to those specializing in emerging markets, from Brazil to Russia. The risk level can also vary greatly, so you'll need to do some careful research or obtain professional advice before deciding which funds are best suited for your plan.

Sector funds. These mutual funds specialize in specific areas of the economy, such as technology, telecommunications, natural resources, and health care. When the target sector is doing well, a fund can produce enormous gains. But when things are going badly, as they were for the natural resources sector through the middle and late 1990s, returns can be dismal.

ETFs. Exchange-traded funds have become a popular way of investing in stocks, both domestic and foreign. The best-known Canadian ETFs are the iUnits from Barclays Global Investors. For foreign market coverage, look at the iShares, operated by the U.S. division of Barclays, which trade on the American Stock Exchange.

Managing Your RRSP

Never forget that your RRSP is a pension plan. If you always approach it from that perspective, you should be able to avoid serious trouble. This money is earmarked for your retirement. If you lose a large chunk of it, you'll pay the price where it hurts most—in the type of home you live in and the kind of food you eat.

That means there is no room in your plan for high-risk investments. If you want to speculate, do so in a non-registered account where the government will cover part of any loss by allowing you to write it off against your taxable capital gains.

Another important rule is to keep your costs low. Managing an RRSP doesn't have to be expensive. Some types of plans cost nothing at all; others charge only a small annual administration fee. But if you're not careful, you can run up some fairly hefty bills that will not be tax-deductible and will be paid from the proceeds of your plan. Here are some examples:

- *Mutual fund commissions.* Avoid them if at all possible. There are lots of great non-load funds out there. If you like a particular load fund, ask your advisor to acquire it on a front-end basis with zero commission. Many now do this because they still collect the annual trailer fees.

- *Mutual fund redemption fees.* If you buy a back-end load (also called deferred sales charge or DSC) fund for your RRSP and then decide to cash in your units, you may be assessed a redemption charge depending on how long you've held it. This will be paid from within your plan. Don't get caught in this bind. Low-load funds are a much cheaper alternative. Ask your advisor about them.

- *Mutual fund switching fees.* Some companies and their sales representatives will charge you for moving your money from one fund in their group to another (for example, from a bond fund to an equity fund). The usual rate is 2 percent but even this can get expensive if you're an avid switcher. If your advisor tries to do this, tell him or her to stuff it or switch to someone else.

- *Broker's commissions.* Every time you trade a stock, you'll pay your broker a commission. You'll also pay when you buy Treasury bills, stripped bonds, and regular bonds. Those charges won't be as obvious because they're built into the price you pay for the security, but they're a drain on your RRSP money nevertheless.

- *Transfer fees.* If you switch your RRSP elsewhere, you'll probably have to pay a fee to the transferring institution.

- *Self-directed RRSP fees.* Annual administration fees typically run between $100 and $150.

- *Trustee and administration fees.* Many RRSPs charge a trustee fee in some form or another. However, in recent years some organizations have abandoned these charges as a competitive move.

Finally, look after your plan. I'm always amazed at the number of people who admit to never looking closely at their RRSP statements. They toss them in a drawer or, worse, in the wastebasket, as if they were so much junk mail. Such indifference can be costly. RRSP trustees make mistakes—not often, but it happens. For instance, both my wife and I have RRSPs with a highly reputable full-service broker, but every so often I find that money that should have been credited to one account has gone into the other one. So be alert for mistakes in your RRSP statements.

For Late Starters

Okay, let's say you're a baby boomer and you're now in your late 40s or even your 50s. You know that you should have gotten serious about retirement planning years ago but something always got in the way. But now it's time to get down to business. What do you do?

To begin with, you need to understand that you can never fully compensate for the lost years. All you can do is mitigate the damage. Second, you'll have to sacrifice more. Because you have so few years remaining until retirement, you'll need to commit a greater percentage of your income to your savings program. Third, you'll need a lot of self-discipline if you are going to succeed. Finally, don't kid yourself. It won't be easy.

If you are prepared to accept all that, here's what you must do.

1. *Open an RRSP now.* If you don't have an RRSP at this stage, open one immediately. That's the first step, and it's an essential one.

2. *Make your maximum allowable contribution.* You've lost enough time already. Contribute the maximum to which you're entitled, this year and every year.

3. *Save, save, save.* You're going to have to put away a lot more of your income than you ever thought possible if you hope to have a comfortable lifestyle in retirement. Some experts contend that people in their 40s should aim at saving at least 20 percent of everything they earn—and that's 20 percent of gross income, not after-tax income. If you don't start until your 50s, 30 percent is your target.

4. *Take more risk.* Older people are urged to become more conservative as they approach retirement in order to protect their capital. But you'll have to ignore this conventional wisdom. The older you are when you begin your retirement planning process, the *more* risk you are going to have to take in your effort to make up lost ground. An older person just starting to save for retirement cannot afford the safety of putting GICs or stripped bonds into a retirement plan the way the person who starts young can do. Equities and income trusts will be the keys to success for the 50-plus starter. If they perform reasonably well, you should end up all right. If they don't, be prepared to cut back on your lifestyle after you retire or make plans to work until age 70.

5. *Consider a catch-up loan.* One way to make up some of the lost time is to apply for a catch-up loan that will enable you to use all your RRSP carry-forward credits immediately. Let's say you're age 40 and you now have 10 years of back credits available. We'll assume you are earning $40,000 a year now and that your income increased by 2 percent a year over the past decade. So 10 years ago, you were earning $32,750 a year. You had no pension plan so your unused RRSP carry-forward in that year was 18 percent of that amount, or about $5,900. Your carry-forward allowance went up two percentage points each year as your salary increased. You are now sitting on almost $72,000 worth of unused RRSP credits.

   If you can swing it, take out a loan for the full amount and put it in your RRSP immediately. Space out your deductions over several years to maximize the refund you receive. Assuming a 10-year repayment schedule at an average interest rate of 6 percent, it will cost you about $800 a month to pay off the loan. That's somewhat more than the 20 percent of salary that you originally targeted, but you are way behind and need to catch up. Yes, you may have to sacrifice elsewhere. No one said it would be easy.

6. *Forget early retirement.* If you haven't seriously begun to save for retirement by the time you're 40, early retirement will never be anything more than a dream. There is no way you can accumulate enough capital to retire comfortably at 55 or 60. Unless your employer comes through with a golden handshake as an incentive for you to depart early, count on staying at your job, or one like it, until at least 65. The financial reality of early retirement is that it gives you

fewer years to save money and more years to spend it. Unless you plan extremely carefully, you run the risk of finding yourself in difficulty before you hit 70.

I know that many boomers will not like to read this. But if you've put yourself into a hole, you're going to have to pay a price. The fable of the grasshopper and the ant was never more on the mark than here.

11

Understanding Income Trusts

Canadians have gone gaga over income trusts, and Americans are jumping on the bandwagon as well. Unfortunately, a lot of people who have added this relatively new type of security to their portfolios don't really understand what they have invested in. Income trusts have added a completely new dimension to the Canadian investing scene and, after a tough fight, have now been granted legitimacy through inclusion in the S&P/TSX Composite Index and the extension of limited liability to shareholders by the provincial governments, which have jurisdiction over most of these entities. So they are here to stay and they can play a valuable role in your retirement plan if you invest wisely and treat them carefully.

To begin with, you need to understand exactly what an income trust is, and what it is not. Basically, it is simply a business that operates under a different legal structure. Instead of being set up as a corporation, it is organized as a trust. Income trusts acquire partial or full ownership of a revenue-producing asset, usually one with limited growth potential. In doing so, the trust may also receive some accumulated tax benefits. It then sells shares (units) in the venture to the public. The attraction is that revenues and the tax breaks flow through to the unitholders, after management fees and other expenses have been deducted.

There is a significant tax advantage in doing this. A corporation pays tax on its profits. If it then declares a dividend on after-tax earnings, those payments are taxed again in the hands of the shareholder, albeit at a favourable rate. So the governments get a double-dip before the investor receives anything. Income trusts, by comparison, are taxed only once. Most of the distributable cash flow is paid out to unitholders, who pay the tax on the income. Under normal conditions, the trust pays nothing. This means more money ends up in the hands of investors, increasing the after-tax return.

The yields on income trusts are higher than those offered by bonds, sometimes much higher. It is not unusual to see an income trust paying annualized distributions in excess of 10 percent. This makes them very attractive to income-seeking investors, such as retirees, particularly during periods of low interest rates.

However, it is important to realize that income trusts are *not* bonds. The payments are not guaranteed and may be reduced or even suspended at any time. This has happened on several occasions. In March 2003, for example, the Halterm Income Fund, which derives its income from a shipping terminal in Halifax, stopped distributions after two important client accounts were lost. Other trusts that have suspended payments in recent years include Atlas Cold Storage Income Fund, which ran into serious accounting problems, and Legacy Hotels REIT, which was hurt by low occupancy rates in the wake of the SARS outbreak in Toronto in 2003.

Another risk is that the market value of trust units may fluctuate considerably. There have been times when income trusts have come under heavy selling pressure, as in 1997–1998 when energy trusts took a pounding after crude oil prices tumbled to the US$10 a barrel range. The trust market was in its infancy at that time and investors temporarily lost confidence in the whole concept.

It was only during the bear market of 2000–2002 that trusts came into their own, driven by the twin forces of low interest rates and a plunging stock market. Desperate investors searched for alternatives, and the financial community was quick to respond by bringing dozens of new income trusts to market during the period. Almost every new offering was snapped up, which of course accelerated the cycle. The growing interest spawned the birth of numerous income trusts mutual funds and exchange-traded closed-end funds, creating an institutional demand. The extension of limited liability to the sector by Alberta and Ontario (Quebec-based trusts already had it) opened the door for pension plan managers to jump on board.

These securities have an important role to play for retirees because of their ability to generate above-average cash flow. But they can also be useful in RRSPs at an earlier stage of the retirement planning process.

Types of Trusts

There is no uniform definition of the various categories of income trusts that are now available. The following division is one that I have devised with the goal of keeping matters simple and easy to understand.

Resource Trusts

The focus of these trusts is the resource sector. The oil and gas trusts are the best known but there are also trusts that specialize in coal and iron ore. All the trusts in this group make their money from non-renewable resources. This means that at some point their wells will run dry or the ore in their mines will be exhausted. For the oil and gas trusts, this is measured by something called a Reserve Life Index (RLI), which tells you how many years remain before the proven and probable reserves are depleted at the current rate of production, assuming no new finds or acquisitions. For the conventional oil and gas trusts, an RLI of around 11 years is about average. Trusts with large investments in the Alberta Oil Sands have a much longer RLI, of about 30 years. Anyone considering investing in an oil and gas trust should check the RLI before doing so.

Some resource trusts offer tax advantages by passing exploration and depletion credits on to their shareholders. However, you can only benefit from these by holding the units in a non-registered portfolio.

Utilities Trusts

This group includes trusts that specialize in power generation and in pipelines. Like utilities stocks, they offer steady cash flow but they tend to be interest-rate sensitive because of the large debt they incur from capital expenditures. The best time to buy utilities trusts is when interest rates are near the top of a cycle and are expected to decline soon. Under those conditions, these trusts will offer the best combination of high yields and low prices.

Business Trusts

In terms of numbers, business is by far the largest category of trusts. Essentially, any trust that doesn't fit into one of the other categories is placed here. The trusts in this group have little in common beyond their legal structure. The underlying businesses are widely varied and cover such diverse fields as advertising, restaurants, manufacturing, entertainment, communications, transportation, food processing, and gaming. It would be hard to name an area of the Canadian economy that is not represented here.

Some of these trusts are extremely large, such as the giant Yellow Pages Income Fund, which has a virtual monopoly on telephone directory advertising in Canada. Others are tiny and would be classed as small-cap stocks if they were set up as corporations. An example is Vancouver-based Swiss Water Decaffeinated Coffee Income Fund, which provides decaf coffee to a number of well-known chains including Starbucks and Tim Hortons.

Real Estate Investment Trusts

More commonly known as REITs, these trusts invest in real property and derive their revenue from rental income. They usually specialize in one particular area of real estate, such as shopping malls, office buildings, retirement homes, apartment buildings, or hotels. REITs were among the original income trusts available in Canada and have always been very popular because of their steady cash flow and the tax advantages they offer by passing through depreciation allowances to their shareholders.

Types of Distributions

I receive letters and emails regularly from investors who are confused by the way in which payments from income trusts are taxed when the units are held outside an RRSP, RRIF, or other registered plan. This confusion is not surprising—there are actually five types of trust distributions, each of which is treated differently for tax purposes. Here's the breakdown.

Interest Income

Interest income will show as "other income" on the T3 form you receive from the trust management each year. The important point is that all income of this type is fully taxable at your marginal rate. There are no breaks at all. Trusts that distribute most or all of their payments as "other income" are best held in a tax shelter, like a RRIF, pension plan, or RRSP.

Dividends

Dividend payments get the benefit of the dividend tax credit, which means your tax rate will be reduced. To give you an example, an Ontario resident with a taxable income of $50,000 in 2004 was assessed 31.15 percent on every dollar of interest income. But the rate for dividends was about half that at 15.86 percent.

Capital Gains

Any capital gains distributions come under the capital gains rules, which means that only half the amount received is taxable. Whether capital gains are more beneficial from a tax perspective depends on your taxable income. For an Ontario resident, the crossover point in the 2004 tax year was $35,000. Below that level, dividends were taxed at a lower rate than capital gains. Above that, capital gains income did better, and the higher the tax bracket, the greater the differential. Capital losses can be deducted from taxable capital gains.

Rental Income

Rental income comes into play when you invest in REITs. Taxable rental income can be reduced by applying depreciation credits earned on properties owned by a REIT, and the benefit can be significant. In 2004, Canada's largest REIT, RioCan, reported that 46 percent of its distributions were sheltered from tax in this way.

Return of Capital

Return of capital is a much misunderstood term. The literal implication is that you are receiving some of your invested capital back, but that isn't necessarily the case. This can be income that has been sheltered by exploration and development allowances (resource trusts), depreciation (REITs), or some other type of tax credit. The important point to note is that all income of this type is tax deferred in the year it is received. You pay no tax on it whatsoever. So any trust with a history of high return of capital payments should be held in a non-registered portfolio.

Tax Considerations

Any trust income that is classified as return of capital has a delayed-action tax obligation attached. As mentioned above, you pay no tax in the year the money is received. But if the units are held in a non-registered account you are on the hook for tax down the road when you eventually sell your units, through the operation of a complex formula called the adjusted cost base (ACB).

Here is a simple explanation of how it works. Let's assume you buy shares in an oil and gas trust for $10 a unit. In the first year, your distributions include a return of capital of 50 cents a unit. This amount must be subtracted from your original purchase price to calculate your ACB. So at the end of year one, your new ACB is $9.50 ($10 − $0.50). In the second year, you receive 75 cents in return of capital distributions. You subtract this from your previous ACB to arrive at a new figure, which in this example will be $8.75 ($9.50 − $0.75). The ACB is adjusted annually whenever a new return of capital distribution is made.

When the units are sold, the amount of taxable capital gain (or loss) will be determined by subtracting the current ACB from the sale price. The original price you paid is no longer a factor. To continue with our example, suppose you sold your units of the oil and gas trust after two years for $11 each. Your taxable capital gain will be $2.25 a unit ($11 − $8.75).

To defer taxes as long as possible, don't sell. However, when the ACB reaches zero there is no tax advantage left because after that all distributions will be taxed as "other income."

Buying Trusts

Buying income trusts can be tricky. Most of the smaller ones are not followed by analysts so there is a dearth of objective advice. Your best sources of guidance for small trusts are a qualified financial advisor or a top-quality newsletter that provides coverage of the sector. *The Income Investor* and the *Internet Wealth Builder,* which are published by my organization, are worth a look in this regard. You will find information at **www.buildingwealth.ca**.

Before you make a decision on adding income trusts to a registered plan, here are some points to consider:

Stability

During the period from 2000 to 2005, some income trusts recorded huge capital gains, in some cases more than doubling in value. Do not be influenced by this; it is not what income trusts are about. Any capital gains should be treated as a bonus; the most important consideration in assessing a trust is the stability of its distributions. Investors are quick to sell off any trust that reduces or suspends its payments. Try to avoid that situation if at all possible. Look at the trust's historic distribution record. See if it has been able to maintain its payments through all conditions or, better still, has increased them on several occasions.

It is also helpful to check the websites of Standard & Poor's Canada and Dominion Bond Rating Service to see if the trust has received a "stability rating" from either or both. Only a handful of trusts have paid the fee required for this, so they are not all listed. But check to see. Both rating agencies use a seven-point scale in determining a trust's relative stability. An SR-1 rating indicates the highest level of stability on the Standard & Poor's scale (hence the least risk) while SR-7 is the lowest.

Dominion Bond Rating Service classifies its highest rating as STA-1 and its lowest as STA-7.

Risk

Income trusts are riskier than GICs, Canada Savings Bonds, or bonds. But the degree of risk will vary from one trust to another. The volatility of commodity prices is one critical variable to consider when investing in a resource trust. Oil and gas prices are highly vulnerable to political, economic, and climatic changes. High prices in 2004–2005 sent the market values of energy-based trusts to unprecedented levels. But a steep drop in the oil price would have the opposite effect, as we saw in 1998.

REITs and utilities trusts are highly sensitive to interest rates. If rates are on the rise, it can have a negative effect on the market value of these trusts, but when rates are at their peak there may be bargains available.

Currency risk is another important factor. Resource trusts price their products in U.S. dollars, so a rise in the value of the loonie will have a negative effect on their bottom line. Some business trusts generate most of all of their revenue in the United States and are subject to the same type of risk as a result.

Next, there is plain old-fashioned business risk. A trust is only as good as its underlying business; if sales and profits falter, the directors may have no choice but to cut distributions, which will have an immediate negative effect on the market price. Trusts that show steady increases in sales, profits, and distributable income will usually demand a premium price in the markets.

Finally, look at the current yield. The higher it is, the more risky the income trust is likely to be. There are exceptions; for example, an income trust that is felt to have strong capital gains potential may command a premium market price (and therefore provide a lower yield) even though it is relatively high risk in nature. But as a general rule, yield is a good guideline to the risk inherent in the security.

Payout Ratio

Always find out the payout ratio of any trust you are considering. This is the percentage of cash flow that was paid out to investors in the prior year or that is expected to be paid in the current year. This is a critical number. The higher the payout ratio, the more vulnerable a trust's distribution may be. Any shortfall in revenue could result in a distribution cut, with all the negative implications that would have. Ideally, a trust's payout ratio will be under 90 percent, which provides a cushion if conditions weaken. A payout ratio of more than 100 percent means the directors are dipping into reserves to maintain their payment schedule. That cannot be sustained for long.

Conversely, a low payout ratio indicates a trust is capable of increasing its distributions. When this happens, investors usually bid the share price higher, so it is good news all around.

Income Trusts Funds

The explosion in the income trusts sector also brought with it a plethora of mutual funds, ETFs, and closed-end funds that specialize in income trusts. I call them "funds of trusts." These funds are well suited for investors who don't want to create their own trust portfolio but would rather buy one off the shelf. They offer professional management, diverse portfolios, and a steady income stream.

However, with all the choices available you need to be selective. Mutual funds are the most popular choice, and some have performed very well. But income trust mutual funds are expensive, with management expense ratios (MERs) averaging 2.29 percent. Actively managed closed-end funds, which trade on the Toronto Stock Exchange, are less costly, with MERs in the 1 to 1.5 percent range. The closed-end funds also tend to have higher monthly distributions than the mutual funds, for those to whom cash flow is important. The Citadel organization offers several closed-end funds. Those from EnerVest and Lawrence Capital are also worthy of consideration.

The cheapest way to buy a portfolio of income trusts is usually through an ETF that tracks a trust index. An example is the Barclays Advantaged S&P/TSX Income Trust Index Fund, which is designed to emulate the performance of the S&P/TSX Capped Income Trust Index. It has an MER of 1.15 percent.

How to Use Trusts

Income trusts and funds should be a core component of a retirement income fund and we'll deal with them in more detail in that context in Chapter 19.

For RRSPs, these securities can add steady cash flow, which can then be used to reinvest elsewhere. If you stick with the soundest, most stable trusts, you will keep your risk to a minimum and give your retirement plan a financial boost. Remember, you are not seeking growth here. Your trusts should be selected on the basis of income and stability. A good RRSP portfolio allocation is about 10 percent.

12

Exchange-Traded Funds

Exchange-traded funds (ETFs) have become increasingly popular among investors in recent years. There's good reason for this. ETFs are easy to understand, readily available, and highly cost efficient. Some investors have abandoned traditional mutual funds and switched their portfolios entirely to them. Others are gradually adding ETFs to their asset mix. However you measure it, ETFs have become hot in Canada.

In fact, we're latecomers to a party that has been going on in the United States for years. South of the border, ETFs are a huge business, with many companies offering them. The iShares issued by the U.S. division of Barclays Global Investors come in more than 100 variations, covering everything from precious metals to Treasury bonds. In this country, ETFs are still the David when compared to the Goliath of the mutual fund industry. But the fund companies may be starting to hear footsteps in the night, even though they won't admit it publicly.

Before we get to the details, there is one point that needs clarification. There is some confusion over the term "exchange-traded fund," and with good reason. Financial professionals tend to include only index-linked securities in this category. These are passively managed funds that track the results of a major market index or a specialized subindex. However, there is a wide range of actively managed portfolio funds that also trade on stock exchanges in Canada and the U.S. These are generically referred to as "closed-end funds," and there is actually a Closed-End Fund Association based in Kansas City that represents the U.S. industry. Its leaders are very unhappy with the "closed-end fund" tag that has been hung on them, especially in the light of the high profile that index-linked ETFs have achieved, and are searching for an alternative.

There are compelling reasons to make a change. The closed-end fund designation suggests an old-fashioned product that usually trades at a deep discount to net asset value. ETFs, by contrast, are seen as new and "in." In fact, many closed-end funds are also relatively new, have first-rate managers, and are posting some excellent returns to go with their attractive MERs. They just need a new image.

I contend that the term "exchange-traded fund" should be used for all portfolio-based securities that trade on a stock exchange. There is nothing in the name that limits it to index-based products. Index securities could be designated as exchange-traded index funds (ETIFs) to highlight their distinctive character.

For now, however, if an index-based security is what you want, check out ETFs. For actively managed portfolios, the closed-end fund moniker still applies, and we will use that distinction through the rest of this chapter.

An ETF Primer

Here are some of the basic things you need to know about investing in ETFs.

Fees

There has been an undercurrent of discontent about high mutual fund management expense ratios (MERs) for several years. However, it has never translated into anything approaching an investor revolt for the simple reason that there was no other easily accessible alternative. Mutual funds offer a combination of portfolio diversification and professional management for a minimal financial commitment. That's a combination that could not be replicated elsewhere, until recently. As a result, some fund companies adopted what amounts to a "charge-what-the-traffic-will-bear" approach. MERs on most equity funds are now somewhere north of 2 percent and in some cases they exceed 3 percent. Charges on segregated funds are even higher because of the guarantees and other extras they offer.

There are exceptions, of course. Some smaller fund companies have resisted the temptation to push fees higher, keeping them at moderate levels for their clients. A few of the larger companies have also made an effort to bring fees down to more reasonable levels. But they stand out as the exception in the mutual fund world. MERs for the iUnits issued by Barclays Global Investors Canada, which are ETFs that trade on the Toronto Stock Exchange, range from a low of 0.17 percent for the i60 units to 0.55 percent for more specialized funds. Only a handful of mutual funds can come anywhere near these numbers.

The MER of any fund is an important factor in determining your profits. These costs are deducted from a fund's total gains to arrive at a net return to the investor. So, for example, a fund with a total return of 10 percent that has an MER of 2.6 percent will leave investors with only a 7.4 percent gain. If the same fund had an MER of 0.5 percent, the investor would be left with a net profit of 9.5 percent. That is a big difference, and over time it can add up to a great deal of money. Over a decade, an investment of $10,000 compounding at an annual rate of 9.5 percent will grow to $24,782. At a rate of 7.4 percent, it will be worth $20,419—a loss to the investor of more than $4,300.

Flexibility

Mutual funds were propelled to the centre of the investment stage by the introduction of the deferred sales charge (DSC; originally called back-end load) by Mackenzie Financial in the late 1980s. Prior to that time, most fund companies had charged front-end sales commissions of up to 9 percent, which turned off many potential investors. The bank no-load fund groups were not big players at that time, with most of their offerings being in the fixed-income categories. The equity funds they did have available were mediocre at best.

When people found that they no longer had to pay upfront sales commissions, they began to flock to mutual funds. The growth of the industry accelerated dramatically in the 1990s as more companies adopted the DSC option and booming equity funds drew away increasing amounts of savings from guaranteed investment certificates (GICs). Today, DSC sales are still popular but more investors realize that they are a millstone around their necks because they inhibit freedom of capital movement.

During the bear market of 2000–2002, many people wanted to get out of equity funds and move their money elsewhere. But they were constrained from doing so by the hefty DSC costs they were facing. ETFs offer a solution to that problem because they trade freely on stock exchanges. You can sell at any time with no penalty.

However, what some novice ETF investors don't take into account are the brokerage commissions. If you think of them in mutual fund terms, ETFs actually charge both a front-end load *and* a DSC—you pay a commission when you buy and another when you sell. It is important to keep those charges to an absolute minimum if you want to get the full benefit from an ETF portfolio. Placing your orders online through a discount broker is the best way to achieve that. And remember that the more you trade, the less benefit you will derive from the low MERs.

Choice

There is another problem if you decide that you want to include ETFs in your portfolio: limited choice. Although the Canadian ETF universe is expanding, you can still create a more diversified domestic portfolio with mutual funds. As mentioned, the largest Canadian provider is Barclays Global Investors Canada. Their main product line is known as iUnits. At the time of writing, there were 12 funds available, in four types, as follows:

- *Broad Canadian index funds:* 60 Index, 60 Capped Index, MidCap Index
- *Sector Canadian index funds:* Capped Energy Index, Capped Financials Index, Capped Gold Index, Capped Information Technology Index, Capped REIT Index
- *Bond index funds:* Government of Canada Five-Year Bond Fund, Canadian Bond Broad Market Index Fund

- *Foreign index funds:* S&P 500 Index RSP Fund, MSCI International Equity RSP Fund

The iUnits are not the only ETFs traded on the Toronto Stock Exchange. Barclays offers five other ETFs under the Barclaysfunds brand, and other ETFs are available from organizations such as Scotia Capital. Still, the range of choices is limited. You need to look south to the New York markets where hundreds of ETFs are traded for maximum diversity. The best known of these are the iShares.

All about iShares

The ETFs called iShares are structured in the same way as Canada's iUnits except that there are more choices, they trade on the American Stock Exchange, and in some cases the MERs are lower. You will have to look long and hard to find an index that is not mirrored in a corresponding iShare issue. There are well over 100 from which to choose, covering everything from small stock markets like Austria and South Africa to U.S. Treasury bonds of varying maturities. There are iShares that focus on value-based indexes and those that track growth-based indexes, for investors seeking style diversification. You can buy iShares that track volatile, high-growth sectors such as biotechnology and units that focus on dull-as-dishwater utilities. It is a veritable smorgasbord of index securities.

If you have a specialized investing need, chances are that iShares can provide the solution. For example, in early 2005 I received an email from one of my newsletter subscribers who wanted to invest in euro-denominated securities. He wrote:

It appears clear that the U.S. dollar is heading much lower and, assuming it does, it will likely pull down the Canadian dollar with it relative to the rest of the world currencies. An obvious investment strategy to offset this would be to put a portion of one's investment funds into euro-denominated funds but there are few of these available. There are a large number of Global and Asian offerings and European equity funds with large U.K. holdings which of course are not euro-based. So now that we can put an unlimited amount of our RRSPs into foreign holdings, how should one make a euro play?

The answer was provided by an iShares security. The iShares MSCI EMU Index Fund offers a pure euro-based equity fund that tracks the performance of securities in European Monetary Union (EMU) markets as measured by the Morgan Stanley Capital EMU Index. This means that only euro zone stocks are represented. The majority of the portfolio is divided among five countries: France, Germany, Netherlands, Italy, and Spain. The fund has a low MER of 0.59 percent and a good track record.

One of the big attractions of iShares is the ability to use them to provide access to securities that are difficult for ordinary investors to acquire. An example is the iShares S&P MidCap 400/Barra Value Index Fund, which offers a low-cost way to gain access to a segment of the U.S. stock market that is absent from most portfolios: the shares of medium-size companies.

Mid-cap stocks, as they are called, have historically outperformed large-cap issues by a wide margin. In recent years, value-oriented mid-cap stocks have been among the market leaders. The objective of the fund is to generate returns that correspond to the performance of the companies with the lowest price-to-book ratios within the S&P MidCap 400 Index, as represented by the S&P MidCap 400/Barra Value Index. It was launched in July 2000, just as the bear market was gathering force, and showed a cumulative return of almost 90 percent in its first four and a half years, which covered the great bear market that began this century.

Please note that I am not recommending this fund (or any other examples used in this book) as something you should run out and buy. These are simply meant as illustrations of the variety of options available to you.

Closed-End Funds

So far, we have discussed what are known as passively managed exchange-traded funds. These track a specific index and the returns will reflect what is happening to that index, good or bad. Closed-end funds, by contrast, are actively managed. Someone makes the buy/sell decisions, just as is the case with a mutual fund portfolio. The performance of the fund will depend to a large extent on the skill of the manager, and the results may bear little or no resemblance to any market index.

They're called closed-end funds because, unlike the more familiar mutual funds, they have a fixed number of shares. Following the initial public offering, no new shares are issued except in special circumstances. If you want to buy into an existing fund you must do so on a stock exchange, just as with common shares. Here are some of the main points to consider with closed-end funds.

Termination

Some closed-end funds have a defined lifespan with a specific maturity date. See if this applies to any fund in which you are interested. If it does, avoid paying more than the fund's net asset value for your shares if the wind-up date is near, otherwise you could be hit with a capital loss.

Structure

For a time, a number of closed-end funds were structured so as to provide a guaranteed return of principal to investors at the expiration date. This was achieved by investing in a forward contract or a stripped bond. However, the cost of the guarantee typically consumed half or more of the fund's assets, leaving only a portion of the money available for investing. During the bear market, these guaranteed funds were badly mauled and in some cases the per unit value of the investment portfolio tumbled to less than 20 percent of the original cost. While the guarantee remained intact, many investors did not want to wait until the fund's maturity to collect. They bailed out, driving down the market price further.

The concept of a guarantee is especially appealing to risk-averse investors. But in my view the cost is too expensive, and experience shows these funds have not done well for the most part. If you are so worried about a loss that you need guarantees, stick with lower-risk securities like GICs.

Mandate

Before you invest a penny make sure you clearly understand the purpose of the fund. Most of the Canadian funds invest in stocks but a growing number specialize in income trusts. There are also a few preferred share funds available.

Every closed-end fund operates under a well-defined mandate. Obtain a prospectus and review it carefully. Pay special attention to any restrictions placed on the manager's freedom to select securities. For example, two funds offered by the Citadel organization may look almost the same both in name and mandate and both have the same manager: Citadel S-1 Income Trust and Citadel S-1 Stable Income Fund. However, the mandate of the latter fund is to focus on income trusts with the highest stability ratings in their respective categories. The first fund has no such limitations.

Management Style

As with an equity mutual fund, it is important to understand the style used by the manager of the closed-end fund in selecting securities. A value-oriented style will usually represent lower risk than a growth-oriented approach. Also, see whether the manager has a history of staying fully invested (higher risk) or raising cash reserves (reduced risk) during periods when a market correction is expected.

Cost

The MERs of closed-end funds will usually be higher than those of the passively managed ETFs. However, they will still be lower than those of most comparable mutual funds. Brokerage commissions will be charged when you buy and sell.

Premium/Discount

Because ETFs track indexes, their market price is usually very close to their net asset value. This is not always the case with closed-end funds. Most Canadian closed-end funds trade at a discount to their NAV, which in some cases has exceeded 30 percent. Proponents of closed-end funds compare this to buying a dollar's worth of securities for 70 cents; however, that analogy only holds if the market price of the fund rises at some point to the NAV or the units are called for redemption. Some funds have a long history of trading at a discount and have no termination date, so this might never happen.

Occasionally, a fund will trade at a premium to NAV, although this happens more frequently in the U.S. than in Canada. The usual reason for this is an expectation by investors that the asset value of the portfolio is going to increase significantly in the relatively near future.

Track Record

If a fund has been around for a while, check out its performance over time compared to the most relevant benchmark index or ETF. If the closed-end fund is not doing better it is probably not worth your attention.

Distributions

If regular cash flow is one of your prime objectives, see how frequently the fund makes distributions to unitholders. Some pay as often as once a month; others may make only one distribution a year.

Tax Implications

Some funds, especially those that specialize in income trusts, offer tax advantages. The information for the most recent tax year should be available on the fund's website.

U.S. Closed-End Funds

Closed-end funds in the U.S. date back as far as 1893. There is an amazing variety of choices, with over 600 publicly traded funds at this time. Slightly more than half the U.S. offerings are municipal bond funds, which provide tax advantages to U.S. investors but none to Canadians. But that still leaves many that may be of interest to you. For example, there are more than 80 single-country closed-end funds, some of which offer access to areas of the world that are difficult for Canadians to invest in, such as India, China, and Korea.

There are funds that have no Canadian counterpart, such as the Van Kampen Senior Income Trust, which holds a portfolio of high-yield floating-rate loans made to corporations with low credit ratings. Royce Value Trust, which invests in a portfolio of U.S. small-cap stocks and makes large quarterly distributions, is another example.

Other types of closed-end funds available on U.S. exchanges specialize in high-yield corporate bonds, emerging market income securities, government bonds, health and biotechnology, utilities, and mortgages.

If you're interested in U.S. funds, apply the same general selection guidelines as for their Canadian counterparts. Just keep in mind that there is an additional element of risk when you invest in them: currency exchange. If the Canadian dollar rises, the currency loss on U.S.-dollar assets will reduce your profits.

13

The Role of Bonds

Bonds should be an integral part of every retirement portfolio. Period!

I can't be more categorical than that, but the reality is that many people do not have any bond exposure at all in their RRSPs. The younger you are, the more this tends to be the case. It's almost as if people under 40 have the impression that bonds are only suitable for old folks.

If you also believe that it's all right to expose your portfolio to big losses while you're young then this rationale is understandable. But if, like me, you think that taking big risks with your retirement savings is a poor idea no matter what your age, then bonds should definitely be an important part of your mix.

In Chapter 9, I discussed asset allocation and suggested that the fixed-income portion (which includes bonds) of any portfolio should never be less than 20 percent. The reason is simple: bond prices tend to have a low correlation to stock prices. This is not always the case, but often when the stock market is in decline the bond market is rising. The reason is that a falling stock market is indicative of a weak economy. In that environment, central banks usually reduce interest rates in an effort to stimulate renewed economic activity. A falling interest rate environment is good news for bonds, which generally rise in price in such a situation.

For example, in 2001 the average Canadian equity fund declined in value by 2.5 percent, according to figures published by *The Globe and Mail*. In 2002, the loss was 10.9 percent on average. U.S. equity funds fared even worse, losing ground in every calendar year from 2000 to 2002, capped by an average decline of 23.8 percent as the bear market reached its culmination in 2002. Global equity funds also lost value over each of those three years. The dollar losses were staggering. For every $1,000 you had invested in an average U.S. equity fund at the start of 2000, only $665 remained at the end of 2002!

During that same three-year period, the average foreign bond fund gained 4.8 percent, 5.1 percent, and 15.9 percent. A $1,000 investment in the average foreign bond fund at the start of 2000 was worth $1,277 at the end of 2002. That's almost twice the value of the same amount invested in a U.S. equity fund.

The Canadian example is not as dramatic but shows a similar pattern. A $1,000 investment in the average Canadian equity fund at the start of 2000 was worth $970 at the end of 2002. That same money held in the average Canadian bond fund would have grown to $1,226.

Clearly, having a portion of your portfolio in bonds during the bear market would have helped to offset stock market losses. Depending on your allocation, you might have been able to eliminate those losses entirely.

A great software program called Your Retirement Planner, which was developed by Ativa Interactive of Hamilton, Ontario, enables you to see exactly what would have happened to an investment portfolio over the period from August 2000 to September 2002, using various assumptions. During that period, which represented the worst phase of the bear market, a portfolio that consisted of 80 percent stocks and 20 percent bonds would have lost 30.7 percent of its value. Adjusting the mix to 60–40, still in favour of stocks, would have reduced the loss to 18.1 percent. Here's the entire table; you can see at a glance the protection that bonds offer in down stock markets.

Asset Mix	Portfolio Gain/Loss
80% stocks, 20% bonds	–30.7%
70% stocks, 30% bonds	–24.4%
60% stocks, 40% bonds	–18.1%
50% stocks, 50% bonds	–11.7%
40% stocks, 60% bonds	–5.6%
30% stocks, 70% bonds	+0.7%
20% stocks, 80% bonds	+7.0%

Source: Ativa Interactive, *Your Retirement Planner* (software), 2003.

If this table doesn't prove the case for including bonds in your portfolio, I don't know what will. I suspect the resistance many people show is largely psychological. Bonds are perceived as dull and unexciting. The stock market is where the action is. Well, guess what? There are times when dull is delightful. If you don't believe me, just wait until the next bear market!

Investing in Bonds

The first thing that novice investors think of when they hear the word "bond" is likely to be Canada Savings Bonds. Perhaps that's because there was a time when CSBs were popular birthday gifts to young children from relatives who couldn't think of anything else. However, CSBs are *not* bonds at all. They're cash-equivalent securities, like money market funds. Genuine bonds are issued by governments or corporations. They usually (but not always) offer a fixed interest rate and mature on a specified date. They cannot be redeemed at face value until maturity; however, they can be bought and sold in a manner similar to stocks on the bond market. That means their value can rise or fall depending on certain variables, the most important of which is the movement of interest rates. This is what differentiates them from guaranteed investment certificates, which do not fluctuate in value under normal conditions.

The basic rule of bond investing is that when interest rates go up, bond prices fall. Conversely, when interest rates go down, bond prices increase.

It doesn't always happen this way and government bonds are more likely to follow this pattern than low-quality corporate bonds, but as a rule of thumb it's important to keep the bond/interest rate relationship in mind when making investment decisions.

Now let's look at some bond basics. Here are four terms you need to know.

Coupon. This refers to the interest rate the bond pays, based on its face value. Bonds are normally sold to individual investors in $1,000 units (although they are priced in $100s for reasons too arcane to get into here). So a bond with a coupon rate of 6 percent would pay $60 a year interest, usually in semi-annual payments.

Maturity. This is the date at which the bond matures and you can cash it in at face value. No interest is payable after that date. Generally, the longer the term to maturity of a bond, the more its market value will fluctuate up or down with interest rate movements.

Yield to maturity. This is the annual rate of return you'll receive on a bond you buy today and hold until its maturity date. It includes both the interest paid on the bond and the capital gain or loss that will result if you keep the bond until it matures. The yield to maturity may be very different from the coupon rate, depending on the price of the bond, time left to maturity, and the general interest rate picture.

Rating. A measure of the safety of the investment, expressed in letters. A rating of AAA (or A++) means the chances of the issuer going belly up and leaving you holding a worthless certificate are almost nil. A bond with a B rating or below, on the other hand, is a signal to run quickly in the opposite direction unless you're prepared to take big risks in hopes of a spectacular return.

You'll sometimes come across bonds that appear to offer great yields. Usually, these wonderful values are issued by shaky corporations. When you encounter such situations, be wary. No one gets something for nothing in the bond world. If a bond is offering an unusually high return, there's probably something wrong with it. That something is usually risk. The greater the chance that the issuer will default on payment, the higher the interest rate must be to attract investors—a danger premium, if you like. If the issuer defaults, investors are left with pennies on the dollar, at best. That's the last thing you want to happen to your RRSP. So make inquiries about the safety of a bond issue before you decide to buy.

There are two agencies in Canada that rate most bonds issued in the country for safety: the Dominion Bond Rating Service and Standard & Poor's Canada. They use slightly different symbols in their ratings, but they're usually in close agreement. Here's how to interpret their ratings.

- **AAA (A++):** Top of the line. These are the Rolls-Royces of bonds. This rating is usually reserved for the issues of senior governments and their Crown corporations, plus a few rich and powerful private companies. A default on any bond with this rating would be a financial shock of tremendous magnitude. Buy with confidence.

- **AA (A+):** Excellent prospects. These bonds don't quite make it to the top rank but they aren't far off in safety terms. Many provincial governments have this rating. Given the slightly higher return these bonds usually pay, they're well worth considering.

- **A:** Solid citizens. They aren't Government of Canada or Province of Alberta, but the issuers are stable and well respected. They should be okay for your retirement plan.

- **BBB (B++):** Worth considering. Bonds with this rating are more susceptible to changing economic conditions but should be all right for RRSPs. I wouldn't go any farther down the scale, though.

- **BB (B+):** Some risk. Now we're starting to move into what the rating companies consider to be speculative territory. These bonds shouldn't carry a high degree of risk but they do have some.

- **B:** Risky. This is the point at which yields can sometimes start looking very seductive. After all, these companies have to do something to raise money.

- **CCC (C):** Pure speculation. When you get down to this level on the bond scale, you're really rolling the dice. Save your gambling instincts for the craps tables.

- **CC (D):** In default. If your bond slips into this category, the issuer has stopped making interest payments. You'll be lucky if you recover your principal. Don't say you weren't warned!

- **C:** Suspended. These issues have dropped off the scale as far as the rating companies are concerned.

Each category is subdivided into high, middle, and low groups, to provide greater precision for the financial community, but you generally don't need to be concerned about that.

As you learn more about bonds, you'll find you can use these variables to improve returns. But the most important thing to remember is the relationship between time and risk. The longer the time to the bond's maturity, the more risky it will be—it's as simple as that. Bonds with 20 years to maturity will move more sharply in price, up or down, than those with five years left.

You don't have to spend a lot of time worrying about which type of bond to choose if you don't want to. That's what makes bond trading so different from the stock market. With stocks, you not only have to consider which way the broad market is moving but you also have to look at specific industries and then at individual stocks within those industries. Bonds aren't as complicated. Most bonds with similar maturity dates and ratings will tend to move in the same direction in the market. You don't normally expect to find one 20-year Government of Canada bond moving up while another is going down.

If you're just starting out in the bond world, stick with Government of Canada issues. Don't consider anything else until you have a clear understanding of what you're doing. Decide whether you prefer short-term bonds (those with maturity dates no longer than five years from now), medium-term (5 to 10 years), or long-term (over 10 years). Short-term bonds are less risky because their maturity date is relatively close. At that time they can be cashed at face value. So if interest rates rise, causing bond prices to fall, short-term bonds won't usually suffer as great a loss as long-term bonds will. Conversely, long-term bonds offer the potential for large profits if interest rates decline. Prices of those bonds will increase more because the holders can collect the coupon interest rate, which will be substantially more than new bonds are paying, for a longer period of time. So if you believe interest rates are in a downward trend, and you're willing to accept a higher degree of risk, buy some long-term Government of Canada bonds.

If you decide to add some corporate bonds and you're not familiar with the issuer, ask your broker to supply current rating information. Also ask if the issuer has been put on watch, which means the rating services are reassessing its position as a result of recent developments. As well, see if the bond is "callable" any time soon, which means you could be forced to redeem it at the issuer's option. A *Financial Post* annual publication titled *FP Bonds: Corporate* is an invaluable reference tool for the serious corporate bond investor. However, like other FP publications, it comes with a hefty price tag.

One easy way to buy bonds for an RRSP is to use a "bond ladder" approach. This is a carefully selected portfolio of bonds with varying maturities. Many brokerage firms offer packaged bond ladder portfolios specifically designed for this purpose.

Bond mutual funds and exchange-traded funds are another option if you want to buy into a ready-made portfolio. But be careful of the high MERs on some bond mutual funds.

Stripped Bonds

I mentioned stripped bonds briefly in Chapter 10. Now let's look at them in more detail. Strips have a sort of Jekyll and Hyde personality, appealing to both ultra-conservative investors and fast-buck artists. Conservative investors see them as one of the most effective ways to lock in guaranteed returns for a long period—10, 20, even 30 years! Speculators buy them with the idea of scoring big capital gains in a short time, a strategy I don't recommend for your RRSP.

To understand how one security can appeal to investors so far apart on the risk spectrum, you need to know something about how strips work.

When a bond is issued by a government or corporation, semi-annual interest coupons are usually attached to it. These used to be real coupons that were clipped by the bondholder and cashed as the interest came due. Now the process is done electronically. Somewhere along the way, a smart financial dealer figured out that by separating the coupons from the bonds—hence "stripping" the bond—he could sell two securities instead of one: the couponless bond and the coupons themselves. A bond without coupons doesn't produce any interest for its owner. The only time it will generate a return will be at maturity, when it can be redeemed for full face value.

Of course no one is going to pay $1,000 today for a bond with a $1,000 face value that doesn't mature for several years and pays no interest. So stripped bonds are sold at a discounted price. The more time that remains until maturity, the less you'll pay. The difference between your purchase price today and the value at maturity is expressed as an annual yield.

The big attraction of strips to conservative investors is that the yield is locked in for many years. There is no other way to ensure an annual compound rate of return over such a lengthy period of time. GICs rarely run more than five years. Ordinary bonds provide a predictable return, but you may not be able to reinvest the interest at the same rate, especially if rates were high when you bought in.

Stripped bonds should never be held in a non-registered portfolio. The government treats the imputed interest as taxable immediately, even though you won't see a penny of it for years to come. Avoid that trap at all costs. Within an RRSP, however, strips can play a useful rule provided they are chosen carefully and the timing is right. Here are some guidelines.

Compare Yields

As with other types of bonds, you don't pay a brokerage commission when you buy strips. The broker's profit is built into the price of the bond. Unfortunately, that makes it impossible to know if you're being gouged— some brokers have been known to add exorbitant markups to strips. So I advise you to phone the bond desks at several brokerage firms and get quotes on strips of comparable term and quality. Ask for the yields to maturity and see how they compare. The higher the yield the less you are paying for the strip. If the quote from your own broker appears to be inflated by an unacceptably high markup, go back with a more competitive quote and see what he or she says. Chances are your broker will match it for fear of losing your business.

Buy When Rates Are High

There is a right time and a wrong time to aggressively add strips to your RRSP. The wrong time is when interest rates are at or near their cyclical low. Strips are much more susceptible to interest rate movements than ordinary bonds, so when rates start to climb the price of long-term strips will decline disproportionately. The best time to invest is when interest rates are high and the media is full of news about the economy slowing down. That's a sure tipoff that central banks will start to ease rates soon, which will drive the price of strips higher.

Plan Your Maturity Dates

If you're within 15 years of retirement, plan your strip maturity dates to coincide with your income needs. For example, instead of buying $100,000 worth of strips that mature in 2015, buy five strips of $20,000 with each maturing from 2015 to 2019. This allows you to extend the period for which you'll receive the current interest rates while ensuring there is always new cash flowing in to your portfolio.

Real Return Bonds

As we've seen, investing in bonds at a time of rising interest rates can be tricky and potentially dangerous. Real return bonds, however, offer a way to protect fixed-income assets against inflation and generate a decent return in the process.

They work like this. Semi-annual interest payments are adjusted to reflect increases in the Consumer Price Index so that you're always getting an inflation-adjusted return equal to the original coupon of the bond. As well, at maturity the bond holder receives a payment equal to the face value ($1,000) plus an inflation bonus that protects the purchasing power of the original investment.

When inflation is quiescent, these bonds produce a steady but unspectacular return. But when the CPI starts to rise, real return bonds come into their own. They were especially strong during 1999–2000, when inflation began to resurface as a growing concern for the first time in several years. In fact, during a time when most bond prices were weakening, real return bonds were rising in value.

The federal and provincial governments are the main issuer of these bonds so there is a decent supply. There are many issues of real return bonds available, with differing interest rate guarantees and maturities.

In summation, bonds are an essential ingredient in every well-balanced retirement plan. You'll need to decide on the most convenient way to buy them to suit your personal goals, but whatever you do, don't ignore them. They could be a lifesaver for your portfolio when stocks turn sour.

14

GICs and Guaranteed Securities

There was a time when guaranteed investment certificates (GICs) and term deposits (TDs) were the core holdings in many RRSPs. That was back in the days when interest rates were high and people felt they were receiving a generous return for a risk-free security. It was largely an illusion, of course. High interest rates normally go hand in hand with high inflation. A GIC paying a 7 percent yield only provides a real return of 2 percent if inflation is running at a 5 percent rate. A 3 percent yield produces exactly the same real return at 1 percent inflation but many people can't seem to get their heads around that.

So as interest rates declined, investors began to look at other options. Mutual funds were the big beneficiaries during the 1990s. With stock markets performing well and inflation waning, money poured in to fund coffers, transforming the industry into a financial powerhouse within a decade.

In the meantime, banks, trust companies, and credit unions, the primary GIC issuers, struggled to regain market share. In an effort to recast the image of staid old GICs into go-go securities in tune with the bullish markets of the so-called New Economy, they retooled the product line in much the same way as automobile manufacturers relaunch ailing models with a new look and more gimmicks. By the late 1990s, the market-index GIC had emerged as the banking industry's answer to mutual funds. You have to give the marketing departments credit; the products had a visceral appeal. They allowed cautious investors to participate in the red-hot high-tech stock market boom while at the same time protecting their principal against loss. What could be more Canadian— a security that allowed for risk-taking without risk! A perfect fit with the national psyche!

The idea worked, too—for a while. Then came the stock market crash of 2000–2002. People who had put money into market-linked GICs in 1999 and early 2000 began to realize that they were likely to get zero return on their investment at maturity. The principal would be repaid, sure. But a three-year or five-year commitment would end up producing nothing in the way of profit. Once the effect of inflation was factored in, they would lose money in purchasing power terms. Sales of market-linked GICs plummeted.

But by now a new dynamic was at work. People who had invested heavily in stocks and equity mutual funds saw the value of their portfolio decline on a monthly basis. It became so painful that many investors couldn't bear to read their financial statements; they were tossed into the nearest wastebasket, unopened. Fear overtook greed as the prime motivating force as Canadians contemplated the damage being wrought on their retirement savings by a relentlessly falling stock market.

In this environment, traditional GICs re-emerged as an attractive alternative for many. Yes, the rates being offered were at levels unseen in half a century. At one point the major banks were paying only 2.5 percent on five-year deposits. But hey—it was better than big losses in the stock market, right? Everything old was suddenly new again.

Then the cycle turned again. In 2003, the markets turned back up. It took a while for investors to realize that the bear had truly been sent back into hibernation, and memories of the savageness of the tech bust lingered. But gradually people began to venture into the markets again, albeit more cautiously. Greed staged a comeback but this time it was tempered by a fear that had not been evident at the end of the 1990s. This attitude resulted in a veritable deluge of guaranteed products that warrant to return at least the original amount invested at maturity. Although they vary in the details, they all operate on the same principle—we'll protect your capital while at the same time giving you an opportunity for profits far beyond what you could earn in a regular GIC.

The variety of guaranteed offerings was staggering. Some companies, such as Mulvihill Capital Management, sponsored closed-end funds that guaranteed a return of principal at maturity, usually 10 or 12 years in the future. Several mutual fund companies made deals with banks to issue guaranteed notes that calculated profits on the basis of how a specific fund or group of funds performed. Banks began to aggressively sell a range of market-linked GICs that gave people an opportunity to play stock markets around the world with, supposedly, no risk. When income trusts emerged as the hot product of the day, guaranteed securities were created to allow still-wary investors to obtain exposure to that sector.

One example was the DARTS Income Fund–Linked Deposit Notes issued by the Canadian Imperial Bank of Commerce in March–April 2005. It's worth taking a close look at how these work as an example of the pros and cons of guaranteed securities.

How DARTS Work

DARTS stands for derivative adjustable ratio securities. They are performance-linked securities, a group that bases payouts on the results achieved by a pre-defined target index, security, or group of securities within a specified time frame. For DARTS, the return on the notes is determined by the performance of a basket of 11 income trusts. Five of the trusts are resource-based (e.g., Canadian Oil Sands Trust, Fording Canadian Coal Trust), three are REITs (e.g., RioCan Real Estate Investment Trust), and three are business trusts (e.g., Yellow Pages Income Fund).

The notes mature on April 21, 2013, eight years after issue (by comparison, five years is standard for regular GICs). At maturity, investors receive their principal back ($100 per note) plus any capital gains and accumulated distributions.

It's worth noting here that guaranteed notes are almost always tied to a high-performance sector of the market. In this case, income trusts had been the strongest segment of the Toronto Stock Exchange in 2004, outperforming stocks. Although experience tells us that all high flyers eventually fall, that didn't stop the marketing machines of CIBC and other organizations from promoting the historical results in selling this and similar products.

One aspect of DARTS that is especially interesting is the potential use of leveraging—borrowing money to add to the number of units held in the portfolio. This could significantly enhance returns if the target trusts perform well over time.

Offsetting that on the downside is something called a "protection event." If the trusts decline and the net asset value of the notes falls to a certain level, all the units are sold and the entire fund is invested in a zero-coupon bond to protect the principal. Think about what this means. Suppose there was carnage in the income trusts sector, for whatever reason. It happened in 1997–1998 when oil prices fell to US$10 a barrel, so there is precedent. Let's say the situation was serious enough to trigger the "protection event" in early 2009. There would be no trusts left in the portfolio and therefore no possibility of profit for the next four years. Your money would be tied up with a certainty of zero return at the end of the day. If you tried to sell before maturity in the secondary market that CIBC promised to maintain, you would incur a large loss. The guarantee only kicks in when the notes mature.

So what's the bottom line? These are the pros of DARTS as I see them:

- *Capital protection.* Your principal is safe if you hold to maturity.
- *No limit on profits.* Some market-linked notes and GICs have a cap on the return they will pay. DARTS did not impose a limit.
- *Leveraging.* The use of leveraging if certain conditions are met would increase the profit potential if the trusts do well.

And these are the cons:

- *Potential for zero return.* Your money could be tied up for eight years with nothing to show for it.
- *High fees.* CIBC charges 2.5 percent annually on the trust portion of the portfolio. That's very high, especially when you consider the basket

of securities is set at the outset and the various action points are triggered by a predetermined formula.

- *No distributions.* The rationale for income trusts is to provide cash flow for investors who need income. DARTS make no payments, reinvesting the distributions instead. (Note: some guaranteed products do offer distributions, so review the terms if this is important to you.)

- *No stock exchange listing.* CIBC said it would maintain a secondary market for DARTS but would not list them on a stock exchange. An exchange listing is by far the best way to provide liquidity.

- *Tax disadvantage.* One of the big attractions of income trusts is the tax advantages they offer. These are not available in DARTS. Any profit at maturity will be taxed as regular income.

The bottom line is that I am not a big fan of DARTS or any other guaranteed product that has come across my desk. While I understand their appeal, I have yet to find one in which the pros outweighed the cons, and not a single reader has ever reported to me that they made a lot of money on a guaranteed security. So be very skeptical if something like this is offered to you.

Market-Linked GICs

DARTS and similar index-linked notes are being heavily promoted, but the more traditional market-linked GICs are often the better choice for investors who really like this concept. There are two reasons: lower cost and a shorter term to maturity. Paying a high management fee for an index-linked note (or indeed paying any management fee at all) is irksome. Given the passive nature of the investment, there is no justification (other that the issuer's profit) for attaching a high cost to it. You can avoid that by using market-linked GICs, if this is what you really want to do.

The shorter term to maturity of market-linked GICs is a big advantage. It means you won't have your money tied up for as long a period if stocks tumble. For example, at the time of writing Royal Bank was offering a three-year market-linked GIC that was tied to the performance of the

S&P/TSX 60 Index, which tracks the 60 largest public companies in Canada—our equivalent of the Dow Jones Industrial Average, if you like. Investors also had the option to lock in gains at the second anniversary. The bank also had a three-year global market-linked GIC with the payout based on returns from the German, French, Japanese, British, and U.S. markets over the period. You can find similar offerings with somewhat different terms at other financial institutions. Like regular GICs, the market-linked variety is protected by deposit insurance to a maximum of $100,000.

If you want to invest in market-linked GICs, here are some important variables to bear in mind.

Method of calculation. Some GICs base their returns strictly on the movement of the underlying indexes between the time of the investment and the maturity date. So, for example, if the index of choice was the S&P/TSX 60 and it rose 25 percent over the term, that's the return you'll earn on your investment. Of course, if it dropped 25 percent, all you'd get back is your original investment. Other GICs use a monthly average in determining the rate of return. This can work out to be much less advantageous to the investor if the markets move up considerably.

Cap on returns. Some market-linked GICs place a limit on how much you can earn over the term of the security. If the cap is, say, 20 percent and the market rises 40 percent, you're still stuck with the 20 percent. Stay away from any index-linked GICs that limit the potential return.

Locking in. A few market-linked GICs allow you to lock in your profits along the way, such as the Royal Bank products just mentioned. That can be a very useful feature, so ask about it.

I don't recommend this type of GIC for retirement plans at times when stock markets are high. When there is a major correction, such as experienced in 2000–2002, you could find your money tied up for several years with zero return. That runs completely contrary to the principle of using the tax-sheltering advantages of an RRSP to maximize the effect of compounding. If you must use this type of GIC, the time to buy is when stock market values are down. Unfortunately, you probably won't find these GICs being offered (and certainly not heavily promoted) during such periods because no one wants to hear about stocks in a pessimistic climate. No financial institution was aggressively selling these products in 2002, for example, when stock indexes were enduring triple-digit losses day after day. If you think stocks are going to rise, a well-managed equity fund will give you a far better payoff.

Royal Bank has a useful market-linked GIC calculator on their website. To see how profitable these securities might be, I ran several scenarios. Here are the results. The profit column shows the gain over and above the return of principal as of late March 2005. Note that this represents the total cumulative return, not the average annual compound rate of return.

PROFITABILITY OF ROYAL BANK MARKET-LINKED GICS

Type of GIC	Purchase Date	Term	Profit (%)
Canadian	March 31, 2000	5 years	0.00
Global	March 31, 2000	5 years	0.00
Canadian	March 31, 2002	3 years	3.58
Global	March 31, 2002	3 years	0.00
Canadian	March 31, 2003	3 years	18.33
Global	March 31, 2003	3 years	17.35
Canadian	March 31, 2004	3 years	4.03
Global	March 31, 2004	3 years	1.77

It's worth taking a moment to study these numbers because they illustrate what a crapshoot market-linked GICs really are. Anyone who invested in a five-year certificate at the end of March 2000 ended up with a return of zero. After that, Royal dropped the five-year option and only issued three-year certificates, so I plugged in the numbers for an investment in both the Canadian and Global GICs on March 31, 2002. At maturity, the Global GIC paid nothing. There was a small profit on the Canadian GIC but it worked out to slightly over 1 percent a year over the term.

The lucky investors were those who put their money in at the end of March 2003. In both cases they were sitting on nice gains two years later, at which time they had the option to lock in if they wished. But anyone who did so closed the books and their investment earned no profit over the next year. In the end, they are left with an average annual compound rate of return of between 5.5 percent and 6 percent. That's not a lot when you consider the risk involved.

Other Types of GICs

If you don't like market-linked GICs but want something with a few more bells and whistles than the plain vanilla type, here are some of the other choices available. Not every financial institution will offer all these types, so you may have to do some shopping.

Interest-Linked GICs

The return on interest-linked GICs is linked to the prime rate. If it moves higher, so does the yield. If the prime rate drops, the return will as well. This type of GIC can be cashed at any time. The catch is that the starting interest rate is less than that of a standard GIC. In March 2005, Royal Bank was paying 1.5 percent on these GICs. The rate on a standard one-year GIC was a quarter-point higher at 1.75 percent.

Redeemable GICs

Redeemable GICs can be cashed at any time but your interest rate will be reduced if you redeem before the maturity date. They provide maximum flexibility, but rates of return are lower than for non-redeemable certificates.

Escalating GICs

Escalating GICs are designed for long-term investors who are unhappy with present GIC rates. The idea is seductively simple: your interest rises each year (or sometimes after the first two years) over a five-year term; by the time you get to the fifth year, your GIC is paying a rate that looks impressive by today's standards.

It seems great, but if you analyze things carefully, it actually isn't. What really counts is the blended rate you'll receive over the full term. You'll probably find that figure isn't much more than you'd receive from a regular five-year GIC. To obtain that, you'll have to accept two disadvantages.

First, you're locked in for five years. It's never a good idea to tie up your money when interest rates are low; the probability is that they will rise during that time. Second, if the certificate is held outside an RRSP or RRIF, you'll be taxed on the blended interest rate over the five-year term. That means you'll pay disproportionately higher taxes in the early years. Since it usually works to your advantage to defer tax for as long as possible, that's not exactly a great idea.

For these reasons, only use this product within an RRSP or a RRIF—and then only if you get a clear interest rate advantage over a standard five-year GIC and there is a high probability that interest rates are set to decline.

If you like the idea of an escalating GIC but don't relish the idea of locking your money away for a long term, there is another alternative to consider. To compete with Canada Premium Bonds, some companies are offering escalating GICs with a cashable feature attached to them. This, in essence, gives you the option to cash them in on each anniversary of the term. Check with your financial institution to see if they offer this product.

Staggered Maturity GICs

Financial advisors are always telling people that the best way to beat volatile interest rates is to stagger the maturity dates of their GICs. By having 20 percent of your GIC assets roll over each year, instead of the whole amount coming up for renewal every five years, you smooth out interest rate variations and ensure you won't see your investment income suddenly nosedive. Some financial institutions now put that advice into practice by offering GICs that can be divided into separate components, each with a different maturity date. So, for example, you could invest $10,000 in a five-year GIC but have $2,000 come due on the anniversary date of each year. Although all use the same concept, the product names vary so ask at your financial institution if these interest you.

Monthly-Pay GICs

If you need regular monthly payments, you can invest in a GIC that will provide it. But the interest rate you receive will be lower than that of a GIC that makes annual or semi-annual interest payments.

There's one more important point to remember when investing in GICs: most bank and trust company branch managers have the discretion to improve on the posted rates. All you have to do is ask. They can usually give you up to a quarter-point more, but I've heard of some bonuses of up to 1 percent where a lot of money was involved, the term was for five years, and the financial institution wanted to keep the business. So don't be afraid to do a little hard bargaining.

15

Shattered Dreams

The stock market can make dreams come true. It can also shatter them. That's exactly what happened during the Millennium Crash, which began in 2000 and finally came to a climactic end in the fall of 2002. By the time it was over, many people had been forced to put their retirement plans on hold as the value of their savings melted away.

The losses incurred during those three traumatic years were truly mind-boggling. A study done by Elroy Dimson, Paul Marsh, and Mike Staunton of the London Business School and published in the 2003 edition of ABN AMRO's *Global Investment Returns Yearbook* estimates that worldwide equity losses during the bear market totalled US$13 trillion, or US$2,000 for every man, woman, and child on Earth! Those are staggering numbers and they dramatically illustrate how quickly years of carefully accumulated wealth can be wiped out. There are no statistics that tell us how many families in Canada and the United States had their retirement put on hold because of the crash or how many extra years they will have to work to make up for the losses. But anecdotal evidence suggests that they number at least in the tens of thousands.

The fallout from the Millennium Crash will gradually fade over time, however, setting the stage for a new round of shattered dreams some time in the future. Don't let it happen to you! This is not to say that you should never invest in the stock market. Not doing so would deprive your portfolio of the most important single engine of growth that we have available. But you must proceed with prudence, discipline, respect, and common sense. There are right ways and wrong ways to invest in equities. Be sure you understand which is which.

The stock market is like an elevator: it goes both up *and* down. I emphasize this because in the late 1990s there was a belief that the down button on the elevator was permanently out of order. This was the era of the internet bubble, when high-tech stocks were driving markets to record levels. Leading the way was Nasdaq, which set record after record during the period from 1998 to March 2000. Some financial experts added to the feeding frenzy by coming out with theories that the old laws governing market valuations had been rewritten. The tremendous growth potential of the internet, fibre optics, biotech, and wireless technology had made long-standing measures like price/earnings ratios and even profits meaningless. Growth rates were what mattered.

The last time this mentality took hold was in the late 1980s, when some people tried to tell us that Japan's soaring stock market could not be measured in conventional North American terms. By 1988, the capitalization of the Japanese market was 40 percent of the world total, well ahead of the U.S. at 29 percent. Everyone assumed the ride would go on indefinitely.

Well, it didn't! The Nikkei Index began a long tumble in 1989 and by the end of 2002 had lost more than 70 percent of its value in real terms. It's a lesson you must never forget. Stock market euphoria inevitably leads to a hangover.

Protecting Your Wealth

No matter what stock you buy, it will eventually drop in price. The decline may only be temporary, but it will happen, and when it does you may tend to become surprised, miserable, angry, frightened, or any combination of the four. You shouldn't. It's a natural part of the process. Wise investors will take steps to protect themselves and their wealth against this kind of disaster. Here's how.

Let Your Age Guide Your Investments

Unless you're extremely knowledgeable, I do not recommend a large stock portfolio for people who are within 10 years of their planned retirement date. The time element is too short. If you run into a prolonged bear market, such as the one we saw in 2000–2002, you may be forced to sell at a huge loss or face going into retirement with a large portion of your assets tied up in unproductive holdings. A younger person can wait out the down cycle and benefit when the inevitable upturn occurs. Older folks no longer have that luxury.

Diversify

Make sure your portfolio is properly balanced. We saw in Chapter 14 how including bonds in a portfolio would have reduced losses during the bear market by a significant amount. Proper asset allocation is critical to protecting your retirement savings, and the older you are the more important it becomes. See Chapter 9 for more details.

Invest in Quality

The stock market is not a casino, although some people tend to see it that way. You don't have to speculate in penny stocks to reap big rewards. A careful, well-informed investor can do very well by sticking with good-quality companies. I've seen many blue-chip stocks double and triple in just a few short years. For example, in the *Internet Wealth Builder* newsletter, which I publish, we recommended shares in Brascan Corporation, a multi-billion-dollar conglomerate with interests in real estate, financial services, power generation, and resources, in April 1997, when they were trading at $13.79 (price adjusted for subsequent splits). Brascan is about as blue-chip as a stock gets in Canada. In late March 2005, the shares were trading in the $45 range and paying a nice dividend as a bonus. You'll find similar stories with banks, insurance companies, utilities, and railroads. Plus, these stocks will usually suffer less in market downturns.

Avoid Speculative Leveraging

The people who were hardest hit by the market crash were those who had succumbed to the siren song of investment advisors who told them in the late 1990s to mortgage their homes to the hilt and put all their money into stocks and equity funds. The numbers were compelling—huge profits could be earned while the interest on the mortgage would be tax-deductible because the money was being used to acquire an investment portfolio. In the overheated climate of the day, it all seemed to make perfect sense. But leveraging magnifies losses as well as gains. When the market went south, portfolio values collapsed. People who expected to have a mortgage-free home going into retirement found themselves burdened with a big loan that would take years to repay. Speculative leveraging can be a financial minefield. Using borrowed money to invest in a low-risk, income-producing portfolio is one thing, but taking big risks should be avoided.

Be Careful of Cyclical Stocks

Many cyclical stocks are resource-based, which means we have a lot of them in Canada. Mining companies, forestry firms, and oil and gas companies all qualify. Like the economy itself, they go through boom and bust periods. When they're hot, they can produce huge profits, as we saw in the energy sector when oil prices hit record highs in 2004–2005. But when the world economy slumps, cyclical stocks tend to drop faster than other sectors of the market. Timing therefore becomes critical if you want to own them.

The best time to buy is when these stocks are off-cycle, and therefore cheap. This means the particular industry is not in favour with investors. Usually, that's because the prices for the commodities it produces (e.g., aluminum, gold, crude oil, lumber) are low so the profitability of the company is reduced. Typically, stocks in such companies rise and fall in tandem with the international price of the commodities in which they specialize.

Another entry point occurs when the cyclical upturn appears to be in its early stages and has a while to run. The rebound in the energy sector actually began in early 1999. It soon became clear that supplies were tightening and that the profits of oil and natural gas companies would continue to strengthen for some time to come. By early 2005, energy prices were at record levels and the stocks were doing very well.

It's important to take profits periodically in cyclical stocks and to leave the party before they start turning out the lights. Otherwise, you'll give back all your gains when the sector again falls out of favour (which it will) and share prices go into a slump.

Use a Value Approach

Most of the world's greatest stock market investors select their securities by using value-based criteria. If it's good enough for Warren Buffett and Sir John Templeton, it should be good enough for the rest of us! Value investing is based on a very simple philosophy—never overpay for a stock. But the process of measuring what is good value and what is not will vary from one investor to another.

One of the most basic criteria used by value investors and money managers who employ this technique is to look at a company's net asset value per share (NAVPS). That's what it is worth on a per share basis when all of its assets are added up and all of the liabilities subtracted. A stock that is trading below its net asset value is considered to be a good buy with limited downside risk. However, NAVPS can sometimes be difficult to ascertain. For example, a company such as a supermarket chain or a large retailer may own a lot of property in urban areas that is being carried on its books at cost. In fact, the market value of the land and buildings is worth much more, creating hidden value. Smart investors are always on the watch for such situations.

Other common ratios studied by value investors include price to earnings (the famous P/E ratio), price to cash flow, and price to sales. Irwin Michael, founder of the ABC Funds and one of Canada's main proponents of value investing, also looks for what he calls a "value catalyst"—a trigger that can act to push up a stock's value. These might include new management, the lack of a control block, which would make the company a potential takeover target, and the sale or purchase of an important asset.

Value stocks typically will not increase in value to the same extent as high-growth securities, especially in a strong market. But they will likely suffer less of a hit when markets retreat. When it comes to your retirement savings, that is an important consideration.

Tune Out Hot Tips

Over the years I've observed that when a broker gives you a recommendation, 7 times out of 10 the stock will drop in price before it goes up again. That's because you aren't the only one hearing about it; if it's a hot issue there will be a lot of action in the market. So don't be too quick to plunge in. If you like the look of the stock, ask your broker to send you some information on it—the analyst's research, the latest annual report, and anything else that's relevant. Read the material carefully and see if the company fits your investment objectives. Also, take a look at how it will fit into your portfolio; would it overweight you in bank stocks, for example. If on close scrutiny it seems like a stock you should own, then set a realistic entry level and monitor its price movements over a period of time. When it comes within buying range—and more often than not it will—make the commitment.

Set Target Points

You should always buy a stock with the idea that you will one day sell it. Even though the market may move up over the long haul, there are times when it's prudent to take profits on even your most cherished stocks with the idea of buying back when the price drops. To do this, you need to set target points at which you'll sell, both on the profit side and on the loss side. Your upside targets will depend on the state of the market and your personal objectives. If the market is strong and shows no signs of weakening, a profit gain of 50 to 100 percent over your purchase price is not unrealistic. If the market is moving sideways and you're looking for a fast trade, you may target a profit as low as 10 to 20 percent. Just be sure when you set a low selling target that there will be enough profit left after commissions to make the whole transaction worthwhile.

While you can be flexible on the high side, you should be quite rigid about taking losses. If the stock drops 25 percent from your purchase price, it's time to revisit it and see whether you should stick with it. Ask yourself this question: Would I buy it now? If the answer is no, it's time to sell.

I've seen many cases of people holding on to a losing stock in the vain hope that it will turn around and at least come back to their purchase price. What generally happens is that the stock just keeps on sliding, and a 25 percent loss turns into a 50 or 75 percent decline. When things go wrong, take your lumps and move on. Don't compound your misery by hanging on, hoping for a miracle.

Don't Be Greedy

Intelligent investing means taking profits along the way. When a stock doubles in value, I always consider selling half my position even if I am convinced it will go higher. By doing so I take out my original capital, thus ensuring that I cannot lose money on the transaction, no matter what happens after that. If the price doubles again, I'll sell 50 percent of what's left, thereby guaranteeing a healthy profit.

That kind of discipline may sound easy. It's not. People tend to agonize over the sell decision far more than they do when deciding whether to buy. But if you adopt this approach and stick to it, you'll reduce your overall risk and have new money ready to redeploy on a regular basis.

Don't Panic

The worst investment decisions are made at times of high emotional stress. If you are prone to overreact to stock market movements, let someone else make the decisions—an investment counsellor or a mutual fund manager. Just be sure you have full confidence that the person who is making the call will act in your best interests.

Following these guidelines won't guarantee that you'll never lose money in a severe stock market correction. But you will be able to keep any losses at a tolerable level and be in a position to recover when conditions take a turn for the better. What you *must* seek to avoid at all costs is the kind of devastating setback that derailed the retirement hopes of so many people in the Millennium Crash. It *can* be done if you put a strategy in place and hold to it.

16

Mutual Funds—Battered but Unbowed

Recent years have not been kind to mutual funds. The bear market of 2000–2002 caused many investors to pull out their money from equity funds and return to the safety of GICs. The problems were compounded by growing competition from other types of securities such as exchange-traded funds, income trusts, and closed-end funds. Then there was the market timing scandal that rocked the U.S. industry and led to five Canadian firms being required to negotiate multi-million-dollar settlements with the Ontario Securities Commission. It's been a tough slog!

Despite all these negatives, the industry actually grew in size by $117 billion over the five years from the end of February 2000, the last month before the bear market began, to February 28, 2005. That represented an increase of 29 percent in assets under management, as reported by the member companies of the Investment Funds Institute of Canada, the trade association of the industry. Obviously, many Canadians still like mutual funds despite all their problems.

Why? There are several reasons. Perhaps the most important one is that mutual funds still offer the best way to create a well-diversified investment portfolio with professional management at a reasonable cost. The secret to using funds successfully in a retirement portfolio is to pick the right ones and make sure the expenses are in line.

Focus on Low-Risk Funds

The first step in choosing mutual funds is to determine an appropriate asset allocation. If you have not done that yet, reread Chapter 9 and decide on how you want to distribute your money. In doing so, keep in mind that what you're actually doing is creating a personal pension plan. Preservation of capital should rank at the top of your priority list. That doesn't mean you should never invest in a security that might experience a decline—that would be unrealistic and would limit your mutual fund choices to low-return options like money market funds, short-term bond funds, and mortgage funds. You can, and should, be prepared to assume more risk than that. But don't go to the other extreme and overload your retirement portfolio with science and technology or Far East funds. Balance is the key.

This means you should focus on mutual funds that are among the lowest risk of their type. Here are some ways to identify them.

Volatility

The more volatile a fund's performance, the greater the chance it will suffer a big loss at some point. Volatility is usually measured by standard deviation, which is a mathematical measure of the degree to which a fund's performance will vary, up or down, from its average. The higher the number, the greater the volatility. For example, at the time of writing, AGF China Focus Class had a standard deviation of 6.00, which is very high. In contrast, AGF Canadian Conservative Income Fund, which invests in a portfolio of bonds, preferred shares, and mortgages, showed a standard deviation of 0.64. Which do you think would be the best choice as a core RRSP holding?

But standard deviation can be misleading because it reflects variations from the norm both up and down. So a fund that is performing extremely well and registering big gains on a regular basis could have a higher standard deviation than one that is gradually losing ground over a period of time. So don't use standard deviation as your only risk indicator.

Beta

Whereas standard deviation measures a fund's volatility in relation to its own performance, its beta is an indicator of how it has done compared to the market it tracks; the lower the beta, the less the risk. A beta of 1.00 indicates a perfect correlation between fund risk and market risk. The CIBC Canadian Index Fund has such a beta, which is no surprise being that it is designed to track the S&P/TSX Composite Index. The CIBC Dividend Fund shows a low beta of 0.60. The CIBC Global Technology Fund has a beta of 1.26.

Maximum Drawdown

Maximum drawdown is a relatively new measurement that was added to the range of risk factors on The Fund Library website (at **www.fundlibrary.com**) in early 2004. Levi Folk, president and managing editor of fundlibrary.com, introduced it with this explanation:

> Maximum Drawdown [reveals] the worst possible loss endured in a given fund before an investor recovers his or her money. A Drawdown is the loss incurred in a fund from any high point in the fund's value until the fund recovers that value. The Maximum Drawdown is the biggest Drawdown that a mutual fund has experienced historically.... We calculate the Drawdown by finding the lowest point a fund has reached from a previous high and calculating this drop. A fund will have several Drawdowns over time, one for each period between new highs …

The Fund Library website provides maximum drawdown numbers for periods of three years, five years, and 10 years. A money market fund will have a maximum drawdown of zero over all periods. A mortgage fund will typically show a low maximum drawdown—TD Mortgage Fund was at 1.58 percent over all time periods at the time of writing. Technology and precious metals funds will be at the other extreme; the maximum drawdown over 10 years in the TD Precious Metals Fund was 65.55 percent.

Bear Market Record

I always like to see how a fund performed during years when the type of security in which it invests came under pressure. For equity funds, the bear market years of 2000 to 2002 are telling ones. When I look at the record of a conservatively managed fund like Mackenzie Cundill Canadian Security ("C" units) over that three-year span, I see a gain in each calendar year of 19.6 percent, 2.9 percent, and 4.1 percent, respectively. That tells me that this fund is managed with a view to protecting capital in tough times, which is what I want to see in an RRSP.

In the case of bond funds, I check years when rising interest rates knocked down bond prices. One example was 1999, when almost all conventional bond funds lost money. But short-term bond funds were able to withstand the slide. TD Short-Term Bond Fund gained 2.2 percent that year, making it one of the better performers.

Annual Profit/Loss Ratio

Comparing the number of years a fund gained money to the number of years it lost ground is another useful measure. The "15-Year Mutual Fund Review," published annually by *The Globe and Mail*, is very helpful in this regard. Over the 15 calendar years from 1990 to 2004, the TD Mortgage Fund never once lost money—a remarkable run. That gives it a success rate of 100 percent. By contrast, Investors Japanese Equity Fund lost ground in nine of those years for a success ratio of only 40 percent. I would think long and hard before putting that one into a retirement portfolio.

Performance Comparisons

You want mutual funds that aren't going to cause devastation in bad times, but you also want funds that tend to outperform others of the same type. So after you have assessed the risk profile of your candidate funds, look at how they did over time in relation to their peer group.

In doing so, avoid placing too much emphasis on absolute numbers. Sometimes they can be deceiving. In 1999, the National Bank Asia Pacific Fund gained 27.9 percent. Sounds pretty good—that is, until you learn it was the worst result in its category that year. Also, do not be unduly influenced by the most recent 12 months. Sometimes fund companies will strongly promote a fund that is coming off a good year; you want to look beyond that.

Some years ago, I devised what I call an Average Quartile Ranking (AQR). Here's how it works. Find an internet site, such as Globefund or The Fund Library, that provides quartile rankings for every fund. The quartile ranking shows you how a fund performed against its peer group in a specific time frame, say, one year. If it was in the first quartile, that means it was among the top 25 percent in its category. Second quartile means it was above average but not in the top league. Third quartile is below average but not terrible. Fourth quartile is pretty bad—the fund was in the bottom 25 percent of its grouping. By adding the quartile rankings and dividing by the number of periods under review, we get the AQR for the time frame you're looking at.

For example, a fund that was in the first quartile for every period would receive an AQR of 1.00—a perfect score. One that finished in the bottom quartile every year would end up with a rating of 4.00. It's not complicated—you can calculate it yourself for any fund in which you are interested.

A fund that showed a quartile ranking of one, three, two, one, and two (total nine) over the past five years would have an AQR of 1.80 for that period (nine divided by five). That's a very good result—anything under 2.00 tells you the fund has been in the top half of its class most of the time during the period being measured. On the other hand, a fund with a pattern of one, four, three, four, and three would have an AQR of 3.00, which is not very good. Yet many people may be drawn to it because during the most recent year it finished in the top quartile. The rest of the time it was a lousy performer, however, which the AQR reveals.

The Saxon organization is small but the funds it offers are first-rate, with very good AQRs. Saxon Stock Fund, Saxon Balanced Fund, and Saxon World Growth Fund all showed AQRs of 1.71 over the seven-year period ending in 2004, making them good candidates for an RRSP. On the other hand, the 3.29 AQR of the RBC Life Science and Technology Fund might send you fleeing in a different direction.

Applying this overlay to the list of funds you chose based on risk profile will enable you to screen out the mediocre performers. Now you can move ahead to look at costs.

Costs Add Up

There are two parts to the cost equation. One is the commission structure—the amount you pay your advisor when you buy or sell fund units. Many people try to avoid this expense by selecting only "no-load" funds, but in doing so they eliminate some of the top performers from consideration. Although it is possible to create a good no-load portfolio, I prefer to keep open all the options.

There are three types of sales commissions:

- *Deferred sales charge (DSC)*. Buying DSC units means you pay no commission up front. However, you will be assessed a fee if you sell before a certain period of time has elapsed (typically seven years). The biggest concern with DSC funds (also known as back-end load units) is that they lock you in for several years. It's true that the fee can usually be avoided by moving to another fund within the same family, but your financial advisor may charge a switching fee of up to 2 percent. Also, if the fund is performing so badly that you are desperate to bail out, you may find it uncomfortable to stay within the same group.

- *Service charge (SC)*. These are more commonly known as front-end load funds. They require the payment of a sales commission at the time of purchase, usually no more than 5 percent. The amount of the commission reduces the money you actually put to work, so a $1,000 investment with a 5 percent commission actually buys only $950 worth of units. Some financial advisors now offer SC units at zero commission. They do this to "build their book"—add to their assets under management. The incentive to do this is the "trailer fees" that are paid by the fund companies. Typically, these amount to 0.5 percent of the value of the assets in an advisor's "book." That may not seem like a lot until you do some math and realize that works out to $5,000 a year in revenue for every $1 million under management.

- *Low load*. Low-load units are a type of DSC option, but are a more attractive choice. They have a much lower fee structure and usually reach zero commission after three years. Most investors are unaware this choice even exists and, if they know about it, they are under the impression it is only available to high-net-worth clients. Not so. If you are considering buying DSC units, ask your advisor if the fund company also has a low-load option. You can also check the fund prospectus online at Sedar (**www.sedar.com**), a website that publishes financial documents for all mutual funds and public companies.

The other main element of fund cost is the management expense ratio (MER). There has been a steady but somewhat muted chorus of complaints about the high MERs of Canadian mutual funds, and to some extent this is justified. Logically, one would expect MERs to decline as funds grow larger because of economies of scale, but this rarely seems to happen.

Some investors have become so obsessed with MERs that they will only buy units in funds that have below-average annual costs or they have abandoned mutual funds altogether in favour of ETFs and closed-end funds. That effectively eliminates some fine mutual funds from consideration. There are many excellent low-MER funds—just because they're cheap does not mean they're bad. There are also many higher-MER funds that are chronic underperformers. So this is not a case of you get what you pay for. A high MER doesn't mean the fund is any better than one with a low MER. It may just be less efficiently managed or the fund company is boosting its profits.

Also, be aware that some MERs appear to be unusually high because they are inflated by performance bonuses. These are extra fees paid to management when certain targets are surpassed. Most funds don't have this provision but some of the smaller companies include it in their prospectus. An example is the Sprott Canadian Equity Fund, which had an MER of 5.63 percent at the time of writing. The fund's average annual compound rate of return of 32.2 percent for the five years to March 31, 2005, made the high fee easier to swallow for investors.

You can see the MERs of all mutual funds on websites like Globefund and compare them to others of the same type. The "15-Year Mutual Fund Review" that I mentioned earlier includes the average and median MERs of all the funds in each category. At the end of 2004, it showed the average Canadian equity fund with an MER of 2.83 percent, with the median being 2.87 percent. Here are the numbers for some of the most popular categories.

MUTUAL FUND MERS (AS OF DEC. 31, 2004)		
Category	Average (%)	Median (%)
Canadian equity	2.83	2.87
Canadian dividend	2.54	2.46
Canadian balanced	2.55	2.73
Canadian income trust	2.29	2.13
Global balanced	2.91	2.93
Global equity	2.94	2.94
U.S. equity	2.72	2.81
Canadian bond	1.81	1.96
Canadian money market	1.07	1.08

Source: *The Globe and Mail Report on Mutual Funds*, February 14, 2005.

When it comes to MERs, the bottom line is how much is left in your pocket after the fees and expenses are deducted. A fund with a high MER that has produced above-average returns over a long period of time should certainly not be dismissed out of hand. That said, experience shows us that the majority of over-achieving funds have below-average MERs. Low costs and higher returns tend to go hand in hand.

Some fund companies that are well known for low MERs include Saxon, McLean Budden, Phillips, Hager & North, Mawer, Leith Wheeler, Chou, ABC, Beutel Goodman, and Sceptre.

Other Factors

Risk, performance, and cost are the three most important considerations in selecting mutual funds for a retirement savings program. But there are some other factors to take into account. They include the following.

Future Prospects

No one can predict the future, but there are some clues that can help you make an informed judgment on how a particular fund is likely to perform over the next year or so. Although your retirement portfolio is a long-range venture, that does not mean you should blithely ignore short-term prospects. A fund that loses 15 percent in the first year after you acquire it must gain 18 percent in the next year just to get back to break-even. Even if that happens, you've gone for two years with zero profit. So your choice should always favour a fund with a good chance of advancing over the next 12 months. That builds in a cushion against future losses. If the short-term prospects for a fund you like appear to be weak, hold off on the commitment until things improve.

Key indicators, which are closely watched by economists, can offer some useful investing clues. If the numbers are indicating a slowing economy, falling corporate profits, rising unemployment, and a decline in the growth rate, the chances are that central banks will begin to ease interest rates. That would be good news for bond funds, income trusts funds, and monthly income funds. Conversely, a rising inflation rate and runaway growth, such as we saw in the late 1990s, would be a signal that interest rates are likely to rise: bad news for bond and dividend funds.

To show you how this works in practice, in late June 2004 the U.S. Federal Reserve began raising interest rates from their half-century lows. The process continued through the rest of the year and into 2005. By the end of May 2005, the Fed had raised its key rate by a quarter-point at each of eight consecutive meetings, with more hikes expected. Historically, this pattern of gradual but steady rate increases has resulted in a slowdown in the stock markets and a retreat in bond prices, with long-term government bonds being the most vulnerable. In light of this, a prudent person would have minimized new investments in equity funds and certain types of bond funds during this period and focused instead on lower-risk funds such as mortgage funds and short-term bond funds.

The Management Team

The fund manager is the person who calls the shots. He or she makes the investment decisions that will determine the fate of your money. You should therefore make every effort to learn something about the person or team to whom you're entrusting your capital. As in every other profession, there are good managers, mediocre managers, and bad managers.

Of course, no one comes out and publicly says a manager is bad—not unless they want to incur the risk of a libel suit. So you have to use your own judgment and sometimes read between the lines.

Good managers are somewhat easier to identify. The stars are often written about and quoted in the media and sometimes win major awards. However, many top-notch managers labour in relative obscurity. Few people, for example, could name a single manager in organizations like Phillips, Hager & North, McLean Budden, or Beutel Goodman, yet their funds perform consistently well, year after year. In situations such as that, you have to look at the overall team and the track record of the company in ensuring that quality leaders are always in place.

It's also important to determine whether a manager's approach is consistent with your investment philosophy. For example, look at the Mavrix funds. Some of their funds (although not all of them) show risk characteristics that are way out of line with their peer group. For example, Mavrix Growth Fund, managed by Marvin Spooner, showed a beta of 1.51, a standard deviation of 8.99, and a maximum three-year drawdown of 92.38 percent at the time of writing. The Mavrix Strategic Small Cap Fund, also run by Mr. Spooner, had a beta of 1.28, a standard deviation of 7.80, and a three-year maximum drawdown of 86.81 percent. You might reasonably conclude from this that Mr. Spooner is a very aggressive money manager. You can then decide if you are comfortable with that type of style.

At the other end of the scale, you'll find managers who are very conservative in their approach, such as Jerry Javasky of the Mackenzie Ivy funds, Gerald Coleman of the CI Harbour funds, and Kim Shannon, who runs the CI Canadian Investment Fund. Investors who prefer less risk may find the cautious, value-driven style used here to be to their liking, but those who are more aggressive may see it as too tame.

The Fund Family

Don't choose mutual funds in isolation. Look at the total family and determine its strengths and weaknesses. There may come a time when you want to switch part or all of your assets to another fund within the organization, or to add other funds from the company to your portfolio. So you want to know a good deal about the other options available to you and how strong they are.

Start by examining the product range. Does the organization offer funds in all the categories that interest you? Or is it limited to only a few choices? This is especially important to know if you're planning to build your portfolio using only one or two fund families.

Next, find out how good the other funds are. Some fund companies are strong almost across the board. Other companies may only have a few standouts in an otherwise mediocre lineup.

While you're at it, look for areas of weakness within a company. Some organizations are very strong in, for example, equity funds, but have a poor record when it comes to fixed income. In other cases, a company may offer several good Canadian funds while displaying a pronounced weakness internationally. Phillips, Hager & North, one of the most respected firms in the business, has suffered from that problem for years. Over the years, they've tried different approaches to remedy the situation, without much success. In fall 2004, they tore down the whole structure and started yet again. The jury is still out.

A major plus is a mutual fund company that provides style options. If you can choose a good value fund and a good growth fund from the same company, it makes the decision-making process easier. Several organizations now offer this kind of style diversification, including Mackenzie, CI, Franklin Templeton, Dynamic, and AIM Trimark.

Taxes

Tax considerations come into play if you are investing outside a registered plan. Several companies offer "umbrella" funds with a corporate structure. These allow you to switch from one "class" to another without incurring capital gains tax liability. (Normally a switch from one fund to another is deemed to be a sale by the Canada Revenue Agency and therefore taxable if there has been a gain.) Among the firms that provide for this sort of tax-deferred switching are CI, Mackenzie, AGF, AIM Trimark, Clarington, and Franklin Templeton.

Funds Have a Place

Despite the troubles the industry has experienced, I still believe that mutual funds offer the easiest way for investors to build a comprehensive retirement portfolio, especially in the early years when the amount of money available is likely to be limited. If most of the money is in an RRSP, using a self-directed plan will give you access to the widest possible range of fund choices.

This is not to say that mutual funds should be the only type of security in your plan. There is certainly a place for ETFs, closed-end funds, and GICs, and, when you have gained enough investing experience to be comfortable adding them, for individual stocks, bonds, and income trusts.

So by all means, don't ignore mutual funds. They should play an important role in building your nest egg. Just choose with care.

17

Warning Lights

Despite all the careful planning, there are myriad ways in which a retirement savings program can be set back or even derailed. Some are outside your control, such as a major recession. But most of the potential obstacles are avoidable or containable. It's a case of knowing where the dangers lie and taking precautionary measures.

In earlier chapters, we've looked at how asset allocation can be used to insulate your retirement portfolio from the worst effects of a stock market crash. We have also dealt with the impact of succumbing to one of the most costly errors of all, relying too heavily on the RRSP carry-forward. Now let's consider some of the other common ways in which your retirement plan can get sidetracked.

The Home Buyers' Plan

Back in the early 1990s, North America was in the grip of a terrible recession. The housing market was especially hard hit, as real estate values tumbled and buyers vanished. The whole sector needed a shot in the arm and the Canadian Real Estate Association (CREA) came up with a plan to do it. They knew that asking the beleaguered Progressive Conservative government of the day for financial assistance would get them nowhere. Budget deficits had spiralled out of control and there was no money available. So they turned their eyes toward the country's largest pool of liquid consumer wealth—RRSPs.

Until then, RRSPs had been sacrosanct. The money accumulated in the plans could be used for one thing only—providing retirement income. CREA set out to demolish this principle. They lobbied the government to allow people to use their RRSP funds to pay for a house, arguing that it would be a win-win situation for everyone. One of the country's most important economic sectors would receive a much-needed boost. New tax revenue would be produced as a pickup in housing-created jobs. And many Canadians who could not afford to buy a home would suddenly have the required financial resources available to them.

The Tories took the bait. In the 1992 budget, then finance minister Don Mazankowski unveiled a supposedly temporary program that allowed every Canadian to borrow up to $20,000 from his or her RRSP for the purchase of a first home. It was called the Home Buyers' Plan (HBP) and it went on to become one of the most successful government initiatives of the decade. In the 1999 budget, the Liberal government of the day made the HBP permanent and loosened the eligibility requirements to allow more people to participate.

The HBP set an important precedent because it allowed retirement savings to be diverted to other purposes. Once the genie was out of the bottle, other exceptions to the rule have gradually crept in and there are likely more coming in the future. This is both a blessing and a curse. I happen to be a firm believer in the importance of home ownership as a cornerstone to personal wealth, so on one hand I have to applaud any initiative that makes the goal more attainable. On the other hand, I have studied the impact of the HBP on retirement savings. It can cost your RRSP tens of thousands of dollars in lost earnings over time, so using the plan can be detrimental to your wealth.

That hasn't stopped close to 200,000 Canadians from taking advantage of it, however. The ability to borrow up to $20,000 per RRSP (so $40,000 for a couple), interest free, is a huge attraction. And talk about easy repayment terms! You have 15 years to reimburse your RRSP, starting in the second year after the withdrawal. If you don't pay, all that happens is that the amount that was due in that year is added to your regular income for tax purposes. This has to be just about the easiest money you'll ever find.

But nothing is free in this life. There are hidden costs involved in using the HBP, which most people don't even consider. As with every financial decision, there is a trade-off involved. In this case, you may have to sacrifice future retirement income for the benefit of owning a home right now.

The younger you are, the greater the potential impact on the future value of your RRSP. If you're a 25-year-old who plans to retire at age 65 and your RRSP money earns 10 percent a year, the final value of your plan will be reduced by over $26,000 for every $1,000 you borrow toward your home, assuming you reimburse your plan according to the government's schedule. But if you're a 35-year-old, the reduction in the value of your plan at age 65 is only about $11,000 for every $1,000 borrowed. That's because you're giving up fewer years of tax-sheltered compounding.

So the future value of your RRSP will suffer. But the reduction in retirement income may be more than offset by a combination of mortgage interest savings and the appreciation in the value of your property over time. Plus, if you use some smart investment strategies, you could actually end up hundreds of thousands of dollars ahead at the end of the day by using the HBP. It depends on how conscientious you are.

Making Money from the HBP

Let me show you how to turn the HBP to your advantage. In all the examples that follow, we'll ignore any increase in the value of your property, because that's unpredictable and you can't spend it anyway unless you sell. But just to give you an idea of what impact capital appreciation might have, at 2 percent annual growth, every $1,000 invested in a home will be worth about $2,200 in equity after 40 years. If the property were to increase in value at a 6 percent annual rate, every $1,000 invested initially would grow to about $10,300 in equity over that time. Those amounts won't be enough to offset the loss in RRSP growth, but other strategies can do the job.

Let's use the case of a 30-year-old woman who withdraws $20,000 using the HBP. Had she not been able to do this, she would have been carrying a $100,000 mortgage. The HBP loan reduces the principal to $80,000. We'll use an 8 percent interest rate throughout (rates are lower at the time of writing, but over a long period 8 percent is a reasonable average), and assume a 25-year amortization. Let's look at the numbers:

MORTGAGE COST REDUCTION

Annual payments on $100,000 mortgage @ 8%	$9,158.64
Annual payments on $80,000 mortgage @ 8%	$7,326.96
Annual savings	$1,831.68

As you can see, applying $20,000 from the RRSP against the mortgage reduces the annual carrying cost by more than $1,800. Now the issue becomes: What does she do with that money? If she spends it, then yes, using the HBP is going to cut into her retirement savings. But suppose she decides to invest the savings instead? Now she's into a completely different situation. There are several ways she might go about this. In all cases, we'll assume retirement at age 65.

Option 1: Reinvest the savings. We've already seen that the lower mortgage frees up $1,832 (rounded to the nearest dollar) in payments each year. Of that, $1,333 goes back into the RRSP annually to pay off the loan. That leaves about $500 a year available for reinvesting.

Let's say the home buyer has no RRSP room available, so she reinvests that $500 outside her plan at the end of each year until the loan is repaid in 15 years. After that, she invests the full amount of the mortgage savings—$1,832 a year—for the next 20 years, until she retires. Let's assume she puts the money into a diversified portfolio of mutual funds, and receives an average annual rate of return of 8 percent, on which she pays taxes at the rate of 40 percent of each dollar earned.

Note that all she has done in this case is to make use of the money she would otherwise have had to pay each year on her mortgage. She hasn't contributed any additional amounts, even though her income would probably increase (perhaps significantly) over those 35 years. Let's look at the result of this strategy.

REINVESTING OUTSIDE THE RRSP	
(a) Value of $20,000 RRSP with no loan at age 65 (base case)	$295,700
(b) Value of HBP portion repaid at normal rate	$168,742
(c) Value of mutual funds at retirement	$ 86,457
(d) Total value of investments (Option 1)	$255,199
(e) After-tax value (base case)	$177,420
(f) After-tax value (Option 1)	$187,702
(g) Option 1 advantage	$ 10,282

Look closely at line (a) of this table, the base case. You'll see this repeated through all the examples that follow. It simply shows what happens to the $20,000 if it stays inside the RRSP over 35 years, compounding at 8 percent a year. In other words, this is the situation that will exist if the HBP isn't used and the money is simply left to grow within the RRSP.

Line (b) shows the end value if $20,000 is borrowed under the plan and then repaid at the prescribed rate. For simplicity, we've left out the effect of the time lag between the time of the loan and the first repayment, because that will vary, depending on the individual.

Line (c) shows the value of the investments that have been built up over the years under the option we're considering here. Remember, this is an after-tax number, using a 40 percent marginal tax rate throughout.

Line (d) shows you the total value of the investments under this scenario—Option 1, as we've called it—both inside and outside the RRSP.

At first glance, our home buyer seems to be worse off at this stage by about $40,000. But remember, money coming out of an RRSP is taxed. Her investment fund outside the RRSP is already fully tax-paid. So we have to equalize the two. Again, we've applied a 40 percent tax rate across the board, assuming that the money won't come out of the RRSP in a lump sum but will be received as income over time. Lines (e) and (f) show the after-tax values on this basis.

You can see at line (g) that, on an after-tax basis, our home buyer actually ends up with about $10,000 more in her retirement fund by using the HBP and employing our Option 1 reinvestment strategy. Plus, she owns her own home, free and clear.

Option 2: Accelerate the repayments. The second strategy is to accelerate the repayments to the Home Buyers' Plan. For this illustration, let's get a little more aggressive. We'll assume our home buyer had already budgeted to repay her HBP loan at the prescribed rate. Now she decides to take her annual mortgage payment savings and throw that into the pot as well. In other words, she decides to pay off the loan at an annual rate of $3,165. That's the total of the HBP repayment plus the $1,832 she saved in annual mortgage costs.

On this basis, she repays the HBP loan in about 6.3 years. Once that's done, she puts the HBP repayments into her pocket but continues to contribute her mortgage savings of $1,832 a year to the RRSP, where she invests it in mutual funds earning an average of 8 percent a year. Let's see the result.

ACCELERATED REPAYMENTS

(a) Value of $20,000 RRSP with no loan at age 65 (base case)	$295,700
(b) Value of HBP portion with accelerated repayment	$243,638
(c) Value of additional $1,832 to RRSP over 28 years	$174,661
(d) Annual tax savings over final 28 years	$ 733
(e) Reinvested value (4.8% after tax)	$ 41,481
(f) Total value of investments (Option 2)	$459,780
(g) Total value added	$164,080
(h) After-tax value (base case)	$177,420
(i) After-tax value (Option 2)	$292,461
(j) Option 2 advantage	$115,041

As in the previous table, line (a) is a restatement of our base-case scenario, not using the plan. Now look at line (b). Because of the accelerated HBP repayment, the loss to the RRSP from using the plan is reduced significantly. But there's more. The extra $1,832 going into the RRSP after the plan is repaid generates almost $175,000 in additional retirement savings, so she's now way ahead of the game. Then suppose she reinvests the tax savings produced by the RRSP contribution of $733 a year. As you can see at line (e), this builds into a tidy $41,481 nest egg, tax-paid, outside her plan. At line (g), the end result is a total value added to her retirement savings of slightly over $164,000. After accounting for taxes, this option gives her a net advantage of about $115,000 (line j).

Option 3: Increasing the RRSP contribution. In this case, the HBP loan is repaid at the normal rate. But our home buyer contributes $1,832 a year to her regular RRSP—the amount of her mortgage savings. So she's tossing the same amount of money into the pot for the first 15 years as in Option 2, a total of $3,165 (the additional $1,333 being her regular HBP repayment). However, in this case, she produces an annual RRSP tax deduction based on $1,832 for the full 35 years (remember, there's no deduction for HBP repayments). And she reinvests her full tax savings outside the RRSP.

Let's see what happens, assuming the same mutual funds investment pattern.

INCREASED RRSP CONTRIBUTION	
(a) Value of $20,000 RRSP with no loan at age 65 (base case)	$295,700
(b) Value of HBP portion repaid at normal rate	$168,742
(c) Value of $1,832 per year @ 8% after 35 years	$315,684
(d) Annual additional tax savings over 35 years	$ 733
(e) Reinvested value after 35 years outside RRSP	$ 63,526
(f) Total value of investments (Option 3)	$547,952
(g) Total value added (Option 3)	$252,252
(h) After-tax value (base case)	$177,420
(i) After-tax value (Option 3)	$354,182
(j) Option 3 advantage	$176,762

Again, line (a) is our base case. Line (b) shows the effect of a normal HBP repayment. At line (c), we see the effect of the regular RRSP contribution, which we assume she continues to make over 35 years. At line (e), we see the value of her tax-paid investments, using her tax savings. The final after-tax result shows up at line (j). The difference in the final value by using Option 3 is over $176,000.

Option 4: Paying down the mortgage. In this case, we assume the HBP loan is repaid at the normal rate. In addition, our home buyer decides to use the $1,832 she has saved each year to pay down her mortgage principal. She makes a lump-sum payment for that amount on December 31 of each year. Once she has the HBP and the mortgage paid off, she directs the full amount she was spending on housing costs into her RRSP and reinvests the tax savings.

Let's see what happens in this case.

PAYING DOWN THE MORTGAGE	
(a) Value of $20,000 RRSP with no loan at age 65	$295,700
(b) Value of HBP portion repaid at normal rate	$168,742
(c) Interest cost on mortgage (25-year amortization)	$103,172
(d) Interest cost (accelerated paydown—15 years)	$ 57,631
(e) Interest savings	$ 45,541
(f) Value of $9,159 per year @ 8% after 20 years	$419,134
(g) Annual additional tax savings over 20 years	$ 3,663
(h) Reinvested value of tax savings (4.8% after tax)	$118,611
(i) Total value of investments (Option 4)	$706,487
(j) Total value added (not including interest saved)	$410,787
(k) After-tax value (base case)	$177,420
(l) After-tax value (Option 4)	$471,337
(m) Option 4 advantage	$293,917

You've seen lines (a) and (b) before. Line (c) is the total interest cost on the $80,000 mortgage if our home buyer takes the full 25 years to pay it off. But the annual prepayments reduce the time needed to pay off the mortgage to 15 years and she saves over $45,000 in interest charges as a result (line [e]).

Now that the mortgage is fully paid off, she directs the full amount of her annual savings, plus the original $1,832, to RRSP contributions. This continues for 20 years, until she retires. On top of that, she reinvests her tax savings outside the plan. You can see the end result at line (m). We're looking at $294,000 in additional after-tax retirement capital by using this option. That does not include an assumption that the interest savings were put into the bank or reinvested. Nor, again, does it include the value of the equity in the home, which is owned free and clear.

Of course, all these scenarios imply a lot of discipline on the part of the HBP user. But so does paying down a mortgage or having an RRSP in the first place. The point of this rather lengthy exercise is that using the HBP does not have to cut into your retirement income, provided you're prepared to adopt a strategy and have the willpower to stick to it.

The Lifelong Learning Plan

Given the immense popularity of the Home Buyers' Plan, it did not come as a great surprise when the federal government decided to allow Canadians to dip into their RRSPs for another purpose. From one perspective, however, the wisdom of further diluting the original goal of these plans is questionable, especially when the main objective of this initiative seems to have been to take some political heat off the federal cabinet of the day.

The Lifelong Learning Plan was unveiled in the 1998 federal budget. Since January 1, 1999, Canadians have been given the option of borrowing from their RRSPs to help pay the costs of post-secondary education. The stated goal is to provide an alternative means of raising capital to allow people to upgrade their skills in order to retain their current job or obtain a new one. The rationale is that retraining or further education is often vital to ensuring future employment income and, subsequently, retirement income.

I have no argument with the importance of a good education. However, as with the Home Buyers' Plan, the federal government has made absolutely zero effort to educate Canadians as to the very real cost to their future retirement savings of using the Lifelong Learning Plan. As with the HBP, if you don't adopt a strategy to offset the loss of capital in your RRSP, the end result will be a much-diluted capital base when it comes time to retire.

The maximum amount that can be withdrawn from an RRSP under this program is the same as for the HBP, $20,000. However, in this case there is a maximum limit of $10,000 a year. As with the HBP, no interest is charged. The repayment is more accelerated, spread out over 10 years instead of 15. This has the effect of reducing the loss to the RRSP's future capital but, of course, not eliminating it. This loss could result in a significant reduction in your retirement income. The upside is that improving your education could result in an increase in employment income that will offset any lost retirement income from the original withdrawal.

In addition to the numbers, you should also consider quality of life and the career choices that would be available should you choose not to continue your education. If you are young enough, and if there is no other way to fund your education, you may well decide to forgo some future retirement income now, with the hopes of more than making up for it in the future.

Unlike the HBP, there are no mortgage interest savings to reinvest to help offset the negative impact of an LLP loan on the future value of your RRSP. So the best advice I can offer is to use part of any extra income earned as a result of your enhanced education to repay the RRSP loan on an accelerated basis.

Home Equity Lines of Credit

In recent years, the home equity personal line of credit (PLC) has become a popular way to tap into the value of your house. Not surprisingly, financial institutions have promoted them heavily, and why not? The line of credit is secured by a solid asset—real estate—and the structure of the plan encourages people to continue to draw money from it, thereby increasing the interest they pay.

Let me be very clear up front—I am not opposed to lines of credit. They can be extremely useful, if they are used properly. But it would be remiss of me not to point out the potential dangers in these plans as they relate to retirees or people coming up to retirement.

One of the cornerstones of financial independence when you stop work is to own your own home free and clear. That means no mortgage payments and no line of credit interest charges. All you need to worry about is property taxes and maintenance. And if you need additional income later, the equity in your home is available.

Carrying a large home equity line of credit into retirement will compromise that. The monthly payments will suddenly look much bigger when they come out of your pension income than they did when you were working. Moreover, the interest rate on PLCs is usually tied to prime. If rates rise, your monthly payment may increase depending on the terms of your plan. For people living on a more or less fixed income, that can spell trouble.

Above all, avoid taking out a PLC to leverage a high-risk investment portfolio. That can lead to financial disaster, as people who tried this strategy in the late 1990s discovered when the bear market hit. Of course, if you plan to invest the money conservatively in order to generate income in retirement, that's another matter. The interest on the PLC becomes tax-deductible for that purpose, thereby decreasing the ongoing cost of the loan. Just be sure that the after-tax income your portfolio creates exceeds your after-tax interest cost, otherwise there is no point to the exercise. Also consider a reverse mortgage as an alternative; see Chapter 21 for details.

Other Debt

If possible, try to avoid carrying any significant debt into retirement. Credit card debt will be the most debilitating to your retirement income because of the high interest rates charged on the cards. If you can't pay off all your credit card debt prior to stopping work, see if you can obtain a consolidation loan to reduce the carrying costs.

Car financing payments are another common type of debt that people sometimes carry into retirement with them. The interest rate is probably lower than that charged on the credit cards but you should make an effort to pay off the loan if at all possible.

Your ultimate goal should be to arrive at retirement with the maximum amount of financial resources and the minimum amount of liabilities. Some thoughtful advance planning, particularly in the area of debt repayment, should help to make that possible.

18

Getting at Locked-in Money

There is nothing I find more distressing than receiving a letter or an email from someone who is in desperate shape financially but unable to access thousands of their own dollars saved over many years because the money is in a locked-in account. Here is an example:

> I have a locked-in RRSP that I took out about 16 or 17 years ago where I worked. Then I was laid off. I took the RRSP funds and transferred them to a GIC and then to a mutual fund, but it's still called an RRSP. I am now having serious financial problems. Is there any way I could access that money under the hardship clause? It no longer belongs to the company I used to work for. Is there any help you can give me? –S.V.

The answer, unfortunately, was no. Upon further inquiry, it turned out that S.V.'s money was in a locked-in RRSP that was under federal jurisdiction. Anyone with a locked-in plan that comes under Ottawa's purview is absolutely out of luck. To quote from the website of the Office of the Superintendent of Financial Institutions: "The PBSA (Pension Benefits Standards Act) does NOT allow access to locked-in funds due to financial difficulties at any time."

This is just one example of the many, many messages of this kind that I receive. The matter falls under both federal and provincial jurisdiction, depending on who had responsibility for regulating the original pension plan. So it's beyond the control of Ottawa to impose a national policy even if it wanted to—and there is no evidence that it does. Although there has been a great deal of liberalization by most provincial governments in the rules for getting at locked-in money in recent years, the federal government remains in the Stone Age on this issue and our national politicians clearly don't see this as a priority.

I think this is deplorable. People are being forced to endure severe financial hardship because paternalistic governments insist that the money that was put aside for retirement cannot be used for anything else. It is also hypocritical. The federal government does not allow any access to locked-in plans under its jurisdiction but it lets people with regular RRSPs borrow from them for other purposes like buying a home or going back to school, both of these programs having been politically motivated. Where is the equity in that? A person who is on the verge of losing the family home because of being laid off cannot use locked-in money to save it, but young people just starting out in life can borrow up to $20,000 to enter the housing market! We've always known the poor have little political clout but this is ridiculous!

Forgive the rant but I have seen and heard about too many hardship cases over the years. More needs to be done, and soon.

Let's look at the facts. Locked-in RRSPs (also known as locked-in retirement accounts or LIRAs) are usually created when an employee leaves a company pension plan and the money vested in his or her name is transferred to a personal RRSP. In their wisdom, lawmakers decided to make it very difficult to gain access to these funds unless the plan is converted to a life income fund (LIF), life retirement income fund (LRIF), or the assets are used to purchase an annuity. LIFs and LRIFs are very restrictive and there is a ceiling on how much can be withdrawn from a plan each year. Lump-sum withdrawals from locked-in RRSPs, which are permitted without limit in regular RRSPs, are prohibited in some jurisdictions and subject to rigid conditions in others.

The rationale appears to be that Canadians need to be protected from themselves. If they could withdraw these savings, they would do so. The only solution is to freeze the assets in locked-in plans to ensure they are used only for the purpose of generating retirement income.

While Ottawa drags its feet on this issue, several provinces have taken steps to ease the rules. Quebec allows unlocking under a plan for phased retirement. In 2001, New Brunswick regulators moved to give account holders one-time access to 25 percent of their locked-in assets (using a transfer to a regular RRIF, which has no limit on withdrawals). In the most radical move yet, Saskatchewan's new rules, introduced in 2002, allow locked-in money to be transferred to a prescribed RRSP or RRIF, essentially giving plan holders unrestricted access. In British Columbia, you can obtain access to your locked-in money if you are diagnosed as having shortened life expectancy or if it is a small plan. In fact, most provinces allow people to unlock a LIRA if the assets are relatively small, although conditions vary across the country. See a financial advisor in your area for more details.

Ontario and Alberta have also relaxed their restrictions to allow people suffering financial hardship or shortened life expectancy to access their accounts, but only under certain circumstances. The rules are similar in both provinces; here are the Ontario provisions:

- *Low income.* If your pre-tax income in the next 12 months will be less than $27,400, you can apply for a withdrawal. This is the 2005 figure; it changes annually. Note that only *your* income is relevant here; the income of your spouse or partner does not count. The higher your income, the less you will be allowed to withdraw.

- *Risk of eviction from your home or rental accommodation.* For a home-owner to be eligible under this provision, that person or a spouse or same-sex partner must have received a demand in writing for payment of money owed on a debt secured by the residence. This could include a mortgage, property lien, or property taxes. In the case of a rental unit, a written demand for the payment of rent owed will do. In either case, if you need money from a locked-in plan to avoid eviction, you can apply.

- *To rent a new place.* This provision applies to those who need money to pay the first and last months' rent on accommodation.

- *Medical treatment.* This allows you to obtain money for medical treatment for yourself, spouse or partner, or for a dependant. The expenses cannot be covered by a provincial health plan, private health insurance, or any other source. You're allowed to claim for expenses you have already paid as well as for future costs. A doctor's letter is required.

- *Home renovations.* Only residential renovations relating to a disability or illness are eligible, and that illness or disability must affect you, your spouse or same-sex partner, or a dependant. The renovations can be made to your home or the dependant's home. You can also use money from this source in the construction of a new home if special features to accommodate an illness or disability are included in it. Here again, a doctor's letter is needed.

If you own other assets, you may be required to sell them first before a withdrawal from a locked-in plan is permitted. However, there are a number of important exceptions, including your house, car, business (up to $50,000), and personal items like clothes and jewellery.

If you live in Ontario and want to apply for a withdrawal under any of these conditions, send a letter to Financial Hardship Unlocking Section, Financial Services Commission of Ontario, 5160 Yonge St., Toronto ON M2N 6L9, or phone 416-226-7889. You can download the 19-page (!) application form at **www.fsco.gov.on.ca/pdfs/Pensions/Form6.12005_Eng.rev.pdf**. If your application is approved, you'll be assessed a fee of 2 percent of the amount withdrawn (minimum $200, maximum $600).

There are also three other circumstances under which Ontario residents can make withdrawals from locked-in plans, but in these cases application should be made to the financial institution that handles the account. They are:

- *Shortened life expectancy.* If your doctor tells you that you have less than two years to live, you can withdraw some or all of the money from a locked-in account.

- *Small accounts.* If you are 55 or older and the value of all assets held in Ontario locked-in accounts is less than 40 percent of the year's maximum pensionable earnings (MPE), you can withdraw all the money in the accounts. The MPE in 2005 was $16,440, so if the plan is worth less than $6,576 you can take out the whole amount.

- *Excess transfers.* If you transferred more money from a pension plan into a locked-in account than was allowed under the federal Income Tax Act, you can withdraw the excess amount plus any investment earnings on that portion of the money.

In Alberta, an application can be filed by anyone faced with eviction or mortgage foreclosure, requiring first and last months' rent, facing heavy medical bills, requiring funds for home renovations due to disability, facing legal action to collect back income taxes, if you are a registered debtor under the Maintenance Enforcement Program of Alberta, your income is less than $27,400 (2005 figure), or you have some other type of financial hardship. The last rule gives a wide degree of flexibility but you have to explain your reasons to the satisfaction of the office of the Alberta Superintendent of Financial Institutions. The form can be downloaded at **www.finance.gov.ab.ca/publications/pensions/pdf/f_hardship_unlocking.pdf**.

Before you take steps to initiate a withdrawal from a locked-in plan, here are some points to consider:

1. Once the money comes out of the plan, it is no longer creditor-proof. If you have a lot of people clamouring to have their bills paid, be careful.

2. You'll have to pay tax on the money you withdraw, some of which will be withheld when the application is approved.

3. In most cases, you need the written consent of your spouse or same-sex partner before you can proceed.

4. Before you make an application, be sure you're dealing with the right people. Find out what legal jurisdiction is actually responsible for the plan. For example, if the locked-in account originated from pension credits obtained while working for a federally regulated industry (e.g., banks, airlines), then provincial rules won't apply.

As you can see from the foregoing, several provinces have made a significant effort to enable those in financial distress to obtain relief by accessing locked-in accounts. That makes the federal government's foot-dragging even more disgraceful. Will someone in Ottawa please wake up!

19

Claiming Your Rewards

When you're just starting out, retirement seems a long, long way in the future—so far that it is more of an abstract concept than concrete goal unlike, say, home ownership. But the older you grow, the more real it gets until you reach a stage in the final years before you stop work when it becomes one of the top priorities in your life.

There are many facets to retirement. It is as important a life step as entering the workforce for the first time or getting married or having a baby. You need to be prepared to deal with it from both a psychological and a financial perspective. There are many sources of information to assist you with the psychological side of retirement planning. Our focus here is on the financial aspect.

The first step is to understand the rules and the options as they relate to your retirement savings, especially your RRSPs.

You may start drawing income from your retirement savings at any time, but by law, you must wind up your RRSP no later than December 31 of the year in which you celebrate your 69th birthday. This rule also applies to pension plans and deferred profit-sharing plans (DPSPs). As well, you may not contribute to an RPP or DPSP after age 69, and you must start to draw payments at that age.

When the time comes to close your RRSP, there are four ways in which you can convert your RRSP capital to a monthly cheque or other source of income:

1. *Withdraw all the money in cash.* Unless the RRSP is very small, I don't advise this. The money you receive will be treated as income and taxed accordingly. You could end up giving half of it to the government.

2. *Use the capital in your plan to purchase an annuity.* This will provide regular income until age 90 (a term annuity), or for life (a life annuity), depending on which type you select.

3. *Transfer your RRSP assets into a registered retirement income fund (RRIF).* This is the preferred choice of most Canadians, at least in the early years of retirement.

4. *Convert to a life income fund (LIF) or locked-in retirement income fund (LRIF).* These options are available to someone with a locked-in RRSP, also known as a locked-in retirement account (LIRA). The LRIF is likely the best option for most people as it allows more flexibility—an LIF must be converted to an annuity after age 80, while an LRIF can continue for life. However, not all provinces allow LRIFs.

These options are not mutually exclusive. You might choose to combine an annuity with an RRIF or an LIF or even cash in some of your RRSP assets at age 69, if your personal situation makes it desirable. Indeed, combining your conversion options could be the best strategy.

Converting to a RRIF

A RRIF differs from an RRSP in two fundamental ways: First, you cannot make new contributions to a RRIF. Additional money can only come from other registered plans. Second, you must make taxable minimum annual withdrawals from a RRIF, according to a formula laid down by the federal government. These withdrawals must begin no later than the calendar year following the date the plan is set up. So, if you open your RRIF at any time in 2005, you must start making withdrawals no later than 2006. Otherwise, a RRIF functions in much the same way as an RRSP. You can hold the same kind of assets, you may have a self-directed plan, and you'll pay similar fees.

Some of the benefits of a RRIF include:

- *Control of capital.* You keep the capital you've built over the years. If you purchase an annuity, the money is paid over to a life insurance company.
- *Withdrawal flexibility.* While you must take out a minimum amount each year, you have the flexibility to withdraw as much as you wish from the plan. This allows for large lump-sum withdrawals in the early years of retirement, when you may wish to travel more. You may also change your withdrawal formula at any time to meet current needs.
- *Inflation protection.* You may set up your income stream from a RRIF in such a way that the amount you draw increases each year. This will enable you to keep pace with higher living costs.
- *Estate planning.* Assets remaining in a RRIF after death will form part of the estate (unless they pass to a named beneficiary of the plan). They will therefore be available to your spouse, children, other relatives, or your favourite charity once appropriate taxes (if applicable) have been paid. Unless you have purchased a guarantee clause, annuity payments cease when you die or, in the case of a joint annuity, when the remaining spouse dies.

If you decide to go the RRIF route, here are three important points to consider:

How much income do I need from my RRIF? Review your planned expenses and other sources of income. See how much you need from your RRIF in order to maintain your desired standard of living. Your goal should be to withdraw as little as possible from your retirement fund.

How often do I need this income? If you require a monthly cheque in order to pay the bills, that can be arranged. But if you can wait until year-end and receive just one annual payment, you'll continue to maximize the tax-sheltered growth in your plan. If you have more than one RRIF, or you and your spouse each have one, you may wish to set up a different payment schedule for each to ensure regular income.

Will my investments provide the cash flow I need? A five-year compounding GIC won't generate any income for you because it's locked in. Neither will shares in a growth company that pays no dividends. At this point in your life, income needs must take precedence over growth in your investment decisions. Adjust the plan accordingly. More on this later in the chapter.

Minimum RRIF/LIF Withdrawals

The government requires you to withdraw a minimum amount from a RRIF or LIF annually, and this amount is fully taxable at your marginal rate. There is no way around this rule. I receive several questions every year from people asking how to minimize the taxes on RRIF withdrawals and the answer is always the same: you can't. There are various schemes for offsetting the tax payable by deductions of different types, but these tend to be quite complex and in some cases legally questionable. Be careful.

The method of calculating the minimum withdrawal requirement depends on your age. If you are under age 71, apply the following formula:

$$\text{Minimum withdrawal} = \frac{\text{Value of RRIF at start of year}}{90 - \text{Your age at start of year}}$$

So if you had $100,000 in a RRIF at the beginning of 2005 and you were age 70, the minimum withdrawal would be calculated as follows:

$$\frac{\$100,000}{90-70} = \frac{\$100,000}{20} = \$5,000$$

Once you reach age 71, the formula no longer applies. Instead, the minimum is a percentage of the capital in the plan at the beginning of each year, as shown in the following table.

Age	Minimum Withdrawal
71	7.38%
72	7.48%
73	7.59%
74	7.71%
75	7.85%
76	7.99%
77	8.15%
78	8.33%
79	8.53%
80	8.75%
81	8.99%
82	9.27%
83	9.58%
84	9.93%
85	10.33%
86	10.79%
87	11.33%
88	11.96%
89	12.71%
90	13.62%
91	14.73%
92	16.12%
93	17.92%
94+	20.00%

At age 94, the minimum annual payment reaches 20 percent of the value of the RRIF at the start of each year, and remains at that level for the rest of your life. Although this ensures there will be money available after 90, the formula poses another problem. The large percentage of the RRIF's assets that must be paid each year will quickly erode the capital base of the plan. As a result, the amount you'll receive each year will steadily decline as you reach your mid-90s, as the table below shows. For this illustration, I've assumed the RRIF is worth $100,000 at age 90, and that income is earned on the capital at the rate of 10 percent a year. For simplicity, it is assumed the minimum annual withdrawal is made in one lump sum at year-end (it won't often happen that way in real life, but this is just an example).

	WITHDRAWALS AFTER 90			
Age	RRIF Value Jan. 1	Income Earned	Minimum Withdrawal (%)	Payment
90	$100,000	$10,000	13.62	$13,620
91	96,380	9,638	14.73	14,197
92	91,821	9,182	16.12	14,802
93	86,201	8,620	17.92	15,447
94	79,374	7,937	20.00	15,875
95	71,436	7,144	20.00	14,287
96	64,293	6,429	20.00	12,859
97	57,863	5,786	20.00	11,572
98	52,076	5,208	20.00	10,415
99	46,869	4,687	20.00	9,374
100	42,182	4,218	20.00	8,436

For a retiree relying solely on RRIF income to live, this type of scenario could be financially devastating. As you can see, by the time you reach the ripe old age of 100, your income is about half what it was just six years earlier. Your reaction may be: "So what! If I live that long I won't care anyway." Maybe not, but your family will certainly be affected if faced with an increased financial burden because you didn't plan for this contingency.

So as you get older, don't put all your retirement eggs in the RRIF basket. You'll need some other sources of income if you live to a ripe old age. One alternative would be to convert part or all the capital in the RRIF to a life annuity when you're in your late 80s. This will ensure regular income for as long as you live.

Note: You may, if you wish, use your spouse's age for the minimum RRIF withdrawal calculation, if he or she is younger. However, you must make arrangements for this at the time the RRIF is set up.

LIFs and LRIFs

RRIFs, LIFs, and LRIFs have the same minimum withdrawal formulas. However, LIFs and LRIFs also have a maximum withdrawal limit in any given year, and the formula is different for each.

In the case of an LIF, the maximum annual withdrawal is calculated by multiplying the assets in the plan at the start of the year by a specific percentage based on the plan holder's age. The percentages are set by provincial governments; in Ontario, for example, a 71-year-old with an LIF is limited to a maximum withdrawal of 8.4548 percent of the plan's value on January 1.

Calculating the maximum allowable withdrawal from an LRIF is more complicated. Here again, the rules are established by each individual province. For example, Ontario retirees with LRIFs may base their withdrawals on the previous year's investment returns. (If the return is negative, the most they can withdraw is the minimum amount set by the CRA.) LRIF plan holders are also allowed to carry forward unused withdrawal room.

One of the main complaints concerning LIFs often heard from seniors is the requirement that the remaining capital in the fund be used to purchase an annuity at age 80. In the 2005 budget, the federal government abolished this provision as it relates to plans under its jurisdiction. Since Ottawa does not make provision for LRIFs, this was a welcome move that provides greater financial freedom for older people. However, many LIFs under provincial jurisdiction still have the annuity conversion requirement.

Unlike some provincial LIFs, LRIFs do not have to be converted to annuities at age 80. The rationale for LIF conversion is to ensure that the LIF's assets, which are intended to provide income support for life, are not depleted. This regulation strikes many people as being overly paternalistic, which is why several provinces have introduced LRIFs as a way around it. Check with the government department or agency that administers pensions in your province to see if LRIFs are an option where you live or if LIF conversion at age 80 is still a requirement. The laws governing LIFs and LRIFs are rapidly evolving and patchwork in nature so you need to stay informed. LRIFs are similar to RRIFs in that they can continue past age 80 and give plan holders a higher degree of flexibility and control over their retirement income than annuities or LIFs do.

If you have the option in your province of residence, the issue of whether to choose an LIF or an LRIF for your locked-in money is a complex one. A number of assumptions and variables have to be considered. If you want to withdraw more than the allowable maximum from an LIF each year, the LRIF offers the possibility of doing so, but only if the return on the investments in the portfolio are sufficient.

For example, in Ontario the maximum annual withdrawal from an LRIF is the greater of the federal government's RRIF minimum and the rate of return on your LRIF in the prior year. Let's assume a 70-year-old has an LRIF and the money in the plan earned 12 percent last year. If the market value of the LRIF on January 1 was $100,000, that person could withdraw up to $12,000 this year. But if the LRIF earned less than 5 percent last year, the federal minimum withdrawal requirement of 5 percent for someone age 70 would apply and that person could take out only $5,000. With an LIF, the maximum withdrawal allowed at age 70 would be $8,225. So if your goal is to take out as much money as possible each year, the choice between a LIF and an LRIF will depend to a large extent on how confident you are about your investing skills, or those of your advisor.

The following table shows the maximum allowable withdrawal from an Ontario LIF in 2005. These amounts may change annually (they are based on a formula) and may vary from province to province, so check the rules that apply in your case.

2005 MAXIMUM ANNUAL PAYMENT AMOUNT FOR AN ONTARIO LIFE INCOME FUND (LIF)

Age on January 1	Maximum % Withdrawal
48	6.19655
49	6.23197
50	6.26996
51	6.31073

Age on January 1	Maximum % Withdrawal
52	6.35454
53	6.40164
54	6.45234
55	6.50697
56	6.56589
57	6.62952
58	6.69833
59	6.77285
60	6.85367
61	6.94147
62	7.03703
63	7.14124
64	7.25513
65	7.37988
66	7.51689
67	7.66778
68	7.83449
69	8.01930
70	8.22496
71	8.45480
72	8.71288
73	9.00423
74	9.33511
75	9.71347
76	10.14952
77	10.65661
78	11.25255
79	11.96160

Setting up a RRIF

Setting up a RRIF is relatively simple, at least on the surface. Just visit the financial institution, broker, or planner who handles your RRSP, say you want to convert to a RRIF, and sign the documents that will be provided. Presto, it's done.

But creating a RRIF that will do exactly the job you want it to do is something else again. That process requires some careful planning and preparation, and there are several steps involved. Here's my Seven-Step RRIF Creation Strategy:

Step 1: Decide what you want your RRIF to provide in the way of cash flow. If you have ample income from other sources (employer pension, CPP, investments, consulting work, etc.), aim for the minimum withdrawal to minimize the tax bite and keep as much money tax-sheltered as possible. However, if the RRIF will provide a significant portion of your retirement income, you may have to take out more than the minimum to allow you to maintain your standard of living. Any RRIF advisor should be able to provide a computer printout showing the effect of various levels of withdrawals on your plan. Assuming a constant rate of investment return within the RRIF, the more money you take out, the faster the capital in the plan will be depleted. Be sure to study the figures carefully, checking to see when the income from the plan starts to decline at the withdrawal level you're considering. If the plan's assets will be depleted too quickly, see if there is some alternative, perhaps by cutting living expenses or supplementing your income with a reverse mortgage.

Step 2: Consolidate your RRSPs into a single plan. Most people have several RRSPs scattered around. You could convert each to a separate RRIF if you want, but it's not a good idea. Several RRIFs are harder to manage and you have to take a minimum payment from each plan. In this situation, choose your RRIF provider with great care. Every company with which you have an RRSP will want your business, but be selective. Have discussions with a representative of each organization before you decide. Ask about the RRIF services they offer and the fees you'll be charged. Insist on seeing a sample account statement and study it carefully to make sure it contains all the necessary information. This should include the current balance of the account, a record of withdrawal, and an itemized statement of assets, including the book value and current market price. Find out how often the statement is issued (monthly is best). If you plan to travel a lot, see what snowbird services the company provides.

Step 3: Decide if you want the RRIF assets to be professionally managed. Most financial institutions and brokerage firms now offer this service. Charges are usually based on a percentage of the RRIF assets. This will cost more than doing it yourself, but it should save a lot of time and headaches.

Step 4: Decide what type of RRIF you want. Like RRSPs, there are several different types of plans. You'll get maximum flexibility from a self-directed RRIF. For minimum maintenance and lowest cost, a RRIF based on GICs or Canada Premium Bonds will be most effective, although not the most profitable.

Step 5: Make the "fine print" decisions. When you set up your RRIF, you have the choice of basing the minimum annual withdrawals on your own age or the age of your spouse if he or she is younger. If the younger-spouse situation applies, you should always select it because it provides more flexibility and lower tax liability. There is no limit on how young the spouse can be. If you're a 70-year-old retired teacher who has just married a 30-year-old former student, use his or her age by all means. On a $100,000 RRIF, you'd have to withdraw (and pay tax on) $5,000 in the first year if you use your age. By using the 30-year-old spouse, the minimum withdrawal would be only $1,667. Of course, this is an extreme example but it dramatically illustrates the point. If you don't need the money right away, better that it stay in the plan and continue to earn tax-sheltered income. Using the age of a younger spouse is the best way to achieve this, even if the differential is only a few years.

You should also designate your spouse or partner as the "successor annuitant" to your plan. This is a technicality that could save a lot of problems later when you die. As a beneficiary, your spouse will inherit the assets in the plan tax-free. But the RRIF would have to be collapsed and the money reinvested in his or her RRIF. As a successor annuitant, your spouse continues to receive payments directly from the original plan.

Step 6: Decide on your investment portfolio. The big difference between a RRIF and an RRSP is that your emphasis switches from growth to income. So the assets in the plan will have to be structured to provide the cash flow needed for the RRIF to dispense regular payments to you.

The frequency of the cheques or direct transfers is up to you; it need be only once a year if you wish. You should also place more importance on capital preservation than you may have in the past. You cannot contribute any more money to a RRIF, so it's essential to ensure that your capital isn't eroded by unwise investments.

Step 7: Consider tax-reduction strategies. Payments from a RRIF will be taxed at your marginal rate. No tax breaks are available, regardless of the original source of the money. So, for example, dividends earned inside the RRIF will not qualify for the dividend tax credit when withdrawn. Therefore, be sure to maximize the tax efficiency between your registered and non-registered portfolios. If you are holding dividend-paying stocks or income trusts inside your RRIF and have interest-bearing securities outside the plan, do a swap. The net effect will be to reduce your tax bill and to leave more cash for you to spend.

Building an Income Portfolio

The traditional asset mix formulas for RRSPs and non-registered growth-oriented accounts don't work when cash flow becomes the primary concern, as it will after you retire. A completely different asset mix is required for that purpose.

Complicating the issue is the question of risk. It would be easy to put together a portfolio that generated cash flow of 8 to 10 percent. Simply throw in a lot of high-yielding income trusts and you've got it. But that would also entail a large measure of risk, which many income investors would be unwilling to accept. So the challenge is to find the right balance.

Before we consider portfolio composition, let's look at the different types of income securities that are available to us. These are listed in ascending order of risk.

Cash-type securities. These include Treasury bills, money market funds, bankers' acceptances, term deposits, high-yield savings accounts, Canada Savings Bonds, and similar securities. The return potential depends on what interest rates are doing. When they are low, the returns from this category will be minimal, as was the case in the early part of this century. Offsetting that is the fact that these securities rank at the top of the safety scale.

Mortgage-backed securities (MBS). These are just about as safe as T-bills because they are guaranteed for principal and interest by Canada Mortgage and Housing, a Crown corporation. As long as you hold them to maturity, you won't lose your capital, and, unlike GICs, there is no limit on the guarantee. MBS are useful for those seeking steady income with very little risk so they are well-suited for retirees.

An MBS certificate represents a share in a pool of residential mortgages. These pools are put together by financial institutions, and vary in size. Each pool is self-contained, with its own coupon rate and payment schedule. MBS units always are dated as of the first of the month and start paying returns on the fifteenth of the month following the issue. Most have five-year terms, although terms can range from as little as 6 months to as long as 25 years. Minimum investment is usually $5,000, but that can vary depending on where you buy. They're eligible for registered plans. Many retirees aren't familiar with them so here are some of their main features:

- *Safety:* Residential first mortgages have always been low-risk investments. But these certificates are as close to no-risk as you can get. Canada Mortgage and Housing Corporation (CMHC) guarantees you'll receive full interest and principal payments on the due dates, even if there are defaults within the pool. Since CMHC is a Crown corporation, your guarantee is backed by the Government of Canada.

- *Decent yield:* MBS, like bonds, are priced daily, and your yield will depend on the price you pay. According to brokers, these securities normally yield about 15 to 30 basis points (a basis point is 1/100 of a percent) more than five-year Government of Canada bonds.

- *Liquidity:* There's an active secondary market for MBS. You can sell them through a broker before maturity if you wish, giving them a clear advantage over locked-in investments such as GICs. Although MBS prices tend to be more stable than those of government bonds, you could suffer a capital loss if interest rates rise after your purchase. If interest rates fall, on the other hand, you'll enjoy a capital gain, albeit not a large one.

- *Availability:* MBS issues are available through major stockbrokers. If you don't have a broker or don't wish to open an account, you can buy them through some of the chartered banks.

- *Monthly pay:* Very few securities offer monthly payments, especially combined with decent interest rates. That makes MBS particularly appealing to retired people, either inside or outside a RRIF. But be aware that the monthly payment is not interest-only—it's a blend of interest and principal. And it can vary, sometimes substantially, depending on the extent to which the mortgage holders within the pool make early payments.

There are some drawbacks to MBS investments. The return they offer is very low, reflecting the high safety level. Capital gains potential is limited. And there is a 15-day period between the maturity date of a certificate and the date the final payment is due. No interest is paid during that time, which could mean a loss of several hundred dollars on very large investments.

In making an MBS investment, it doesn't matter much whether you buy a new issue or one being traded in the secondary market. The yield will be about the same in either case; the only difference is that older issues have a shorter maturity.

Guaranteed investment certificates. Traditional GICs are very safe, especially those covered by deposit insurance, which is any certificate from a Canada Deposit Insurance Corporation (CDIC) member institution with a value up to $100,000. For cash flow purposes, monthly-pay GICs are the best choice, although they offer a lower return.

Short-term bonds and funds. Short-term bonds have a maturity date of no more than five years from the time of purchase. These bonds are highly defensive, which means their market value is not severely affected by interest rate movements, up or down. As a result, these funds offer good protection in a rising interest rate climate. As a general rule, the shorter the term to maturity, the lower the risk. Canada bonds are the safest, but AA- or AAA-rated corporate issues are almost as good and will give you a better return.

Mid-term bonds. Here we are looking at maturities of 5 to 10 years. The yields are higher but so is the risk.

Long-term bonds. This is a classic case of higher returns, higher risk. Bonds with a maturity date of more than 10 years in the future normally offer the highest yields, but if interest rates move higher, their market value is likely to decline.

High-yield bonds. These so-called junk bonds don't follow the general pattern of government and highly rated corporate bonds. Interest rate movements aren't the primary force here. What counts is the creditworthiness of the issuing companies. In times of economic stress, the risk of default mounts as credit ratings are downgraded.

Preferred shares. They normally provide a better yield than the dividends paid by common shares and are eligible for the dividend tax credit.

Income trusts. You can expect better cash flow from an income trust than from a bond but the risk is much higher. These trusts trade on the stock exchange, which tells you immediately that they are more akin to equities than to bonds.

Dividend-paying common stocks. Generally, investors buy these for their capital gains potential, not for cash flow, although some stocks do pay decent dividends, notably banks and utilities.

Now let's put all this together in sample portfolios. I have created both registered and non-registered portfolios with three levels of risk in each.

REGISTERED PORTFOLIO			
Security	Low Risk	Mid Risk	Higher Risk
Cash-type	20%	10%	0%
Mortgage-backed securities	20%	15%	10%
GICs	20%	15%	10%
Short-term bonds	20%	15%	10%
Mid-term bonds	20%	15%	10%
High-yield bond funds	0%	15%	15%
Dividend funds/preferred shares	0%	0%	0%
Income trust funds	0%	15%	25%
Selected income trusts	0%	0%	20%
Common stocks	0%	0%	0%

As a general rule, the more risk you are prepared to assume, the higher the likely cash flow. However, even in the case of the higher-risk portfolio, I have built in a significant amount of capital protection in the form of mortgage-backed securities, GICs, and short-term bonds. You could increase the yield by reducing or eliminating those categories. I have not included any dividend funds or common stocks here as they are better held in a non-registered portfolio.

NON-REGISTERED PORTFOLIO

Security	Low Risk	Mid Risk	Higher Risk
Cash-type	20%	10%	0%
Mortgage-backed securities	15%	10%	5%
GICs	15%	10%	5%
Short-term bonds	15%	10%	5%
Mid-term bonds	15%	15%	5%
High-yield bond funds	0%	15%	15%
Dividend funds/preferred shares	20%	15%	15%
Income trusts funds	0%	15%	25%
Selected income trusts	0%	0%	20%
Common stocks	0%	0%	5%

The cash yield in this portfolio will probably be about the same as for a comparable registered portfolio (e.g., a RRIF). However, the tax efficiency in this case is better because I have reduced the positions in some of the interest-paying securities and replaced them with dividend funds, preferred shares, and high-yielding common stocks, all of which qualify for the dividend tax credit.

The Annuity Option

An annuity is a contract with a financial institution, usually an insurance company, to provide you with a set amount of regular income for a specified period of time, using the proceeds of a lump sum that you pay to the annuity provider. The payments are made up of capital and interest.

Annuities can be used in conjunction with RRIFs as part of your retirement income strategy. One major advantage of converting to an annuity is the fact that, once you've chosen the terms of your annuity, it requires little decision making or maintenance.

There are several types of annuities available, but only two can be purchased with RRSP money. One is a life annuity, which, as the name suggests, will provide payments for as long as you or your spouse survives. These are offered only by life insurance companies, although they can be sold by other firms acting as brokers. The other is a term certain annuity, which makes payments to age 90 (or until your spouse turns 90 if he or she is younger), then cuts out. These can be obtained through insurance firms or financial institutions such as banks and trust companies.

Non-registered assets may be used to buy a prescribed annuity, which will provide regular income for the period you select. These are available from a variety of financial institutions.

The advantage of a life annuity over a term certain annuity is that you can't outlive it. An increasing number of people today are living past age 90. The last thing you need if you are among the long-lived is to have your income suddenly cut off. The Canadian life insurance industry uses this as a major selling point for life annuities and it's certainly worth thinking about.

A word of warning before you venture into the world of annuities. Like most other life insurance company products, they have been made far more complicated than they need to be. Be prepared for all kinds of variations and combinations, each carrying a different price tag, each guaranteed to make your head spin. That seems to be the way the insurance industry likes to operate: dazzle the client with numbers and get them to sign while they're still reeling. Don't be bamboozled; find out exactly what is being offered and at what price. Then take your time assessing the relative merits of the income products available to you.

The amount you'll receive from an annuity will be determined mainly by five factors: the amount of money you have to invest, your sex (men get higher payments than women because they tend to die sooner), your age when payments begin (the older you are, the more money you'll get), the number of bells and whistles you select, and the level of interest rates at the time you make your purchase (the higher, the better). By using these variables properly, you can develop an annuity strategy that will give you the maximum possible payback.

Annuity Terminology

Before you start, here are some terms you need to understand when shopping for a life annuity.

Single annuity. An annuity that is issued to you personally. Payments will be calculated on the basis of your life expectancy.

Joint life annuity (also called last survivor annuity). A guaranteed payment for both you and your spouse (or partner) that will continue for as long as one of you remains alive.

Guarantee. A promise from the issuing company that you or your estate will receive a specified amount of money, no matter what happens. Think of it as a form of insurance. If you die without a guarantee the month after you purchase an annuity, your heirs will receive nothing. With a guarantee, they'll at least get a return equal to the amount you would have been paid over the guarantee period. This may be paid either in instalments or as a lump sum, depending on the terms you choose. A typical guarantee will run for 5, 10, or 15 years, although some companies offer them for longer periods. The longer the guarantee you choose, the less your income payments will be. In effect, you'll pay a higher premium for a longer guarantee.

Many financial advisors recommend you take a guarantee, especially if you're buying a single annuity. But it's very costly, and the amount of protection you're receiving declines every year. It's also one of the few forms of insurance I'm aware of where the premiums continue long after the coverage runs out (you'll continue to receive the lower payment even after the guarantee expires).

Only you can decide if it's worth it, but the younger you are and the better your health, the less chance your heirs will ever benefit from the guarantee. If you're buying a joint annuity and you and your spouse/partner are in good health, I suggest you seriously consider bypassing the guarantee; the odds are at least one of you will outlive it.

Impaired annuities. If you're in poor health when you apply for a life insurance policy, the odds are you won't get coverage. If you do, you're likely to be charged a premium rate. With an annuity, however, poor health can translate into a financial advantage. If your medical report indicates that your life expectancy is below normal, some companies will issue what's known as an impaired annuity. You'll receive higher monthly payments (perhaps by as much as 15 percent) for your money. The trick is to then turn around and surprise them by living far longer than anyone expected!

Increasing income and indexed annuities. In the old days, annuity payments were fixed for life. But high inflation in the latter part of the twentieth century plus competition from RRIFs forced the insurance industry to come up with alternatives that protect annuity buyers from cost of living increases. There are two basic types of income-protection annuities available. One is known as an increasing life annuity. This type of plan increases your payment by a set percentage each year, usually between 1 and 4 percent, regardless of movements in the Consumer Price Index. Alternatively, you can choose an indexed annuity. This plan will increase your payments each year in line with the inflation rate, although some companies put a cap on the amount of annual increase that's allowed.

With both these annuities, your initial income will be much lower than you'd receive with an ordinary, level-payment plan. However, you'll make up for that initial shortfall over time, as your payments increase— assuming, of course, that you live long enough.

If you don't have any other inflation protection in your retirement income program, you should look carefully at these annuity options. No one should begin retirement with an income that will remain relatively constant, unless it's much more than you initially need and you can afford to keep adding to your savings.

Income-reducing annuities. Payments from these joint annuities decline when the first spouse dies, on the somewhat dubious theory that one can live more cheaply than two. The income for the surviving spouse may drop by anywhere from one-third to three-quarters of the original payment. There's potential for genuine financial hardship for your loved onc in arrangements like this. Suppose, for example, he or she needs expensive medical care in old age or has to live in an assisted-care facility. Cutting the annuity payment substantially may make that difficult or impossible. These plans aren't particularly popular, with good reason.

Integrated annuities. These are structured in such a way that the payments are reduced on a dollar-for-dollar basis as Canada Pension Plan and Old Age Security benefits kick in. The result is a level income for life. Integrated annuities are most useful to people who retire early and need higher monthly payments to tide them over until they are eligible to begin drawing government benefits (age 60 for CPP and 65 for OAS).

Variable annuities. These plans invest your money in a fund, with your payments based on the fund's performance. Because of this unpredictability factor, they shouldn't be considered if you're relying on this money as the prime source of your income.

Cashable annuities. At one time, an annuity, like a diamond, was forever. Once you were in, there was no going back. The decision was made and you had to live with it. Now, however, you can keep your financial options open with a cashable annuity. If you decide you want to get out, you can arrange to have your annuity cashed in (the technical term is "commuted") at its current value. At that point, you can use the money to buy another annuity or to invest in a RRIF, in which case no tax will be payable. Or you can have the cash paid directly to you, as long as you don't mind paying tax on it at your top rate.

As with everything else in the annuity world, you have to pay for this flexibility in the form of lower monthly payments.

Renewable annuities. Normally, the interest rate on which your annuity payments are based is locked in for the duration of the plan. However, it is now possible to buy an annuity for which the period of the rate guarantee is shorter than the term of the plan. At the end of each interest rate period, you can use your remaining cash value to buy another renewable annuity, a life or fixed-term annuity, or a RRIF.

This type of annuity is worth considering if interest rates are low at the time of your purchase. Rather than lock in a low rate for the rest of your life, a renewable annuity enables you to choose a shorter term in the hope rates will be higher when the time comes to renew. Usually, however, the shorter the term you select, the lower the interest rate paid and, therefore, the less income you'll receive. Again, you pay for flexibility.

Deferred annuities. One way to avoid the problems created by annuity shopping when interest rates are down is to buy a deferred annuity when rates are high. This is the life insurance industry's equivalent of a guaranteed investment certificate. The primary difference from an ordinary GIC that you'd buy from a bank or trust company is that with a deferred annuity, the proceeds from the plan must be used to purchase an annuity (or be redeemed) by a specific date. This may be a specific number of years, or it may relate to the investor's age.

There are also some other differences between a deferred annuity and an ordinary GIC of which you should be aware:

- *Beneficiary.* You can designate a beneficiary for a deferred annuity, who will continue to receive payments if you die. This is not possible with regular GICs.
- *Pension tax credit.* Income from a deferred annuity is eligible for the pension tax credit. Ordinary GIC interest is not.
- *Creditor protection.* If the beneficiary of the deferred annuity is your spouse, a child or a parent, creditors cannot make a claim against the invested principal. They can, however, go after payments made to you.
- *Liquidity.* Most deferred annuities can be redeemed prior to maturity, with an interest rate adjustment. Ask the company with which you're dealing about its policy in this regard. In most, but not all, cases, bank and trust company GICs cannot be cashed before maturity.
- *Security.* GICs from banks and trust companies are protected by deposit insurance up to $100,000, as long as the term does not exceed five years. Life insurance companies are not members of the Canada Deposit Insurance Corporation. However, CompCorp protects deferred annuities to the same dollar limit as deposit insurance. There is no maximum term.

Shopping for an Annuity

A deferred annuity enables you to lock in your interest rate when rates are high, but to delay receiving payments until you need them. So you can go shopping for an annuity several years before you actually expect to draw the money. This is an important advantage that allows you to set up the maximum possible income flow from your annuity.

The level of interest rates is an extremely important factor in buying an annuity. If you lock in for a long term at a time when rates are low, you'll end up sacrificing thousands of dollars in retirement income. So time your annuity purchases for maximum return. If interest rates are low when you're shopping, postpone the decision or buy a renewable annuity, which will allow you to get back into the market under more propitious circumstances.

Although I generally don't recommend them in the early years of retirement, if you decide to convert to an annuity, here are a few tips that may help:

1. *Do some comparison shopping.* The rates paid on the same annuity will vary from one company to another at any given time, sometimes substantially. The problem is that, despite some diligent searching, I have not been able to find any independent source for comparative rates. So you may have no choice but to ask for quotes from several different companies. Alternatively, you can call an annuity broker. There are usually a number of them in major cities who will do a computerized search to obtain the best rate, usually at no charge (they're paid a commission by the insurance company that gets the business). You'll find them listed in the Yellow Pages under Annuities. You can also view one set of real-time quotes by going to Cannex Canada at **www.cannex.com/canada/english** and clicking on Annuities. This will give you an idea of current payouts per $100,000 invested and the companies that offer the best rates.

2. *Wait as long as you can.* The older you are when you buy an annuity, the greater the return. The reason, of course, is that the actuaries calculate you won't be around as long to collect.

3. *Understand the tax consequences.* Although annuity payments are a blend of principal and interest, the full amount will be taxed at your

regular rate if the plan has been purchased with registered funds (e.g., your RRSP savings). You are, however, allowed to claim the pension tax credit for the first $1,000 you receive each year. Annuities purchased with non-registered funds are treated differently. In this case, only the interest portion of the payment is taxed. This interest is deemed to be averaged over the full term of the annuity for tax purposes, resulting in a tax deferral that can be significant on a long-term contract. Payments from these annuities are also eligible for the pension credit.

4. *Be clear about the variations.* There are many variations of annuity products in the marketplace. Often, these are offered in combination with RRIFs, with the goal of achieving a more attractive combination of steady returns, flexibility, and inflation protection. Some of these plans can be extremely complicated. If you're not clear on exactly what you're getting for your money, I suggest you pass.

5. *Consider converting RRIF assets.* You might want to convert part or all of your RRIF to a life annuity when you reach a point when the capital in your plan starts to decline. The reason is that as the assets in the RRIF decline, so will the payments you receive. (You could always increase them, of course, but that would only speed up the capital erosion process). By moving to an annuity at this point, you'll ensure a steady income stream for the rest of your life. And because you'll likely be quite old when this happens, your annuity payment will be higher.

In summary, annuities can be complicated but they also can be of great use in the right circumstances. Don't write them off because they seem like an old-fashioned concept. Just be sure that you use them efficiently, and that you get the best possible return for your money.

20

Effective Tax Planning

I wish I could begin this chapter by telling you that the tax aspect of your retirement program is relatively simple. Unfortunately, I cannot. There are ways to legally reduce the amount of tax you pay, both during the accumulation years and the withdrawal years, but it requires some careful planning. Further complicating matters is the fact that the strategies that work while you are building your retirement fund will no longer apply once you start to receive income from it. So you have to go through the whole process twice.

The Accumulation Years

All the money you contribute to a registered plan is tax-deductible, as long as you don't exceed your allowable amount. This applies to registered pension plans (RPPs), registered retirement savings plans (RRSPs), group RRSPs, etc. As well, any income earned within these plans is tax-sheltered.

Individuals don't have much control over RPPs, but RRSPs are another matter. There is a lot of flexibility with these plans and the potential to run into some serious tax problems if you don't handle things properly. Here are some of the potential problem areas from a tax perspective with some tips on how to deal with them.

Withdrawals

Any time a person runs into financial trouble, the first instinct is to dip into the RRSP for some extra cash. I receive more questions about RRSP withdrawals every year than about any other aspect of retirement planning. So let me first say that if it is at all possible to deal with a crisis in some other way, leave the RRSP money alone. Don't touch it unless it is a dire emergency.

That said, you can take money out of your personal RRSP at any time, unless it is a locked-in plan. However, be prepared to pay tax. RRSP withdrawals are treated as income in the year they're made and you don't get any special tax concessions, such as a lower rate for any capital gains in your RRSP. You'll pay tax on your RRSP withdrawals at your marginal rate—the rate that applies to the last dollar you earn in any given year. And, if you withdraw a large amount, you may find yourself in a higher bracket as a result.

The trustee of your RRSP is required by law to withhold tax at source on any withdrawals you make from a plan. The rate of withholding tax increases with the amount you take out; in 2005 rates were as follows:

WITHHOLDING TAX FOR RRSP WITHDRAWALS		
	Federal	Quebec Residents
Up to $5,000	10%	21%
$5,001–$15,000	20%	30%
Over $15,000	30%	35%

When you file your tax return, you may claim any tax withheld as a credit. But keep in mind that the actual rate at which you are assessed may be higher (perhaps significantly higher) than the withholding rate. So with large withdrawals, you might end up owing several thousand dollars more in taxes when it comes time to file your return.

And here's a special warning. Be especially careful when dealing with labour-sponsored venture capital funds in an RRSP. I had a situation recently in which a family wanted to withdraw money from an RRSP to see them through a difficult time. When I looked at the plan, I found it was almost entirely invested in labour-sponsored funds. If they had gone ahead with the plan and cashed them in, they would have ended up with almost nothing. They would have been required to repay the tax credits earned when the funds were purchased, plus a deferred sales charge, plus tax on the money taken out of the RRSP. Needless to say, they dropped the idea.

Spousal Plan Withdrawals

Early withdrawals from a spousal RRSP are subject to hefty tax penalties, so be careful about dipping into your mate's plan. Under the rules, there has to be a gap of at least three years between the last contribution to any spousal RRSP and a withdrawal. Otherwise, the amount withdrawn is attributed back to the spouse who made the original contribution and is taxed as income at that person's marginal rate.

For example, suppose you made a $2,000 contribution to your spouse's RRSP in 2005. Neither you nor your spouse can withdraw any money from that plan, or any other spousal RRSPs you own, until 2008 without creating a problem. Nor are you allowed to make any contribution to a spousal plan in 2008, even after a withdrawal has been made, without attracting a penalty. If the spousal RRSP is converted to a RRIF in the same three-year period, any withdrawals in excess of the minimum required will also be subject to the attribution rule. If either of you makes any premature withdrawals, the money is treated as income in the hands of the person who made the original contributions, up to the total amount claimed as tax deductions during the three-year period.

This rule makes income splitting difficult, but it also ensures that taxes are not avoided altogether. Without it, a high-income spouse could claim a tax deduction for an RRSP contribution and then have the lower-income spouse withdraw the money immediately. If the withdrawing spouse had no other income, he or she might be able to escape paying taxes entirely on the withdrawal.

Occasionally, a situation may arise in which the spousal plan rules can be turned in your favour. Take the case of a high-income executive or professional who makes maximum annual contributions to her husband's spousal RRSP. She then decides to retire, taking a big drop in income as a result. The husband, on the other hand, continues to work and, in fact, sees his income go up. He decides to make a big withdrawal from his spousal RRSP before the three-year period has lapsed. But, because of the special rules, the income is attributed back to his wife, the original contributor. Since she is now in a much lower tax bracket, the so-called penalty actually works in the couple's favour, reducing the tax that would otherwise be payable.

RRSP Loans

Financial institutions aggressively promote special low-rate loans during RRSP season. These can be useful if you don't have the cash available to make a contribution but the interest on these loans is *not* tax-deductible.

RRSPs as Collateral

You may not use your RRSP or any property held within a plan as security for a loan. If you do, you're supposed to include the value of the property you've pledged as security in your taxable income for that year. However, you are not required to take the money out of your plan.

Non-Qualified Investments

There are only a few types of investments that don't qualify for an RRSP. But if you make a mistake and put one in a self-directed plan, the tax consequences are significant. The Canada Revenue Agency will require that the fair market value of the non-qualified investment be included in your taxable income in the year the asset was acquired. If you have any doubts, review the criteria carefully before going ahead. If your plan owns a qualified investment that, for whatever reason, becomes non-qualified later, a special tax of 1 percent per month of the asset's fair market value when it was acquired must be paid as long as it stays in the RRSP.

Overcontributions

You may overcontribute up to $2,000 to your RRSPs over your lifetime (as long as you are age 19 or older). Any amount beyond that will attract a special tax, at the rate of 1 percent a month on the excess amount. However, if you overcontributed up to $8,000 between 1991 and 1996, different rules apply and you won't be subject to penalty.

Home Buyers' Plan

If you borrow from your RRSP to make a down payment on a new home and then fail to repay the plan on schedule, the amount owed in any year will be added to your income and taxed accordingly.

Transactions at Other Than Fair Market Value

If your RRSP pays more than fair market value for an asset, the difference will be included in your taxable income for the year. A similar situation will arise if the plan sells an asset at below fair market value.

Death of an Annuitant

If you should die, the tax impact on your RRSP can be serious for your heirs. In determining your final tax bill (unfortunately, you have to pay taxes even after you're dead), the Canada Revenue Agency (CRA) will treat your RRSP as if all the funds had been withdrawn in your final year. If your plan is a large one, the resulting taxes could be quite high.

There are a couple of ways to beat the tax people, however—at least for a while. One is to make your spouse the beneficiary of your RRSP. This should be done through the financial institution that holds your plan, and simply requires completing a form. If you do this, the money in the plan can be transferred to your spouse's RRSP or RRIF, with no taxes payable. Any income earned by an RRSP between the time you die and the time the assets are transferred to your spouse may be included in the tax-free transfer to your spouse until the end of the calendar year following your death.

If you have no spouse, another way to reduce the tax burden on your heirs is to name a dependent child or grandchild as your RRSP beneficiary.

Final RRSP Contribution

A final contribution may be made to a regular or spousal RRSP by the estate of the deceased. This contribution may be made up to 60 days after the end of the calendar year of the death. Depending on the amount of RRSP contribution room available to the deceased this could reduce taxes on the estate by several thousand dollars.

Maturity

You may not hold an RRSP after the last day of the year in which you turn 69. When you reach the mandatory wind-up age, you must begin paying tax on the money in the plan, one way or another. If you choose, you can pay the whole shot at once by collapsing the plan and drawing out all the funds. In that case, the full amount will be treated as income in the year you receive it and taxed accordingly. Unless your plan is very small, this isn't a good idea. You'd be much better off spreading the tax burden over a longer time frame, by converting to a RRIF and/or annuity.

If you fail to take steps to convert your RRSP to a RRIF or annuity before the age deadline, your plan may be automatically deregistered on January 1 of the following year. All the RRSP assets would be considered as having been taken into income and you'd pay taxes accordingly. Some institutions will automatically convert your RRSP to a RRIF if you haven't given instructions by a specific date, but others will not.

Moving Abroad

Find out the rules governing your RRSP before you take any action. They'll often be determined by the tax treaties between Canada and the country to which you're moving; however, some rules apply no matter where you go. For example, if you move elsewhere but keep your RRSP in Canada, you'll pay a 25 percent withholding tax on any lump-sum withdrawals from the plan. But you can reduce that to 15 percent in the case of periodic withdrawals. Special rules apply if you are moving to the United States, and you can use these regulations to decrease the taxes you'll pay on money coming out of a plan. See Chapter 22.

The Income Years

Once you have reached the point where you begin to draw on your retirement savings for income, the tax game changes. As I said earlier in this book, there is, unfortunately, no way to reduce the tax payable on money coming out of a registered income fund, such as a RRIF or LIF. But here are some tips that may reduce the tax bite in other ways.

Create a Tax-Friendly Non-Registered Portfolio

A non-registered portfolio can be set up so as to produce mainly tax-advantaged or tax-deferred income, and you should make every effort to do this, especially if you are receiving large amounts of money from a pension plan and/or from RRIF withdrawals. The applicable tax rate on investment income can vary greatly, depending on the form in which it is received. Dividends are taxed at lower rates because of the dividend tax credit and are especially tax efficient for lower- to middle-income people. For example, a British Columbia resident with less than $63,309 in taxable income paid a maximum rate of 15.9 percent on dividends for the 2004 tax year. Those with taxable income under $31,654 paid a maximum of 4.52 percent. For those people, dividends were virtually tax free. Capital gains also attract less tax, although for people in retirement this is a less common and less dependable source of income.

Rental income is another tax-effective way to receive money and you don't have to become a landlord to take advantage of it. Instead, invest some of your non-registered portfolio in real estate investment trusts (REITs). These trusts own various types of commercial real estate, from office buildings to long-term-care facilities. They collect rents on the properties and distribute the profits to shareholders on a tax-advantaged basis. This is made possible by the fact that depreciation on the properties owned by a REIT is passed through to the investor so a portion of the cash flow is received on a tax-deferred basis. Note that this is a tax deferment not an exemption. Eventually the CRA will get its share because you must deduct the amount of tax-deferred revenue you receive each year from the original purchase price of your shares to arrive at an adjusted cost base (ACB). See Chapter 11, Understanding Income Trusts, for a detailed description on how this works.

You can also receive tax-deferred income from other types of income trusts, especially those in the energy and mining fields. A financial advisor can help to identify those trusts that are most tax effective.

Deduct Carrying Charges and Interest Expenses

If you have a non-registered investment portfolio, there are several types of expenses that you may be able to deduct. These include interest paid on an investment loan, safety-deposit-box fees, professional money management fees, and accounting fees related to your investment income.

Make Use of Unused RRSP Contribution Room

Just because you have retired, it doesn't necessarily mean that you can no longer contribute to an RRSP—yours or your spouse's. Check your most recent notice of assessment from the CRA to see if you still have unused RRSP contribution room accumulated from years past. If so, you can use up those credits by continuing to make RRSP contributions, even though you no longer have any earned income. I strongly recommend you use them all before your RRSP (or your spouse's) has to be wound up, which is by the end of the year in which you turn 69.

Shelter Money through Retiring Allowances

The term "retiring allowance" covers various types of payments. It may refer to money you receive when you retire, in recognition of years of service to an organization. In this form, it may include payments relating to sick-leave credits you never claimed. A retiring allowance can be a euphemism for severance pay—money you received because you were fired, whether or not as a result of legal action. Retiring allowances do not include any pension benefits, death payments, or benefits received for counselling services that are part of a dismissal arrangement.

Any eligible payments may be transferred directly to an RRSP (or to a registered pension plan, but not to a RRIF) without being taxed, within certain limits. The transfer can be done in one of two ways:

1. *By arranging to have the money transferred directly into your RRSP.* In this type of arrangement, you avoid having income tax deducted at

source. Your company's payroll department will handle this; just let them know that you have the contribution room.

2. *By receiving the money yourself and making a contribution to your RRSP within 60 days of year-end.* In this case, tax will be withheld on the payments when you originally receive them, but you'll get part or all of the money back when you file your return, depending on how much goes into the RRSP. To make a claim, show the total amount of the retiring allowance you received on line 130 of your return. You can then claim a deduction for the amount transferred to an RRSP at line 208. Be sure to attach a receipt for this amount to your return.

The maximum amount of eligible retiring allowances you can transfer directly to an RRSP without leaving contribution room available is $2,000 times the number of years or part years you were with the employer, up to and including 1995. No credit will be granted for any year or part year from 1996 forward. You may also claim an additional $1,500 for each year or part year prior to 1989 for which no money was vested for you in a pension plan or deferred profit sharing plan. The formula looks like this:

($2,000 x Years of service before 1996) + ($1,500 x Non-pension years before 1989) = Eligible retiring allowance

For purposes of this calculation, any part of a calendar year is considered a full year. So, if you joined a company in July 1990 and left in July 2005, you're considered to have been with the firm for 16 years, not 15, as it might first appear. However, since no credit is granted for service from 1996 to 2005, you may use only six years—1990 to 1995—as the base for your calculation. As an example, if you had been with an employer from 1980 to 2005 and had no pension plan, your maximum retirement allowance eligible for RRSP rollover would be:

($2,000 x 15) + ($1,500 x 9) = $30,000 + $13,500 = $43,500

If you were fully vested in the company pension plan for all those years, your maximum would be:

$2,000 x 15 = $30,000

But what about the portion of a retiring allowance that is not considered to be eligible for direct RRSP transfer? With eligibility only available for years up to 1995, more people find themselves faced with a heavy tax bite on these lump-sum payments. Fortunately, there is a solution—if you have contribution room in your RRSP, perhaps as a result of carry-forwards. If you provide evidence that you have unused contribution room, your employer may agree (note the word "may") to transfer an equivalent sum from a retiring allowance directly into your RRSP, without deducting tax. There is no obligation on employers to do this, however, and it's up to you to provide the evidence.

Here's an example of how this might work. We'll use a fictional retiree named Bill. He gets a retiring allowance of $50,000 in recognition of long service. Of this, Bill can transfer $21,000 directly to an RRSP by applying the credits available for service prior to 1996. He also has $10,000 in unused RRSP deduction room available and asks his boss to also transfer that amount to the plan, providing a copy of his latest notice of assessment as evidence the room is available. The amount subject to tax deductions at source will be:

Retiring allowance:	$50,000
Amount eligible for direct transfer:	$21,000
Amount transferred based on contribution room:	$10,000
Total transferred to RRSP:	$31,000
Amount taxed at source:	$19,000

The employer does not require a letter of authority from the CRA to do this. Of course, if you've used all your contribution room this option won't be available.

Claim the Pension Income Credit

The first $1,000 of pension income qualifies for a special tax credit, called the pension income credit. It's worth $160 off your federal tax. When the provincial tax saving is added, the total reduction is around $225–$250, depending on your province of residence.

Only specific forms of pension income qualify, however. You can claim periodic payments from an employer pension or deferred profit sharing plan, payments from an annuity purchased with RRSP money, and the taxable portion of payments from an income-averaging annuity contract. You can also claim income from a RRIF if you are 65 or older during the tax year, or you received the RRIF money because a spouse died.

You may not claim CPP or QPP payments, Old Age Security, lump-sum withdrawals from an RRSP, lump-sum payments from a pension plan, retiring allowances, a retirement compensation arrangement, and income from a variety of other sources (consult the General Tax Guide if you're unsure).

Contrary to widespread belief, there is no age limit for claiming the pension credit, except in the case of RRIF payments. If you have income from a qualifying source, this credit is available to you. Complete the appropriate chart at line 314 in the tax guide to make the claim.

Claim the Age Credit

To be eligible for the age tax credit, you must meet both an age test and an income test. If you were 65 or older before the end of the tax year, you've passed part one. However, your net income must be less than a certain amount, which changes from year to year (it was $29,619 in 2005). You'll find a form at line 301 of the tax guide that will lead you through the calculation.

Transfer Unused Credits

You're allowed to claim certain tax credits for yourself if your spouse is unable to use them, including the pension credit and the age credit, as well as credits for disability, tuition, and education. Any amounts not needed to reduce your spouse's taxable income to zero are eligible. You'll have to complete Schedule 2, which comes with the tax return.

Transferring credits can be especially valuable in cases where one spouse has a very low income. Take, for example, the case of a couple in which the 66-year-old wife receives only Old Age Security plus a small private pension of $2,000 a year. She's not liable for any taxes. But she has pension and age credits which she can't use. Her husband can transfer these credits to himself, and reduce his tax bill by over $1,000 in the process. If the wife were eligible for the disability credit (perhaps because of a severe hearing impairment), he could transfer that amount as well, adding another $1,000 and change to his savings.

Claim All Medical Expenses

Your tax-deductible medical and dental costs may increase after you retire. This can be as a natural consequence of the aging process or because you no longer have a group health and dental plan, or both. The medical credit will provide some relief. But, unfortunately, you'll only be able to recover a portion of your total costs. You'll receive no credit for expenses up to 3 percent of your net income, to a maximum of $1,844 (2005 tax year). For anything above that, you get a 16 percent federal tax credit. With provincial taxes taken into account, you'll end up recovering about a quarter of your costs above the threshold.

That's small compensation for a large medical bill. So know the rules in order to take maximum advantage of it. Many people aren't aware of the wide range of expenses that can be claimed for the medical tax credit. They include everything from premiums paid for private health insurance plans (including travel insurance while outside Canada) to full-time attendant care. All the things you expect are on the list: doctors' fees, hospital bills, dental charges, prescriptions, glasses, and the like. But you can also claim a variety of costs you might not regard as truly medical. For example, if you begin to lose your hearing, which is common as you get older, the cost of hearing aids is deductible, as is the cost of any repairs. If you're physically disabled, the costs of modifying your home to make it more convenient for you to function may be claimed. A blind person may include the cost of a seeing-eye dog. You can even claim medical expenses incurred abroad. The rule of thumb is: if it's a genuine medically related cost, claim it. The worst the CRA can do is say no.

You may claim expenses that occurred in any 12-month period ending in the tax year for which you're filing a return, as long as they weren't deducted in the previous year. Since the tax credit is the same no matter who claims it, have the lower-income spouse do so. The 3 percent net income threshold will be less and you'll end up with a larger tax refund.

For example, if a wife has a net income of $50,000 annually, she'll have a medical expense threshold of $1,500 (3% x $50,000 = $1,500). If her husband has net income of $30,000, his threshold is only $900 (3% x $30,000 = $900). They'll be able to claim an extra $600 in expenses if he includes the bills on his return.

There is one problem here if you use tax preparation software. Some programs automatically default the medical credit to the higher-income spouse, which can cost a couple money. Moreover, this can be difficult to override. If you use such software, check this aspect carefully.

See if You're Eligible for the GST/HST Credit

You may not be claiming the GST/HST credit now because your income is too high. But if you expect it to drop in retirement, you may be entitled to receive a regular cheque from the government. Remember, if you are eligible for the credit you have to make a new claim every year.

Check Out Provincial Tax Credits

Most provinces offer their own tax credits to seniors. Although in virtually all cases only lower-income people can make use of them, it doesn't hurt to check them out when you're completing your tax return. You might get a pleasant surprise.

Don't Miss Your Instalment Payments

Once you stop receiving a regular salary, you may have to begin remitting tax to the CRA on an instalment basis if a significant portion of your income comes from sources that do not withhold tax at source (e.g., investments). Payments are due quarterly, on the fifteenth of March, June, September, and December. The tax department usually won't hit you with interest and penalty charges in the first year, but once you've received official notice of your obligation to pay quarterly, you'll have to send in a regular cheque, set up an electronic transfer (by far the most convenient way), or make the quarterly payments through your bank. You can find more details on the CRA website.

You may also wish to ask the federal government to withhold tax from your CPP and OAS payments. This is not something I normally recommend—it's always best to defer paying taxes for as long as possible. But having tax withheld at source will reduce the amount you will have to pay by instalment and will help to ensure that you don't find yourself cash-short when tax filing time comes around.

21

Alternative Income Sources

Uh-oh! You've retired and started to enjoy the so-called golden years, but things aren't going quite as you expected. It's been sneaking up on you gradually but one day you sit down, take a close look at the finances, and realize you're having trouble making ends meet.

It's a common problem. A poll conducted by Ipsos-Reid for RBC Financial Group in the fall of 2004 found that 47 percent of the retirees surveyed felt they could not afford to maintain the standard of living they had when they were working. Almost two-thirds agreed with the following statement: "Since retiring, managing my cash flow has been the top priority."

This should come as no great surprise. Prices don't stand still. As the years pass, it costs more to operate the family car, to fill the grocery shopping cart, to enjoy a meal out. Property taxes keep going up. The medical expenses are higher than you anticipated because you need to change your glasses more often and your spouse requires a hearing aid. Your kids continue to produce offspring, which is a great joy but means more money for birthdays and holidays. The cost of travel insurance for a winter vacation in the sunny south is more than the airfare and hotel combined. Meanwhile, your pension income stays the same and your CPP and OAS deposits increase by only a small amount.

You feel the first twinge of panic in your tummy and struggle to fight it off. What are you going to do? Will you need to start cutting back on some of the pleasures you enjoy? Ask the kids for financial help? Sell the house? You know that unless you do something soon, the situation is just going to get worse until it reaches a crisis stage. So what are the options?

Actually, there are quite a few of them. It's a case of being creative and looking carefully at all the possibilities. Here are some of the areas you might consider.

Go Back to Work

We spend most of each winter in south Florida. At the local supermarket I have noted that many of the baggers are obviously retirees, working for minimum wage and a few dollars in tips to try to make ends meet. Of course, this is always an option but when I talk about going back to work it is not really what I have in mind. There are many more interesting and more lucrative ways to supplement your retirement income through work.

Working past retirement age is becoming more popular. A poll released by TD Waterhouse in December 2004 found that one-third of those responding said they expected to work past 65, not just because of financial need but also because they want to. This growing trend has led to legislative action in a number of jurisdictions to remove mandatory retirement age statutes and to legal challenges where such laws are still on the books.

So what sort of work should you consider? Here are some ideas.

Consulting

If you have special knowledge or skills, you may be able to continue to profit from them in retirement by taking on consulting work. It is not uncommon for senior executives to continue to provide services to their former companies after officially retiring but, unless you have a contractual agreement, you're not limited to your ex-employer. A close friend of mine provided consulting services to a number of major companies for several years after his retirement as a senior executive of a big energy firm. He earned a substantial income in the process but, even more important, he greatly enjoyed the work and it helped to ease his way into full retirement.

Part-Time Work

You may be able to continue working at your old job on a part-time basis after you start drawing your pension. Many employers prefer this kind of arrangement to hiring new staff. It reduces costs while eliminating the necessity of training a new person, who may or may not work out. Ask about the possibility before you actually leave.

Some people take on part-time work so they can afford a particular lifestyle. Every year we get a phone call from Tom, a Chicago retiree who likes to spend six weeks in Florida every winter. He pays for it by riding around Fort Myers Beach on his bicycle, washing windows. He returns to the same regular customers each year, earning just enough to pay for his southern holiday.

Become an Entrepreneur

The number of 50-something retirees out there is astonishing. It's become an invisible growth industry. In January 2005, *USA Today* ran a front-page story in which it reported that 5.6 million Americans over age 50 are self-employed, a 23 percent increase from 1990. They bake cookies, build furniture, sell real estate, renovate homes, publish books—you name the business and you will probably find a retiree doing it.

Some friends of ours actually went through three different entrepreneurial stages once they retired. Stage one was buying and renovating homes in a fast-growth area of Florida, which they then sold for a profit. Stage two was doing the same thing with a small motel, supplementing their income through rentals until the work was completed. Stage three, which they are still doing, is breeding show-quality puppies that they sell all over the U.S. for hundreds of dollars each.

Another friend, a retired policeman from the Northeast, moved to Florida and turned his interest in computers into a business that he runs out of the garage of his home. He builds machines-to-order for clients, does repair work, and supplies equipment at a modest mark-up over wholesale, which earns a little extra for him and makes the customers happy.

There are thousands of other stories like this, so if the idea appeals to you, go for it. Just remember these cardinal rules:

1. *Do something you enjoy and are good at.* Don't take on a lot of stress at this point in your life.

2. *Start small.* Don't overextend yourself. Find out what your limits are and work within them. Leave adequate leisure time for golf, tennis, fishing, family, travel, or whatever.

3. *Don't invest a lot of money up front.* See if the business takes off and, if it does, use your cash flow to expand if you wish to do so.

4. *Have a back-up.* You're not as young as you used to be. Have a contingency plan to look after your customers if you are taken ill or want to go on an extended vacation. My friend with the computer company has made arrangements with a local computer store to take care of his clients in such circumstances and to handle overflow work.

5. *Have an exit strategy.* You're not going to do this forever. A study done for CIBC World Markets in early 2005 found that only 40 percent of "seniorpreneurs" have a clear strategy for exiting their businesses. So if you are going to start a business, make sure you can finish it.

Review Your Investments

You may be able to squeeze more money out of your investment portfolio—if you are prepared to accept some additional risk. Many retirees are ultra-conservative in their approach to money management. In one sense, that's good because it reduces the chance that your capital will take a big hit from a stock market correction or a sharp rise in interest rates. The downside is that a safe portfolio won't produce much cash flow. A 3 percent return on a GIC will only generate $3,000 in income from a $100,000 portfolio. You could probably double that by putting the money into high-quality corporate bonds or triple it with a portfolio of income trusts. Yes, there is more risk involved, so you have to decide where your priorities lie: making sure your money is absolutely safe or improving your standard of living. Like everything else in life, it's a trade-off.

If you are uncertain about your investing skills, the best course of action is to sit down with a financial advisor who is knowledgeable about income securities and review all the options. Make sure you understand exactly what risks are involved. Then make an informed decision.

Use Your Home Equity

Before I begin this section, let me make a disclosure. In my earlier books on retirement planning *(Retiring Wealthy, Retiring Wealthy in the 21st Century)* I wrote favourably about reverse mortgages as an excellent way for converting home equity into additional income. Since that time I have appeared in advertising for the Canadian Home Income Plan (CHIP), for which I am paid, and I own shares in Home Equity Income Trust, which generates its cash flow through CHIP reverse mortgages. So I have a financial interest in the company's success.

Now let's look at the home equity options.

Many retirees own their homes free and clear. In fact, I have long regarded going into retirement with an unencumbered home as one of the objectives toward which people should strive. This gives you maximum flexibility as you grow older to make use of the equity in your home as a source of capital, for estate planning, and/or to generate extra income. Your home equity may be worth hundreds of thousands of dollars so it is essential that you use it correctly.

Drawing on your home equity for cash or income has significant advantages over some of the other choices available to you. For example, home equity is not taxable. If you withdraw money from an RRSP or RRIF, it is treated as income and taxed at your full marginal rate. (Of course, you must take out a taxable minimum amount from a RRIF each year but anything in excess of that is at your discretion.) Alternatively, if you sell securities from a non-registered portfolio you may trigger capital gains, half of which will be taxable. Money received from a loan (any kind of loan) does not attract tax.

Another advantage of using home equity is that it does not affect your eligibility for government benefits. Money received from a loan is not "income" for purposes of calculating a claim for the age tax credit nor does it trigger the Old Age Security clawback. (However, if the loan principal is invested, which I recommend, the income generated by the securities does count for these purposes.)

There's an additional tax advantage if you invest the money from a home equity loan: the interest on the mortgage becomes tax-deductible, thereby significantly reducing the real cost to you.

The first thought that comes to the mind of most people when they think about using home equity is simply to sell the property and move into something smaller or into a rental property (for most people, living with their children would be a last resort). That, the thinking goes, would free up a substantial amount of capital, which could then be drawn on or invested to generate income.

But what if you don't want to sell? I know a couple who have always regretted that they sold the family home and moved into a much smaller townhouse immediately after the husband retired. The new place wasn't big enough to hold all their furniture and a lifetime of memorabilia and, because it was located in another part of the city, they lost contact with the neighbourhood in which they had lived for more than a quarter-century.

You also need to think about the costs involved in selling, buying, and moving. The real estate commission alone on the sale will be as much as 6 percent, and expenses like legal fees, land transfer tax, packers and movers, and redecorating will add thousands of dollars more. Plus, if you buy a smaller place, part of your capital will have to be used for that purchase. So before you make a decision, look carefully at all the numbers and see how they shake out. And don't forget to consider the stress involved in selling, finding a new place, and moving everything.

Let's say that at the end of this exercise you decide you really love your existing home and would like to stay in it for as long as possible. But you would still like to make use of the money that's tied up in your home equity to generate more income or for other purposes. What are your options?

Remortgage the House

You've had a mortgage before, so this is nothing new. You go through the standard process, which will include income and credit checks. Since regular repayments are required with a mortgage, the lender needs to be assured that you have the financial capacity to handle the cost. For retirees on a fixed income, this could be a problem. The usual expenses of mortgaging a home will apply, including such things as legal fees and appraisal.

Apply for a Home Equity Line of Credit

You will still have to place a mortgage on the house to obtain a personal line of credit (PLC) that is secured by your home equity, which means the same credit/income checks and expenses as in the previous option. But there are some potential advantages to using this approach.

1. *You don't have to take all the money at once.* You can draw as much as you need and only pay interest on that amount, keeping the rest in reserve.

2. *You can repay the principal at any time without penalty.* With a conventional mortgage, early repayment in excess of 10 percent or 15 percent of the principal (depending on the terms of your loan) will trigger a penalty.

3. *Your interest rate may be lower.* Home equity PLC rates are usually prime or prime plus a quarter. That may be better than you'll get on a conventional mortgage, but do some cost comparisons. Also, remember that the PLC rate will fluctuate as prime moves up or down. You can't lock in.

In both these cases, be certain that you can meet the required payment schedule. Failure to do so could put your home at risk.

Obtain a Reverse Mortgage

If you are 62 or older, you may be eligible for a reverse mortgage. The Canadian Home Income Plan is the largest issuer of these mortgages in the country, operating from coast to coast. In my experience, many Canadians don't really understand how a reverse mortgage works so they tend to overlook this option. That's unfortunate, because it can be a valuable financial tool in the right situation. A reverse mortgage is most appropriate for people who want to convert some of their home equity to cash but do not want to be saddled with monthly repayments. A reverse mortgage will advance up to 40 percent of the value of the equity in your home, which can then be spent or invested as you wish.

You don't have to make any repayments on this type of mortgage. The accrued interest is added to the principal, which means the total amount owing will increase over time. The full balance becomes payable when you sell the house or when the last surviving spouse dies. The amount to be repaid can never exceed the fair market value of the property, so the balance of your estate will not be encumbered. Also, you can never be forced to sell the home prematurely, even if the loan balance rises to more than the property value (that has happened with conventional mortgages during periods when real estate prices fell sharply).

The interest rate on a reverse mortgage reflects the long-term mortgage rate market, so it will usually be higher than the rate on a conventional mortgage or a PLC. As well, there will be the standard expenses associated with a mortgage plus a set-up fee. More information on reverse mortgages can be found at the CHIP website at **www.chip.ca**.

Whichever option you choose, my strong advice is to invest the proceeds, thus making the interest tax-deductible. That means the cash flow generated by the investment portfolio will in all likelihood be received tax free in your hands since the deduction generated by the mortgage interest will probably offset the income received. Investing the money also preserves the principal for estate planning purposes. The portfolio could eventually be liquidated by the estate to help repay the mortgage loan.

If you are seeking more cash flow and use a conventional mortgage or a PLC, make sure that the after-tax income generated by the portfolio exceeds the after-tax interest cost or the whole exercise won't be worth the effort. This may require accepting a higher degree of risk in the securities you select so as to produce greater returns.

With a reverse mortgage, you can take a more conservative approach with your investments since no monthly repayments are required. The entire amount of the income produced by the portfolio will be yours to spend as you wish. In this case, I recommend a mix of government bonds, high-quality corporate bonds, preferred shares, and top-grade income trusts so as to preserve the capital intact.

Draw More from Savings

It's not a good idea to spend your retirement capital, but sometimes it is necessary. However, keep in mind this is not an unlimited source of funds. The more you spend, the sooner the nest egg will be gone and you'll have to look for other solutions.

If you have a RRIF, there is no limit on the amount of money you can take out each year. You simply have to advise the plan administrator in writing and you can have access to the extra money. Keep in mind that the money will be taxed as income when it comes out of the RRIF.

Locked-in plans (LIFs, LRIFs, LIRAs) are another matter. These are governed by strict rules that vary depending on which government, federal or provincial, has jurisdiction. See Chapter 18 for information about getting access to locked-in accounts.

Of course, you can draw on any unregistered investments at any time. But consider the tax consequences before you do. Selling securities may trigger a capital gain or loss. If possible, try to balance off the two to minimize the tax payable.

Apply for Government Assistance

If all else fails and you're in truly difficult straits, consider applying for government assistance. The federal government and most provinces offer support programs of various types for low-income seniors, but you have to be pretty badly off to qualify.

The Guaranteed Income Supplement (GIS), available from Social Development Canada, is the most widely used income support program of this type. However, many people don't know about a related benefit, known as the Allowance, which is also offered to low-income seniors. To qualify, you must be a Canadian citizen between 60 and 64 and living with a spouse or common-law partner who is entitled to receive Old Age Security and the Guaranteed Income Supplement. The amount you can receive is based on the combined income of you and your spouse. The maximum monthly benefit in the third quarter of 2005 was $846.21. Payments are adjusted quarterly for inflation.

There is also a Survivor's Allowance for people between 60 and 64 whose spouse or common-law partner has died. You qualify if your annual income does not exceed $18,624 (third quarter 2005) and you meet the other tests. In this case the maximum monthly payment is $934.24.

22

Living in the Sun

According to a survey done for the RBC Financial Group in the fall of 2004, more than half of the respondents who had not yet retired dreamed of spending their winters in a warm climate. That hardly comes as a surprise; many Canadians love their country dearly but would just as soon forgo the icy blasts of January and February.

What *was* something of a surprise was how few people actually manage to translate the dream into reality. Among the retirees who responded, only 19 percent said that they actually spent winters in the Sunbelt. Presumably the rest found they really didn't want to go south after all or, more likely, that they couldn't afford to do so.

For those who have succeeded in making it happen, Florida, Arizona, California, and Hawaii have become the favourite U.S. retirement destinations. More adventurous snowbirds have flown to places as far afield as Mexico, the Caribbean, the Bahamas, Costa Rica, and southern Europe. If you're inclined to join the exodus to the sun after you retire, you'll need to do some careful advance planning. Financial considerations are important, of course, but there are other matters to take into account such as housing, family, medical facilities, and social ties.

The first, and most important, decision is whether you plan to cut your ties with Canada partially or totally. You can spend your winters in the warmth and still remain a Canadian resident, with all the pluses and minuses that involves. Or you can sever your connection with Canada entirely and take up full-time residency in another country.

You retain your Canadian resident status for tax purposes if you maintain a home in this country and live here over half the year. Even if you are abroad for more than six months each year, the Canada Revenue Agency may take the view you're still a Canadian resident for tax purposes if you retain ties to Canada, such as real estate, bank accounts, investments, club memberships, driver's licence, etc.

Being a Canadian resident makes you eligible for continued coverage under your provincial health care program, a benefit many older people are reluctant to surrender. However, "residency" for purposes of health insurance varies from one province to another, so make inquiries first. Continuing as a Canadian resident also ensures you will receive any social benefits to which you are entitled. Some of these may be lost under certain conditions if you leave the country—Old Age Security benefits, for example, may be discontinued after six months if you take up residency abroad and did not live in Canada for at least 20 years after the age of 18. But if you meet the qualifications for continued payment, you'll be able to draw OAS while sunning on the beach, and you can even arrange to have your money directly deposited to a U.S. bank account if you take up residence in that country. Any benefits earned under the Canada Pension Plan are payable no matter where you live. Direct deposit to a U.S. account can also be arranged for these payments.

Of course, retaining Canadian residency also makes you liable to pay Canadian taxes, which are much higher than those in the most popular snowbird destinations, including the United States. You'll have to weigh the economic pros and cons.

Your country of residence is more than just a matter of money. You may wish to continue to keep a home in Canada because you don't want to spend muggy summers in Florida or the hurricane season in the Caribbean, or because you want to be closer to your family and friends for part of the year—or simply because you love what is, after all, a very beautiful, if normally cold, country.

If you decide to move abroad, make inquiries about residency requirements at the embassy or consulate of the country you're considering. Moving to the U.S. permanently has become easier in certain situations as a result of the Free Trade Agreement, but you'll still need to meet their qualifications. You'll have to obtain a green card, which could take some time, or meet what they call a "substantial presence" test, which is based on a period of residency in that country. Check with a U.S. immigration representative for full details.

RRSPs and RRIFs

One of the greatest areas of concern and confusion about moving abroad is the fate of retirement savings that are held in RRSPs, RRIFs, and other registered plans. It is a complex subject and a lot depends on where you plan to live. There are an estimated 800,000 U.S. residents with Canadian RRSPs or RRIFs, so this is a major issue. If you're planning to join this group, here's what you need to know.

The value of an RRSP when you become a U.S. resident is considered capital, and is therefore not taxable. Any income earned within the plan after you become a U.S. resident may continue to compound tax free. You only become liable for U.S. taxes once you start making withdrawals from the plan, and then only on those amounts that relate to income earned in your RRSP *after* you became a U.S. resident, plus any unrealized capital gains. This makes it a sound strategy to take any capital gains in your RRSP before you leave Canada, thereby reducing the U.S. tax for which you'll eventually be liable. If you've lost money in your RRSP to the extent that the plan's value is less than your total contributions, you'll face no U.S. tax at all.

You will have to pay a withholding tax of 25 percent in Canada when you make withdrawals from your RRSP after you become a non-resident by moving to the U.S. Periodic payments from an RRIF, LIF, or annuity are subject to a 15 percent withholding tax. (Withholding rates may differ if you move to another country; the standard rate on pensions, RRIFs, and annuities is 25 percent, but any tax treaty provisions take precedence.) If you become a non-resident, the CRA will regard the withholdings as your full payment. This means you'll pay tax at a much lower rate than would have been the case had you stayed home. Of course, some tax may be assessed in the U.S. (or wherever else you're living). But if you're in the States, such tax will only be payable on a portion of your withdrawals, as we've seen. Plus, you should be able to claim a credit for your Canadian withholdings against your U.S. taxes payable. These rules make it advantageous to keep your RRSP if you decide to move to the States. Your investments will continue to grow, tax sheltered, just as if you'd stayed in Canada.

To get the tax break, you have to make a declaration to the Internal Revenue Service (IRS) that you intend to make use of the relevant provision of the tax treaty. Doing so requires a special election, which is made with the first U.S. return you file. You'll be required to supply detailed financial information about your RRSP at that time. The specific rules covering this election are complex and somewhat tricky, so I strongly recommend seeking the advice of a tax expert who is familiar with the process if you decide to make this move.

The same rules apply to registered retirement income funds (RRIFs) as well. They're simply regarded as a substitute for an RRSP.

Pension income may also receive a tax break if you move to the U.S. Employee and employer contributions made to the plan on your behalf are considered capital, in the same way as your RRSP, and therefore won't be taxed. Pension payments originating in Canada are also subject to withholding tax if you become a non-resident. The standard rate is 25 percent, but what you pay will be determined in the provisions of the tax treaty between Canada and the country you're moving to. Several other types of Canadian income may also have tax withheld at source if you leave. These include most interest payments, dividends, rents, CPP, and OAS.

One serious disadvantage in moving to the U.S. is that you may find that your RRSP/RRIF assets are frozen. Canadian brokers who are not registered in the U.S. (which is most of them) cannot make trades in your account once you become a non-resident. Even those who are registered are limited in what they are allowed to do. State regulations make matters even more complicated.

So before you leave Canada, make sure you sit down with your financial advisor and discuss exactly what the status of your RRIF/RRSP will be after you depart. If the account will be frozen, you may decide to convert everything to cash and then draw from it as required. If there is a lot of money involved, this is a major decision so explore all the options thoroughly.

Canada's "Departure Tax"

It isn't actually called that, but Canada has what amounts to a departure tax, and it may make it financially difficult for you to take up permanent residence in another country, depending on your situation. It works like this. On the day you leave the country, the CRA takes the position that you sold all your stocks, bonds, mutual funds, and other securities. This is called a deemed disposition. You must declare any capital gains (or losses) that result from this fictitious sale on your final Canadian tax return. If you have a lot of invested money, the tax liability could be huge.

There are a few exceptions to the deemed disposition rule. You don't have to declare any Canadian real estate that you own, any Canadian business property (if the operation is run from a permanent Canadian address), pensions and other rights, stock options, and certain property of short-term residents.

You can, if you so choose, defer paying the tax on property subject to this rule until it is actually sold. The catch is that you have to provide the CRA "acceptable security" to ensure they will eventually get paid. You can also arrange to pay the tax in up to six annual instalments, again with acceptable security.

As you can see, leaving Canada permanently can be expensive, and it will certainly entail a lot of paperwork. Note that these rules do not apply if you are spending only part of the year in another country and continue to maintain Canadian residency for tax purposes.

The Florida Option

Whether or not you choose to remain a Canadian resident, you may decide to purchase a Sunbelt home for the winter months. After all, there's nothing wrong with spending November to April in Florida or Hawaii and arriving back just in time for the spectacular blossoming of May flowers. So let's spend some time looking at Sunbelt real estate and some of the problems that can develop if you're going shopping for a winter residence for the first time. We'll use Florida as our example because it's the most popular choice for Canadians and the area with which I have the greatest familiarity since we own a winter home in Fort Myers Beach. But most of the points that follow will be applicable to other U.S. Sunbelt states as well.

The first thing to understand is that buying a place in a hot climate is not like buying a home in Canada. Many considerations come into play that you've probably never dreamed of. Here are a few examples.

Climate Zones

All of Florida is warm in the winter compared to Canada, but some areas are much warmer than others. Your comfort level will be influenced by which one you choose. The state has three main climate zones.

The North. This is a belt across the top of the state that includes the Panhandle, Jacksonville, and the capital, Tallahassee. It can be quite cool in winter, with even the occasional snowflake. The average daily temperature in January in Tallahassee is only 12°C (53°F). Also, this zone is much more susceptible to the winter and spring storms that track from southwest to northeast across the U.S. You are much more likely to find yourself under a thunderstorm or tornado watch here during the winter and early spring than you are in any other part of the state.

The Middle. The central part of the state encompasses such popular vacation destinations as Tampa/St. Petersburg, Sarasota, and Orlando. Winter temperatures are much milder; the average daily temperature in Orlando in January is 16°C (60°F).

The South. The extreme tip of the state is warmest of all in the winter. It includes Miami, Fort Lauderdale, Key West, Fort Myers, and the lovely community of Naples. Average January temperature in Miami Beach is 21°C (69°F), the same as in Key West.

Housing Considerations

Insects. Insects thrive in the heat. Termites, roaches, fire ants, no-see-ums (my wife's pet peeve)—you name it, it's around. In Canada, many buyers insist on having a house checked by a home inspector before closing a deal. In Florida, a check by a pest control expert is equally important. As well, you will need to pay for year-round pest control maintenance, unless it is covered by condo fees.

Storage areas. Warm-weather homes usually don't have basements (although those built on pilings may have usable space underneath). This makes storage a chronic problem; be sure there's adequate room for all your possessions. Garages, which serve as junk-collectors in Canada, are also rarer in the south; carports tend to be more popular.

Flooding. Florida is nothing more than a big sandbar. If you want to live near the sea, high water should be a concern if you are on ground level. Some coastal communities now require that land be artificially elevated before new homes are constructed or that the lower level not be used as living quarters, to reduce the flood risk. But older buildings have not been subject to these requirements in most cases. Check out the flood risk and the elevation above the high-water mark on any property you're considering before going ahead.

Hurricane shutters. All areas around the Gulf of Mexico and the Caribbean Sea are potential hurricane targets. If the property you're considering does not have hurricane shutters you may have to install them, and they aren't cheap. For our three-bedroom home, the price tag was about US$12,000 a few years ago; it would be more now.

Landscaping. If you're buying a condo, you don't have to worry about landscaping. Otherwise, keeping a property neat and tidy in a subtropical climate can be even more difficult than it is in Canada in June. That beautiful palm tree on the front lawn will have to be sprayed regularly to keep it healthy. An orange tree may seem wonderful—until the fruit falls to the ground and starts rotting, attracting all kinds of unwelcome insects, or an agricultural inspector spots citrus canker and orders it to be cut down (yes, they can do that).

If you're not planning to take up permanent residence, you'll need to hire someone to come in regularly to do the yard work for you. Expect to pay upwards of $100 a month for the service. Alternatively, you can look at places with "maintenance-free landscaping," which basically means your lawn will be pebbles instead of grass. That eliminates the need for mowing, but you may still have the falling oranges to contend with. And not all communities permit this form of landscaping.

Sprinkler systems. Underground sprinklers are much more common in the south than in Canada. They're especially useful if the house is going to be vacant for long periods and you want to keep the vegetation green during the winter dry months. (It rains so much in summer that you really don't have to worry about watering; Mother Nature does the job.)

Pools and pool heaters. Pools are a common accessory in more expensive southern homes. It may not surprise you that many of them are not heated—after all, this is the Sunbelt, right? Unfortunately, even the mildest parts of the Sunbelt can get rather cool at times. If the pool isn't heated, you may find the water too chilly for your liking, especially in January and February. In my experience, a system of solar panels is the least expensive to operate (the sun does all the work). However, even they might not be adequate to keep your pool at a toasty 27°C (80°F) during the depth of winter when even south Florida temperatures can fall below 7°C (45°F) at night. In such cases, a supplementary propane gas heater may be needed, at a cost of about $1,500, or you can consider a more expensive heat pump. So if you're looking for a pool and you find one that's already heated, consider it a plus.

Of course, you will have to have your pool maintained regularly. If you don't, you'll be greeted by a foul-smelling algae pit when you arrive for the winter. You should arrange for weekly visits by a qualified person. Cost will be $50 to $100 a month.

Screening. Most Florida residences have a screened balcony, porch, or lanai. If you look at one that doesn't and the real estate agent insists it's not really needed, don't believe a word of it. Unless you want to retreat inside at sunset when the mosquitoes and no-see-ums emerge in their zillions, you need screening, and even that is not 100 percent effective. If you like the idea of enjoying a barbecue dinner outside on a soft Florida night, a screened lanai is an absolute essential.

Sea/canal frontage. If the place is on tidal water and you've never had experience with the sea before, there are a host of things to watch out for. One is the condition of the seawall, if there is one. If it needs repairs, they can be costly. If the house has a dock, check the pilings. They must be replaced periodically, which is also expensive. Many Florida canal homes have davits or lifts for raising boats out of the water. See if they're working properly. I once encountered a davit that wasps had virtually destroyed by packing it with mud as they built a nest.

Condo rules. If the property you're considering is a condominium, get a copy of the rules and study them thoroughly before you buy. Some of the regulations can be strange. For example, some of my friends purchased a condo home in Boca Raton. After investing a lot of money in hurricane shutters, they discovered that the rules did not permit homes to be shuttered unless there was an actual hurricane warning. Since hurricanes occur in the summer months, when they were back in Canada, it created a big problem for them.

Costs

The financial considerations involved in buying a Sunbelt property can also differ from your Canadian real estate experience. Here are some of the money problems to be aware of.

Prices. Prices will vary depending on where you buy, but if you're used to the prices in expensive cities like Toronto and Vancouver or popular vacation areas such as Whistler and Muskoka, you'll find Florida costs are comparable once the exchange rate is taken into account. Of course, much depends on the area you choose. You can find some wonderful Florida properties for a fraction of what you'd pay in Canada if you go hunting in the Panhandle or some of the less fashionable inland areas. On the other hand, some areas are outrageously expensive. You'll pay a big premium for addresses like Palm Beach, Boca Raton, Fort Lauderdale, Sanibel, Naples, and some parts of Sarasota.

Don't expect to make a killing on your investment. Generally, Florida real estate prices tend to be soft, especially for condos. That's because the market is usually saturated with resale properties, due to the older age of the population in the most desirable resort areas (people become ill or die and the house goes up for sale). A few areas of the state have experienced significant price gains in recent years, however, most notably the south-western area around Naples.

This chronic oversupply makes some parts of Florida a buyer's market. In those areas, you can afford to be choosy and to drive a hard bargain. It's not unusual for properties to stay on the market for a year or more; I've seen some that have gone for two or three years without moving. The longer a "for sale" sign has been on the front lawn, the better your chances of getting a good buy.

The other side of this coin is that it may take a long time to sell the property when the time comes to do so, and you may take a loss in the process. I have several Canadian friends who have owned Florida property at some time in their lives. Most enjoyed the place while they had it, but few ended up making any money when they sold. But let me stress that this is not the case everywhere. In the region where we live, property values skyrocketed in the late 1990s and the early 2000s because a big population influx resulted in a development boom. Waterside residences saw the greatest escalation, with some homes tripling in value in five years.

Mortgages. Mortgage interest rates used to be lower in the U.S. than in Canada, but that has not been the case in recent years. But you can lock them in for a long period if you wish; 15- and 30-year mortgages are common.

You may have to pay more up front when you take out a mortgage in the States. Many lenders charge "points" for initiating a mortgage; these are a percentage (1 or 2 percent is common) of the total value of the loan. The charge is supposed to cover a variety of costs, but it's mainly an inter-est rate buy-down. Usually (but not always), you'll find that the more points you're charged, the lower the interest rate will be.

Since there are many more mortgage lenders in the States than in Canada, you'll have to shop around for the best deal. And you'll need to do a lot of calculations to figure out whether you're better off paying points and taking a lower rate or putting out nothing up front but carrying a higher interest charge. A mortgage broker can be very helpful in cutting through the maze of numbers on your behalf.

Another problem you may encounter is the reluctance of many U.S. financial institutions to lend money to aliens (that's us, folks, not some weird creatures from space). The reason is that many companies sell their mortgage contracts to third parties, and they are reluctant to accept Canadian or other foreign owners because of the potential problems of collection in the event of default. Maybe they think we're bad risks.

Property taxes. Of course, you'll have to pay property taxes on your Sunbelt residence. But the rate of tax may depend on whether or not you're moving there permanently. The state of Florida provides a substantial discount to permanent residents, which is not available to snowbirds (Canadians and Americans) who only come down for the winter. This seems to defy logic, since seasonal residents put less strain on community services, but that's the way it works.

The way the system operates is that Florida residents living in their own home have a cap of 3 percent or the CPI, whichever is less, on their annual property tax increase. Everyone else gets hit for the full amount. Since real estate valuations are based on fair market value and are adjusted annually, taxes can rise very quickly in areas where real estate is hot. Don't think you can beat the system by buying from a permanent resident; when a property changes hands the tax rate is adjusted to current market value.

Insurance. You'll need to carry flood and hurricane protection, which you may not have on your Canadian home policy. These riders can be very expensive. It used to cost about three times more to insure our Florida home than it does our residence in Toronto, even though the values are roughly comparable. After the state was ravaged by four hurricanes in the summer of 2004, the differential went even higher.

Also, you may have trouble finding a company to insure your property, especially if it is an older building and/or located in a coastal community. Make sure you can obtain coverage before you close a deal.

Estate taxes. Estate taxes have been a major area of concern to anyone buying property in the United States. Canadians used to face death duties on U.S. property that could only be described as confiscatory. Changes approved by the U.S. Congress have raised the limits on estates subject to this tax but it is unclear at the time of writing whether the new rules will become permanent. Consult an expert in cross-border taxation for the current rules.

Foreign property declaration. The CRA requires you to report any foreign property you own if the total cost is more than $100,000. Purchasing a Sunbelt property may put you into that category. If so, be sure to make an annual declaration to that effect. You won't pay any extra tax; the measure is mainly intended to prevent Canadians from earning undeclared income from offshore investment accounts.

Renting your house. If you rent your Sunbelt home for part of the year when you're not there, the tax people are going to come sniffing around. If the property is in the U.S., both the CRA and the IRS are going to want their share. As far as Canadian taxes are concerned, income from your U.S. property will be treated in the same way as any other rental income. You'll be allowed to deduct appropriate expenses to arrive at your net rental income, so be sure to keep all your receipts.

If you are a "non-resident alien" (which I'll explain in more detail shortly), any rental income from a U.S. property is subject to a 30 percent withholding tax in that country, with no deductions allowed. However, there is an exception if you want to treat your property as a business. To do this, you have to complete IRS form 1040NR, *U.S. Nonresident Alien Income Tax Return,* and attach a letter providing full details about the property.

Selling your house. If the time comes to sell your U.S. house, the buyers or their agent are required to withhold 10 percent of the gross price and remit it to the IRS. You then have to file form 1040NR to report a gain or loss. If you and your spouse owned the property jointly, you must each file a return. If you want more information about how all this works, get a copy of IRS publication number 519 titled *U.S. Tax Guide for Aliens.*

Income Taxes

So much for housing. There are a number of other matters you also have to deal with if you decide to take up residency abroad. Income taxes are clearly a major consideration. The big issue that will have to be resolved is who you have to pay them to. If you spend a significant amount of time in the States, you may be classified as a "resident alien." To determine if this is your situation, take their "substantial presence test." It works like this:

For the current year, count every day spent in the U.S. as one day.

For last year, count every day as one-third of a day.

For the year before that, count every day as one-sixth of a day.

If the total exceeds 182 days, you meet the substantial presence test. If so, you have to file a U.S. tax return and report your worldwide income.

So, for example, suppose you spent 125 days in the U.S. in each of the past three years. That's about four months a year. Here's the calculation.

This year = 125 x 1   = 125 days
Last year = 125 x 1/3 = 42 days
Prior year = 125 x 1/6 = 21 days
Total   = 188 days

Even though in this case you never spent more than about four months in the U.S. in any one year, you qualify as a resident alien of that country.

You can get around this if you meet three conditions:

1. You were in the U.S. less than 183 days in the current year.
2. Your tax home is in Canada, meaning you are employed in this country or live here regularly.
3. You have a "closer connection" to Canada than to the U.S. This can be determined by a variety of things, from where you vote to the religious institution to which you belong. In this case, you have to advise the IRS by filing form 8840, *Closer Connection Exception Statement.*

There's a useful pamphlet published by the CRA titled *Canadian Residents Going Down South* that outlines your obligations either as a resident alien or non-resident alien in the U.S. If you plan to spend any significant amount of time in that country after you retire, I strongly recommend that you get a copy of it.

If you do end up paying any U.S. income tax as a result of all this, you may be able to claim a foreign tax credit when you file your Canadian return.

RRSPs and RRIFs are another issue that will inevitably come up if you take flight from Canada. Of course, if you remain a Canadian for tax purposes, nothing happens. Your retirement plans are subject to the same rules as before. But if you become a resident of another country, that all changes. Again, everything will depend on which country you choose and the tax treaty that prevails between that nation and Canada.

The Lure of Mexico

A growing number of Canadians are looking beyond the attractions of the American South to the warmth and value to be found in Mexico. One of them is a long-time friend of mine, Ted Turner, who, with his wife, Trish, owns a beautiful condominium on Peninsula de Santiago in Manzanillo where they can sip fine wine on their large terrace and watch the sun set over the Pacific every evening.

Since I have always believed that the best source of information on a subject is someone who has actually experienced it, I asked Ted to provide some guidance for Canadians who might be interested in following him and Trish into what for many of us is unknown territory. Here is his detailed Mexico report.

Choosing Where to Go

Mexico is a very large country and offers many options of lifestyle, geography, weather, cost of living, and access to English-language services. You'll find communities with large English-speaking populations and regions that require a knowledge of Spanish to survive. If you don't know the language and don't plan to learn it (in which case, you are missing a great pleasure), then you had better stick with cities and towns that cater to Americans and Canadians.

Mexican weather is usually much warmer than that of Canada and the northern U.S. states, but don't be misled into thinking that's the case everywhere. Both coasts offer beach communities that are warm to hot during the winter season and often very hot during the summers. But many retirees prefer inland cities, which are at higher elevations and can be quite cool, especially during the winter. We have been in Guadalajara in January when it was 5°C (40°F) every morning, warming to only 20°C (68°F) during the afternoon. Guadalajara is close to the retirement communities of Ajijic and Chapala.

The Gulf Coast has Caribbean weather with significant temperature fluctuations and a tendency to hurricanes during the June to November season. Many communities in that region focus on short-term vacationers with large hotels, nightclubs, and busy traffic. It is possible to find residential communities outside or near the major tourist destinations.

The west coast has more stable weather conditions with warm, dry winters and hot summers, with some rain almost every day. Earthquakes of varying intensity can occur every few years somewhere along this coast. Hurricanes can happen too, but violent ones are exceptions.

Each of the major west coast cities or towns has a distinctive character. For example, Acapulco is one of the oldest of the developed vacation cities and it seems to cater to shorter-term vacationers, although there are luxurious hotels and areas with fine homes and condominiums. Farther south is Puerto Escondido, which was a hippy and surfer haven in the 1960s. Younger surfers still are attracted to the main beach, which is off limits to casual swimmers for very good reason: it has a treacherous undertow. Some of the '60s hippies still return to Puerto Escondido or live there. It has only a few hotels and some newer good residential properties. It is more typically Mexican, with less English than one would find in other communities. Farther south, Huatulco is being developed with larger hotels and is worth considering as it grows.

Going north from Acapulco, the towns of Zihuatenejo and Ixtapa offer two differing styles. The former is an older Mexican fishing town, the latter a developed modern resort centre. Farther north is the spread-out port city of Manzanillo. Its central area (Centro) consists mostly of a very large container port and offers few facilities or services for retirees. The port is one of the largest in Mexico and is also home to the Mexican Navy. However, Manzanillo stretches north for several kilometres and includes many different economic levels of accommodation along the beaches. At the high end currently is the Peninsula de Santiago, home of the well-known and still top-of-the-line Hotel Las Hadas, site of the movie *10*. There are several condo developments of different price levels on the Peninsula and the very exclusive and pricey La Punta gated residential community, home to many of the rich and famous. There are other housing and condo developments as one progresses farther north, such as the gated Club Santiago with upmarket homes and condos. Still farther north you'll find Vida del Mar, a condo development on the cliffs over-looking the Pacific inhabited almost entirely by ex-pats who live there much of the year. The communities of Manzanillo offer many services in English and the expatriate community has many activities to help meet others, although there is less obligation to participate than in other areas. However, the Manzanillo area is still principally Mexican.

North of Manzanillo, there are several small communities along the Costa Alegre—the Happy Coast. This coast features many of the best hotels in Mexico, if not the world. For example, Barra de Navidad is home to the Grand Bay Hotel, recently named the world's best luxury vacation hotel by Travel TV. The small, sleepy town of La Manzanilla is attracting ex-pats who really want to get away from it all, as well as artists and writers. The next large community is the very big and developed Puerto Vallarta (known locally as PV). It bustles with activity and development. There are many options for retirees in condos or homes in and around PV and many English-language services. The expatriate community is very large there.

Other options to consider are the inland communities that have larger ex-pat and retiree populations. The weather in these cities and towns is much more temperate due to the higher elevations, with cool nights and warm but not hot days. Probably the most "American/Canadian" communities are Ajijic and Chapala, on the shores of Lake Chapala, just south of Mexico's second-largest city, Guadalajara. Many Canadian and American retirees live in this area either part or all of the year. Consequently there are many English-language services and things to do, from English movie theatres to English churches. Real estate prices tend to be higher due to this demand.

Farther north and in the mountains is San Miguel de Allende, a well-developed and very art-oriented town. It has a large English-language population including well-known skater and artist Toller Cranston. San Miguel is also pricey but has a very Mexican feel, even with all the Canadian and American residents.

The bottom line is that you can't simply "think Mexico" when considering a retirement place. Rather, think what kind of Mexico. Are you willing to learn Spanish and get to know and converse with Mexicans? Do you need English-language neighbours and services? There are people who live full-time in Mexico who speak almost no Spanish except possibly *"Una cerveza más, por favor!"*

What can you afford? There is a tremendous variance in the price of condominiums and houses from community to community. Do you want a house or a condo? How much security is important to you? What weather do you enjoy? Hot? Temperate? Are the ocean and a view important? If you will be living in Mexico for only part of the year, how important is a car to you? Are you willing to drive down and back each year? It's a four- to five-day trip from most of Canada and the northern U.S.

These are the first of many questions to consider when thinking about Mexico for full-time or part-time retirement living. I suggest that you do a lot of research. Ask anyone who has reliable information about Mexico and decide where you think you would like to live. Then visit the one or two places that interest you for a few weeks or months.

Once you decide on your new retirement community, you will find other ex-pats to be willing sources of information and referrals. This information is often very helpful. However, a word of caution—be careful in selecting your sources as they can be wrong and you may waste a lot of time doing things the wrong way.

You may be able to find sources of reliable information in your community such as the HELP! organization, which is based in Manzanillo with services in Zihuatenejo and along the Costa Alegre all the way up to and including Puerto Vallarta. The founder and general director is the energetic Bonnie Sumlin and you can reach her at 314-334-0977. The website at **www.mexicohelp.com/index.htm** includes all contact information. Her group focuses on providing the information needed by ex-pats and helps them settle into their new country with all its intricacies and legal issues. Many other websites provide useful tips as well.

Immigration—Temporary and Permanent

Mexico welcomes visitors and especially seems to welcome Canadian and U.S. citizens who want to live in Mexico for extended periods or full-time. The formalities are relatively simple if you are visiting for up to 180 days. On the plane or at the border you will be asked to fill out an immigration/customs form. When you pass through Customs and Immigration, you will get a copy of this form. Keep it! You will need it to get out of the country easily.

If you plan to move to Mexico, we recommend you engage the services of a good immigration lawyer or talk directly to a Mexican consulate.

Once you decide to spend large amounts of time each year in Mexico, you may want to explore applying for a non-immigrant visa or FM3. For details of applying for an FM3 see either of the following websites: **www.consulmexny.org/eng/visas_fm3.htm** or **www.mexconnect.com/ mex_/immigration.html**. The non-immigrant visa provides several benefits. For example, if you want to open a Mexican bank account, you will need an FM3. Also, having an FM3 allows you to keep a car in Mexico beyond the permit date. Many ex-pats leave a car in Mexico and fly back and forth. You need to renew your FM3 each year.

Some people use their FM3 status as a prelude to applying for Mexican citizenship, and dual citizenship is possible. If that makes sense for your circumstances, when the time comes to consider citizenship, we recommend that you engage the services of a professional. As a Mexican citizen, you can own property directly even in the restricted areas, so you can avoid the use of, and the costs of, a real estate trust. (See the following section.)

Even as a visitor without FM3 status, there are benefits for which you can be eligible. One is an INCEN card, available to those over 65.

INCEN card holders get free admission to any museum in Mexico, discounts on bus and air travel, and other benefits for seniors.

Rent First

The first time you try a new community, you should rent, at least for a short term. Many Canadian and American retirees find renting for the season a better solution than buying, so it is important to be aware of a few issues when renting in Mexico. The good news is that there is a wide variety of rentals available in all the ex-pat communities we have mentioned. Prices are usually quoted in U.S. dollars. Our experience is that the rental market is not as organized as you would find in Florida, for example. Equipment in a rental unit may or may not be up to the standards you expect. Often you will be dealing directly with an owner who may be hard to contact. This is why we recommend that you use the services of an established Realtor, especially the first time you rent in a community, so that you will get value and the unit will be furnished and equipped to your expectations.

In general, values are excellent, if not exceptional, when compared to the southern U.S. rental market. It is not unusual to rent a condo with an ocean view for about US$1,500 per month for a seasonal rental. You'll pay less in beach communities with no water view. Rents can escalate quickly, however, depending on location, size, and amenities. We have seen large, luxury villas for rent in our area for US$10,000 a week! Inland communities are in the same price range and the better properties are also more expensive, as you would expect.

Finding rental properties is not difficult if you have even basic internet skills. Just search using the community name and the word "rentals" and you will find a large choice.

Buying Mexican Real Estate

Once a decision is made to retire in Mexico, either full- or part-time, and you have selected a community that suits you, the next big decision is whether to continue renting or to buy. Many people who spend less than six months a year in Mexico continue to rent year after year with apparent success. Others prefer to have their own place and buy. If you decide to go that route, you then have to decide between an individual home and a condominium. There are benefits and pitfalls to watch for in both options.

First, let me dispel one myth. It is not difficult for a foreigner to buy property in Mexico. Each community has several thriving real estate agencies, many of which specialize in the expatriate market. They can guide you through the process. We recommend that you invest time in selecting your agent just as you would in Canada or the U.S. Pick a pro with several years of experience in the market. Note that prices in the areas you are likely to want to live are quoted in U.S. dollars.

Now for the principal Mexican difference—you cannot directly own property within 100 kilometres of a border or 50 kilometres of a coast. However, in the interest of foreign investment, Mexico has found a way, albeit costly, to enable foreigners to buy property within these restricted areas. It is done through a *fideicomiso,* loosely translated as a trust. When you find your dream home, you make an offer to purchase to the seller, subject to obtaining a satisfactory trust arrangement with a bank. The trust arrangement is handled by your Mexican attorney, who normally has a relationship with at least one bank. On closing, the bank holds the title "in trust" for you for a 50-year period, which is renewable for another 50 years, and you are buying the trust. Of course, there are set-up charges and annual dues to maintain the trust. For one recent trust, the annual fee was US$522.50 on a US$100,000 property sale, plus set-up and attorney fees of about US$1,500. The offsetting cost is low property taxes—in this case about US$150 per year.

This brings up another problem with Mexican property, low taxes. While it seems to be a benefit, it actually means you can expect very little in the way of municipal services. This is why roads in many places are full of potholes, policing is poor, and many other services that you take for granted in Canada are just not there for you in Mexico. Private communities and condominiums usually contract privately for these services but at a charge to the owners. So watch your overall cost structure. Condo fees for the transaction mentioned are US$4,500 per year, so it all evens out. What you avoid in taxes you pay in fees.

Other concerns for property owners are safety and security. Crime rates have risen in some parts of Mexico over the past several years, which is why you see security gates, barred windows, and high stone and concrete fences. However, the same issues exist in the U.S. and Canada so normal caution is well advised. It may look like heaven but you need to have good security. (For more, see the section on Crime and Personal Safety that follows.)

In condominiums, be sure that the condominium corporation is in solid financial condition. After the peso devaluation of 1995, many in the Mexican middle class were wiped out and defaulted on their condo fees. It seems this is now a bit of a habit and many condominium corporations are carrying large arrears on their books, as assets, because some owners, Mexican and foreign, found that arrears were not pursued too aggressively. This appears to be changing, however, as owners and managers ultimately realize that a well-maintained condo complex is a better investment than a rundown property. It is also not unusual to find condo volunteer presidents using their position to line their pockets. Try to find out how well the condo is run and what improvements are ongoing. Talk to some other owners to get the real scoop.

One final note on taxes: keep your receipts for any renovations and avoid the cash payments offered by many contractors. If or when you sell your property, you may be liable for a capital gains tax. Your Mexican attorney can give you details for your specific situation. This tax is based on your purchase price plus any renovations paid for that, included certain taxes. Otherwise, you will find the capital gains tax deducted from your proceeds. And remember, if you own the property "in trust" you will be selling your interest in a trust, unless you are selling to a Mexican citizen. Then there could be a trust termination fee of up to US$1,000.

Health Care in Mexico

The quality of health care services in Mexico is generally very good, especially in major towns and cities. Many doctors and dentists speak English, but don't count on it. Try to get a referral when looking for medical attention.

Often the costs of medical services are less than you would pay in the U.S. or Canada. One example is the cost of eyeglasses, which can be obtained from reliable optometrists for less than half of the Canadian or American cost. My wife, Trish, had successful laser eye surgery for a fraction of the cost that would be charged in Canada or the U.S. Dentists are often much less expensive as well.

Medical insurance is highly recommended. This is available from several sources and should be purchased before you go. Mexico has a national health plan (IMSS) through its social security system. If you are planning on regular long-term visits or are moving to Mexico, you should explore whether you qualify as this coverage can be purchased separately. In 2004 the cost was less than US$300 per year per person. The system has doctors, hospitals, and most medical and drug services under its mandate. Mexico also has parallel private medical services, including private hospitals.

Even as a visitor, you may be eligible for IMSS. However, as you are an outsider buying into the plan, pre-existing conditions will either be excluded or could result in you being denied coverage. To find out if you qualify you must apply at an IMSS office. Be aware that everything from the staff to the forms is entirely Spanish so you must be able to speak the language or go with a helpful Spanish-speaking person. The decision to grant you coverage will be based on this application and your medical history. In case of any doubt, you will be examined by an IMSS doctor before approval.

Cars in Mexico

There are many sources of information about driving in Mexico, bringing cars into the country, and Mexican car insurance. These include AAA, CAA, Mexican consulates, and websites. Here is a brief overview of what to expect but be aware that if you plan to take a car to Mexico, there is a lot that you need to know.

In general, driving in Mexico is relatively easy for most North Americans. And, contrary to many rumours, we have found Mexicans to be very good drivers. The extensive toll road system *(cuotas)* is excellent, although expensive. Because of the cost, many Mexicans avoid toll highways and take free roads *(libre)*, which means traffic is usually light on the toll roads. There are always free road alternative routes and they are often very scenic. One thing that does not get enough emphasis in most articles on driving in Mexico is the speed bumps, or *topes*. They are found on almost all two-lane roads when entering a town or village and again when exiting, and often there are several in between. There are usually signs to warn you but sometimes local pranksters take them down. You will know it when you hit one at higher speeds! *Topes* also are used as speed controllers in all cities and towns. Drivers beware.

Driving in cities and towns can be a challenge. In small towns, road maintenance is poor and streets can be narrow. Stop signs and traffic lights can be difficult to see. In larger cities, traffic can be very heavy and signs confusing. Caution is urged at all times.

One major difference is that a left-hand turn sometimes must be made from a special right-hand lane. Watch for this, especially in busy towns and cities. Speaking of left-turn signals, if you are caught behind a slow truck on a highway, the driver will often put the left-turn signal on to let you know it is safe to pass.

It is important to know that your Canadian or American car insurance is *not* valid in Mexico. You will need to arrange Mexican car insurance for the time your car is in Mexico, and this must be done before you cross the border. We leave a car in Mexico and buy our insurance from a Mexican insurance broker. It is very reasonable and costs us about US$400 for a year.

If you are involved in a traffic accident, you should be aware that Mexican law is derived from the Napoleonic Code. This means you are considered guilty until proven innocent. This is especially true if there is an injury as a result of the accident. Mexican police generally do not speak English, so have your Mexican car insurance policy handy and the toll-free claims phone number.

If you are visiting Mexico for six months or less, you must obtain a permit for your car. This involves going through a procedure at the Mexican border that involves a lot of detail plus some costs. This permit is prominently displayed on your windshield and you must check back with Customs when leaving Mexico to verify that the car is no longer in the country. We recommend that you get information about these details from a reliable source such as CAA or AAA before you get to the border.

You can keep a car in Mexico beyond the permit date if your immigration status is under an FM3. (See previous section.) FM3 visas must be renewed annually and, at this time, the legality of keeping a car in Mexico is tied to your FM3 being active.

Car services are generally excellent in most of Mexico. All the major manufacturers have a dealer network but you should be aware that your warranties are probably not valid while in Mexico. Good independent mechanics are best found by referral, and it seems that everyone is happy to share the name of a good repair shop.

Finally, Pemex is the only gas retailer in Mexico. There is no competition. Try to keep your tank above half-full because in some areas you may not find a station for many kilometres. There are two other very important differences you must know. First, Pemex stations do not take credit cards. All purchases are paid for in cash. Second, there is no self-service and the person pumping your gas expects a tip, usually in the two to five peso range. Occasionally, you will find a second person cleaning your windshield and they expect a tip as well. We have never found a Pemex station that checked oil or other fluid levels.

Crime and Personal Safety

In the retirement communities mentioned, personal safety is not usually an issue. Just follow your normal precautions as you would at home. No one is safe at 2 A.M. in a bad part of town, especially if they've had too much to drink. That's not just in Mexico—it's anywhere!

Generally, crime is higher in large cities, but not more so than most American and Canadian cities. However, Mexico City is a special situation. It is beautiful and exciting and very much worth a visit, but care must be exercised in everything from public displays of jewellery to hailing cabs. Do your homework first about ways to avoid danger.

Driving at night is discouraged, especially on country and remote roads. Even if safety was not the issue, stray animals, poorly lit vehicles, pedestrians, and potholes add to the danger.

As is usual in most of North America, home security is important. Condominiums are popular as they allow better security than private homes.

Cost of Living

At this time, the cost of living in Mexico is very reasonable. This is due to the fact that the Mexican peso is the only major currency to lose ground to both the U.S. and Canadian dollars since 2000. That represents a big change; only a few years ago, the cost of living was much more expensive for ex-pats. Most items such as groceries, wine and liquor, restaurants, and gasoline have increased in pesos only by the rate of inflation. Therefore, the cost of these items is now much more reasonable when converting dollars due to the weakness of the peso. For example, in the best restaurants, main courses are usually under US$15, often under $10.

Labour rates are also much lower than in the U.S. or Canada, so services that are labour intensive are very reasonable. The one exception to lower costs is real estate, which in retirement communities is always quoted and paid in U.S. dollars.

Taxes

The Mexican taxation system is complex and we will not attempt to go into the details here—it would take a whole chapter on its own. The important thing to know is that residents and non-residents are treated differently for tax purposes and, as you might expect, the rules favour residents.

The country recently changed its laws to say that a "tax resident" is anyone with a home in the country, regardless of how much time they spend there (which could be seen as a reason to rent if you are only going to winter there). However, if you have a residence in Mexico and one in Canada, you will only be considered a Mexican resident if over half your income comes from sources within the country.

For specific details about how your personal tax status might be affected by becoming a Mexican resident, talk to a knowledgeable accountant or lawyer. You will also find useful information by going to the Solutions Abroad website at **www.solutionsabroad.com/a_mexicantaxes.asp**.

Shopping

Shopping in Mexico can be a wonderful experience. Arts and crafts abound in all regions. Mexico has a long tradition of very talented artists and artisans. Colourful markets allow the opportunity to bargain for the best prices. Try to enjoy the process of bargaining, as it is the custom. Also expect that your price may be higher than a native Mexican would pay.

However, over the past several years American-style retailing has gradually moved into Mexico's shopping world. There are supermarkets that look very much like those at home and carry even more varied merchandise. Recently, small motorcycles were for sale at a Mexican supermarket, along with TV sets, appliances, hardware, clothing, and, of course, liquor and a full line of groceries. You will be familiar with most of the brand names. Multinational big-box store retailers have moved in, such as Wal-Mart, Sam's Club, Costco, and a Mexican copy called City Club. There are even Office Depot box stores.

Membership cards from the U.S. and Canada are valid in Mexico and vice versa. Retailers in shopping centres surrounding these stores are unlikely to bargain due to their higher rents.

23

Your Retirement Questions

Every year I receive hundreds of questions from people on all aspects of retirement planning. They come from Canadians of all ages, from new college grads in their early 20s to retirees well into their 80s. I answer as many as I can on my website at **www.buildingwealth.ca** as well as on **50plus.com** and Sympatico/MSN, but I simply don't have time to get to all of them—they have not yet invented the 32-hour day! So I extend my apologies to all those who have sent in questions over the years and did not receive an answer. I assure you, it was not because of disinterest or laziness on my part.

The volume of retirement-related questions far exceeds those for any other topic, which suggests that if this issue isn't the number one financial concern for Canadians, it certainly ranks near the top of the list. Therefore, I have selected a number of the queries received in the past two years to include in this book, since one or more of them may relate to your personal situation. I have categorized the questions by subject matter to make it easier to identify those of special interest to you personally.

RRSPs (General)

Mother Wants to Give Money to Her Children

Q: My mother is turning 70 this year and wants to give each of her children a sum of money. The only "liquid" assets she has are in her RRSP. Because her RRSP will have to be converted to a RRIF this calendar year I wonder if this will be a good time to minimize the tax impact. I understand that if the RRSP is "cashed in," the resulting amount is considered income and subject to applicable taxes, some of which are withheld at the time of withdrawal.

She also wants a rainy day fund for unexpected expenses. Again, this would have to come out of her RRSP when we change to a RRIF. Are the same income tax rules applicable or do you perhaps have some tips to minimize the tax impact? —A.V.D.

A: I sure hope you mean that your mother is turning 69 this year, not 70. The rules are that an RRSP must be converted to a RRIF, an annuity, or cashed in by December 31 of the year in which a person turns 69. If your mother missed the deadline, the plan will consider to have been automatically deregistered by the Canada Revenue Agency. This means the plan would be terminated and all the money in it would be treated as income received in that year. Clearly, this is not desirable. If she is in fact going to be 70 this year, you need to check with the plan administrator immediately to determine its status, and professional assistance may be needed.

Assuming you simply got her age wrong, then she does indeed have the option of cashing out the RRSP. Whether this is the best choice will depend on how much money is in the plan and what other income she has. The proceeds from any withdrawal or from a plan wind-up are taxed in her hands at her marginal rate. A withholding tax of up to 30 percent applies at the time of the withdrawal, with the exact rate depending on the amount of money involved. The tax treatment of money withdrawn from a RRIF is the same as from an RRSP.

As a general rule, the more money that is in the RRSP, the less desirable the cash-out choice becomes because of the high tax it will attract.

Wants to Undo RRSP Transfer

Q: As a result of my ignorance, I transferred some shares of a company into my RRSP at a time when they were trading below my cost for them. I have now found that at the time of transfer into the RRSP, those shares were "deemed" to be sold at their market value and I cannot claim the deemed loss on that transfer. I would like to undo my mistake by taking them out of the RRSP, pay any tax as a result of this withdrawal from the RRSP, and then actually sell the shares to realize an "actual" loss (representing my original cost of purchase less the current market price or the market price at which I contributed those shares to the RRSP). I have suffered a real economic loss and I want to be able to undo it. Please let me know if I can do this. I would really appreciate your input. —M.S., Toronto

A: Sadly, the news is bad. What you've done cannot be undone. I have said for years that the government's policy on this issue is unfair, but unfortunately it's the law and we're stuck with it.

The rule is this. When you transfer any security into a registered plan, it is a deemed sale. If the market value at the time of the transfer is greater than your cost price, you have a taxable capital gain which you must declare on your return. But if it is below your original price, you are not allowed to claim a capital loss—hence the inequity. So an investor should never transfer a losing security into an RRSP or other registered plan. Sell it instead. This creates an allowable capital loss for tax purposes. You can then contribute the cash to the RRSP and use it to buy back the security within the plan, if that's your desire.

As I said at the outset, you cannot undo this by transferring the shares back out of the RRSP. If you do, the Canada Revenue Agency will treat it as a new purchase within your non-registered account at the current market value. At this point, your original purchase price has been wiped from the books. There is nothing that can be done to get it back.

Wants to Give RRSP to Dad

Q: I have a locked-in RRSP and I was wondering if I could give it to my father who is 68 years old and needs the money. Is this possible? Can I just sign it over to him? —A.G.

A: Absolutely not. I receive many variations on this question, all of which basically ask the same thing: Can I give my RRSP to someone else? The answer is a flat no. Your RRSP is your personal property and it cannot be transferred to another person except to a spouse in the event of death or marriage breakdown.

In this case, you can't even collapse the RRSP and give your father the after-tax proceeds because the plan is locked in. I'm afraid that you (and he) are stuck.

Wants to Use RRSP to Pay Off Credit Card

Q: I currently have approximately $17,000 saved in RRSPs. I want to pay off a credit card debt of $5,000. I was going to redeem $5,000 but I am wondering how much tax I will have to pay on the money I redeem. I also wonder what I will have to pay at income tax time. —C.R., Pickering, Ontario

A: As a resident of Ontario, you will have 10 percent withheld for tax if you withdraw $5,000. So you will actually receive $4,500 from the plan administrator, which will leave you $500 short of the amount needed to pay off the bill. If you take out more than $5,000, the withholding jumps to 20 percent so you would have to withdraw $6,250 to end up with the amount you need.

At tax time, you'll be given credit for the amount withheld. You'll be assessed at your marginal rate as if the withdrawal were regular income. So, for example, if your marginal rate is 30 percent and 20 percent was withheld at the time of the withdrawal you will have to pay an additional 10 percent when you file your return.

Bank Won't Transfer RRSP

Q: My husband has been trying to consolidate all his RRSP funds into one account by transferring an RRSP from one banking institution to a different one. The problem he is having is that the bank holding the RRSP keeps denying the transfer, stating that the request was not submitted in time. This is the second time this bank has held onto an RRSP that we have been trying to transfer. Both requests were submitted in sufficient time before the renewal date as we have seen the forms sent into the bank. Is this a common occurrence and is there any way for us to transfer the RRSP so we do not have to wait another year and have it happen again? —P. G.

A: It appears the money is invested in GICs and the bank keeps rolling them over. I recommend that you issue immediate instructions to the bank, in writing, that no automatic rollover should take place in the future and that the current GICs should be cashed in at maturity.

If you have evidence in writing that appropriate notice was given on a timely basis in the past, take it to the bank manager and present it. He or she should agree to redeem the GIC immediately with no penalty. If for some reason the manager refuses and your paperwork is correct, you can always appeal to the bank ombudsman.

Tax Deduction for RRSP Loan

Q: Is it possible to deduct the interest on a loan taken out to invest in an RRSP?

A: No, you cannot claim a deduction for the interest paid on an RRSP loan.

RRSPs at 69

Q: Can you give me an opinion on turning an RRSP into a RRIF at age 69 or cashing in the RRSP? Are there any benefits to either? —H.B.

A: It depends on the circumstances. If the RRSP is quite small, it probably makes no sense to convert it to a registered retirement income fund (RRIF). You'd have to pay the ongoing expense of the plan and the amount of income it would generate would be insignificant. However, if there is a lot of money in the RRSP, cashing it in would attract a hefty tax bill. The entire amount would be treated as income in the year you receive it and taxed at your marginal rate.

Take a fresh look at the RRSP and see what makes the most sense, with these thoughts in mind.

Young RRSP Investor with Questions

Q: I am a young investor in my early 20s and have read your *6 Steps to $1 Million* book and have found it very insightful. Since I'm young I want to take advantage of tax-deferred savings and compounding. I recently opened an RRSP and have embarked on a vigorous savings program. After much research there is one question I cannot seem to find an answer to: Is there a maximum RRSP withdrawal limit? If there is, does it also apply to RRIFs? —R.P.

A: I really enjoy getting questions like this from young people who are starting early to save. If all goes well you'll have your first million before you hit 50.

As to your question, there is no limit on the amount of money you can take out of an RRSP, as long as it is not a locked-in plan. If need be, you can withdraw the full amount although I would not recommend it except in dire emergency. It's the same situation with a RRIF—no limit, as long as the plan is not locked in.

Tax-Free RRSP Withdrawals

Q: Recently my parents and I were looking on the internet for financial information regarding withdrawing funds from their RRSPs as both are retired. Among the many articles we read was one claiming that my parents could withdraw up to $8,000 per year without paying tax. Does that sound correct? Is there a way for them to take out funds without being hammered by the taxman? —R.M.

A: Well, it's sort of correct. It depends on what other sources of income your parents have. The basic personal amount for the 2005 tax year was $8,148 (the federal budget of February 2005 will increase it to $10,000 by 2009). That means that if a person's taxable income did not exceed that amount, the tax owing would be zero because of the effect of the personal tax credit. So, in theory, each parent could withdraw about $8,100 from an RRSP and pay no tax. But note that I said "in theory." That assumes they receive no Old Age Security, no Canada Pension Plan, no pension income, no investment income—in other words, that the RRSP withdrawal is the only income they have. That will not be the case for most people. So before they rush to the bank, have them sit down and calculate what their income from all sources will be. If the taxable amount is likely to be less than $8,100 (or whatever the figure is at the time), then they have some room available for an RRSP withdrawal tax free.

Advice for a Newcomer

Q: I immigrated to Canada in 2002 and have had a permanent job since November 2002. I'm 37 years old, married, with two kids. I don't have any previous knowledge about personal finance because it does not exist in my native country but I have to learn it here.

My friends advise me not to put money in an RRSP because it's too risky and I am too old to start with that. They advise me to buy a house instead of renting. When I retire I can then sell my house and get my money. I calculated that I will pay about $10,000 for the rent this year and I think maybe they are right. Can you give me any advice, please? —S.P.

A: Your friends are both right and wrong. They are wrong about the RRSP. At 37, you are certainly not too old to open a plan, far from it. And too risky? That is plain silly. An RRSP is simply a shell—you can use it to invest in almost anything you want, from very safe to very risky investments. For example, if you decided to invest your RRSP money in Canada Premium Bonds and bank guaranteed investment certificates, you would have a plan that would be virtually risk free from the point of view of protecting your capital. Of course, your returns would not be very high as long as interest rates stay down, but that is the trade-off.

As for buying a house, your friends are right on that score—sort of. I regard home ownership and an RRSP as the two key pillars of financial independence. If you are paying $10,000 a year in rent, you should certainly consider buying a place. However, when they say you could then sell it after retirement and live on the income, where exactly do they propose you live? Go back to renting? That doesn't make a lot of sense.

What I'm saying is that you shouldn't pay a lot of attention to financial advice from friends, well-meaning though they may be. Do some reading and research on your own so that you can better understand the principles of personal wealth building. You'll end up telling *them* what to do.

Meantime, start putting away a little money in an RRSP and begin looking for a house. If you can find a place that you can carry for less than $833 a month (which seems to be your current rent), then you can put the difference toward the RRSP.

Using RRSP for Line of Credit

Q: Are there financial institutions (i.e., banks or trust companies) that offer a secure line of credit based on RRSP holdings rather than house equity? I'm looking for the best rate for a loan. My house is paid up and I don't wish to lose my insurance premium discount. I don't wish to cash in any stocks or other holdings at this time. —G.D.B.

A: Sorry, but you are out of luck. Federal laws specifically prohibit using RRSP assets as loan collateral. So no financial institution can offer the kind of line of credit you are seeking.

RRSP Overcontributions

Wants to Have Penalty Waived

Q: I unintentionally made an overcontribution of $13,000 to my self-directed RRSP last May and I am now facing a penalty of $900. Is there a way that I can reduce or waive this penalty? Besides, my 2005 RRSP deduction limit is only $3,000 because of a 2004 pension adjustment from my employer (my 2004 RRSP deduction limit was $11,000). So it seems that I will have to continuously pay the penalty in 2005. I am in my 30s and currently I am holding stocks and securities in my RRSP account. Should I sell some of the securities (might have to take some losses) and withdraw the overcontribution amount from my RSP? —J.Z.

A: I get more questions about overcontributions than almost any other RRSP-related topic. So before I answer this specific one, a word of general advice: be very careful about how much you contribute to your plan and be sure it is within the allowable limit. The Canada Revenue Agency allows you to go $2,000 over your allotment but after that a penalty of 1 percent a month on the excess will apply.

Can you reduce or waive it? No, not unless you can persuade the CRA to go along with the idea, and that's highly unlikely. You will continue to be penalized on the excess every month so your best bet is to get the money out of the plan and put things right. You can use form T3012A if the contribution was made in 2004. It will take about eight weeks to process, so act now.

Overcontribution in Plan for 10 Years

Q: I have had a $7,500 overcontribution in my RRSP since my husband died 10 years ago. I got caught when the limit changed from $8,000 to $2,000. I have never heard anything from the CRA on this. I can claim the overcontribution as a deduction as I have not worked since. I am still in my 50s. What should I do? Why have I not been penalized? —N.R.

A: You're in luck. The reduction in the overcontribution limit from $8,000 to $2,000 was announced in the 1995 budget and took effect on February 25 of that year. Everyone who had an overcontribution of more than $2,000 but less than $8,000 at that time was grandfathered. It appears your overcontribution slipped in under the wire so you are allowed to retain it for as long as you have your RRSP, with no penalty.

However, you cannot add new money to your RRSP until you draw down that amount to under $2,000 by claiming the extra as a deduction. As long as you have no employment income to create new RRSP contribution room, this can't be done.

I suggest you relax. The $7,500 is earning tax-sheltered income for you and you are not on the hook for any penalties. Timing is everything!

Worried about Warning from Government

Q: I have an RRSP overcontribution of $1,116 from my 2003 income tax. My assessment shows a $0 contribution limit for 2004. Below this line is an addendum stating: "You have $1,116 of unused RRSP contributions available for 2004. If this amount is more than $0, you may be subject to a penalty tax." My question is: Do I have to cash in that amount to avoid any penalties? —F.P.

A: Good news. You can leave that money in the RRSP without penalty. Everyone is allowed a $2,000 overcontribution cushion before penalties cut in. If you exceed that, however, the Canada Revenue Agency will assess a penalty of 1 percent a month until the situation is corrected.

You can claim a deduction for the $1,116 as soon as new contribution room becomes available, if you wish. Or you can carry it forward indefinitely. Just don't make the mistake of contributing more and going over that magic figure of $2,000.

Home Buyers' Plan

Parents Struggling to Repay Home Buyers' Loan

Q: My parents purchased their first house at age 64. At that time my father was still working; he has since retired. When they purchased the house they used $15,000 in RRSP as a down payment since it was their first home.

They are now required to start to pay back this $15,000. They are 68 and 69 years of age now. My question is, due to their age do they still have 15 years to pay this back or is there a way they can avoid paying this back yearly? They are both on a fixed income and are finding it difficult to pay back the required amount. Is there a way to claim this as income and pay one lump sum all at once? The government was not able to help them as we have called them.

They are considering getting a bank loan for the outstanding amount and paying it all back at once, then cashing in the RRSPs to pay back the loan. I do not think this is a wise decision. Can you help?
—C.R., Pickering, Ontario

A: There is no need to get a loan to repay the Home Buyers' Plan and I agree with you that it is probably not a good idea. The fact is that your parents don't have to repay the loan at all, ever. Given the circumstances you describe, it appears they shouldn't do so.

If they don't make the annual payment, all that happens is that the amount due in that year is considered to have been taken into income. In this case, that will be $1,000 a year over 15 years. If the loan came from your father's RRSP, he will be assessed income tax on that amount annually. Since it appears he is in a low tax bracket, the rate should not be very high.

You will have to compare the tax cost of doing this with the cost of cashing in the RRSP to repay a bank loan. The entire lump sum withdrawal will be treated as income in the year it is taken out, which means the marginal rate could be much higher. But check it out.

I should add that both your parents are approaching the stage when they need to convert to a RRIF. Repayments to cover a Home Buyers' Plan loan cannot be made to a RRIF (you can't put any money into a RRIF except from another registered plan), so in this case the $1,000 due each year would automatically be assessed as income.

First-Time Home Buyers

Q: My husband and I are first-time home buyers and are considering taking out money from our RRSPs for the down payment. I have heard that this is not necessarily a good thing, but since we are in our late 20s and this would significantly lower the amount of interest we would pay on a mortgage, should we do it? —S.P.

A: Probably. Years ago, I advised my children to take advantage of the Home Buyers' Plan (HBP) when they were starting out—but with a caution. You have to realize this is a trade-off. You are saving money on your mortgage interest today but you are sacrificing future retirement income. That's because you lose many years of tax-sheltered compounding while the RRSP loans are being repaid. Those years can never be recovered and the reduction of the final value of your retirement plans will be many thousands of dollars. So using the HBP should not be done lightly.

My feeling is that if you can afford the additional mortgage payments and have the down payment without resorting to the HBP you should not borrow from your retirement plan. However, if the HBP would make the difference between buying a home and having to rent, then by all means take advantage of it. Just try to repay the RRSP loan as quickly as possible.

Wants to Eat Cake and Have It Too

Q: I purchased a home this year with my wife. It is our first home purchase. I withdrew $20,000 out of my RRSPs under the Home Buyers' Plan. As I repay the RRSPs do I still get the benefits at tax time on these RRSP amounts? —P.M.

A: If I understand your question correctly, you are asking if you can claim a tax deduction for repaying your Home Buyers' Plan loan. This is rather like asking if you can have your cake and eat it too. You claimed a deduction for the $20,000 at the time you made the original contributions to your plans. Then you took out an interest-free loan, using this same money. I expect you'll understand why the government will not allow you to claim a second deduction for putting it back into the RRSPs again.

Locked-in Money

In Debt and May Lose Home

Q: I am currently unemployed and badly in debt. I cannot manage to remain in my home and pay the mortgage. Is there any way to "unlock" a portion of my "locked-in" RRSP? I live in Ontario. —B.E.

A: You're in luck, as long as your locked-in plan is regulated by the Ontario government and not the federal government. The Financial Services Commission of Ontario (FSCO) handles such requests and you will find the required forms on their website at **www.fsco.gov.on.ca**. One of the accepted reasons for drawing locked-in money is the risk of eviction from a home or rental accommodation. To be eligible, you must have received a demand in writing for payment on a debt secured by the residence. This could include a mortgage payment or property taxes.

The rules are different in every province, and federally regulated locked-in plans make no provision for hardship withdrawals.

What Happens if Locked-in Account Is Moved to Another Province?

Q: I am 59, living in Ontario, and will be retiring within six weeks. I have a locked-in retirement account which I plan to convert to a LRIF for income.

My question is: If my plan is under the jurisdiction of Ontario at the time I convert but I later move to another province which does not have LRIFs, could I be required to convert my LRIF to an annuity at age 80? My choice would be to continue to manage my LRIF for life (or at least have that option).

The various provincial rules seem to vary quite a bit. Is there a source where I can find a summary of the rules in each jurisdiction? —K.S.

A: Wherever you go in Canada, the rules that apply to your LRIF (life retirement income fund) will continue to be those that applied in the original jurisdiction, in this case Ontario. The general rules governing locked-in accounts in Ontario are as follows:

> The key to understanding the rules that determine how any individual transfer amount must be administered is knowing which pension legislation originally applied to the member under the plan; the legislation of that jurisdiction will continue to apply after the transfer. Where the money is being transferred ... to a financial institution in another Canadian jurisdiction, all parties must ensure that the transfer satisfies Ontario's rules, i.e. that the funds in the locked-in account continue to be administered in accordance with Ontario pension law.

I agree that having so many pension jurisdictions is very confusing. However, I am not aware of any source one can go to where all of the provincial and federal rules pertaining to locked-in accounts are summarized. The federal government would be the logical coordinating body but it has taken no initiative in this regard, as far as I know.

Retirement Income

Do I Have Enough to Live On?

Q: I have retired at 56 and have a defined benefit pension of about $17,000 per year (with cost of living adjustments). In addition, we have $170,000 in non-registered investments as well as $540,000 in a defined contribution pension plan from a former employer, along with $214,000 in an RRSP and $78,000 in a spousal RRSP. We have no mortgage or other debts, owning a $400,000 home in Victoria. We have no children or other dependants.... Do we have enough to retire on? —D.L.

A: It sounds like you are very well positioned financially. Lots of people would be happy to trade places with you. However, I can't tell you whether you have enough to retire on because it all depends on how much income you expect to need each year. The various savings you mention total just over $1 million. If you invest that conservatively and earn an annual return of 6 percent, that will add $60,000 a year to your $17,000 pension. You can start claiming a reduced CPP at age 60, which will be worth, say, $5,000 a year. So the question back to you is simply: Is $82,000 annually enough for you to maintain your lifestyle while providing a bit of an inflation cushion for the non-pension income?

How to Manage Retirement Income

Q: I am a 53-year-old divorced man with no dependants and have recently retired. I have a small company pension of $26,000 per annum. I also have a $300,000 house, $400,000+ in non-sheltered equities, and $200,000 in sheltered equities. All of my investments are fairly diversified. When I die, my estate will pass entirely to charity.

My question is this. In order to supplement my retirement income, should I draw from my sheltered or non-sheltered investments first? If from the non-sheltered, at what age should I think about reducing the sheltered portion? Obviously, taxes are a major consideration. —F.L.

A: The general rule is to draw against the non-sheltered portfolio first. There are two reasons for this. First, there is no tax payable except on any capital gains that may be realized when you sell. Second, this strategy allows the assets in your registered plan to continue to grow in a tax-sheltered environment until the money is needed.

There is no magic age for switching from the non-registered to the registered assets. Of course, by law you have to start drawing down the registered portfolio after age 69, but you are a long way from there.

There is one more thing to consider. You say that your non-registered assets are in equities. Why not move some of the money into tax-advantaged income-producing securities such as REITs and preferred shares? The income that is generated may be enough to minimize or even eliminate the need to draw against capital, depending on your needs, and the tax breaks will increase your after-tax return.

Planning Retirement Income

Q: In our younger days, many financial planners gave us advice on how to plan our retirement. My wife and I are now a little over 50 and plan to retire in the next two to three years. We are now holding some stocks, some mutual funds, and some cash.

When we retire, we mean to enjoy our life. We do not want to spend so much time listening to advisors on how to manage our investments in our golden years. So, Gordon, I would like to know if there is any institution that can provide an investment scheme that by putting in a fixed amount one can get a monthly return (something like a fixed-rate deposit, but a lot better rate of return.) —P.T.

A: I understand that you don't want to spend a lot of time managing your money but I hope you are not being short-sighted about this. No investment is perfect and conditions change. The right choice today may be the wrong choice five years from now. Plus there is the little matter of taxation. You want to be sure that your money is invested in such a way as to minimize your tax payable, thereby giving you more cash with which to enjoy those golden years.

There are all kinds of ways in which money can be invested to generate monthly income. The amount of income you receive will be directly proportionate to the risk you are prepared to take. You could put everything into a monthly-pay GIC for absolute security. You could invest in one or more monthly-pay mutual funds—there are many of them out there. You could build a portfolio of income trusts. You could invest in equity funds and use a systematic withdrawal plan.

There is no "one-size-fits-all" choice when it comes to investing, especially when retirement income is involved. So the best suggestion I can make is to get over this idea that you can retire to a lake for the rest of your life and forget about your money. You may live to regret it. Instead, find a financial advisor you can trust, set up an income portfolio, and meet with the person once or twice a year to review it. Surely you can afford to take that much time to ensure the money will always be there for you.

Pension Plans

Buying Past Service in Pension Plan

Q: Do you recommend purchasing service time to put into a government-funded pension plan versus investing the money on your own? —P.B.

A: As a general rule, yes, particularly when a government plan is involved. These are among the most generous pension plans around from the point of view of guaranteed benefits, plus they offer a lot of bells and whistles, such as indexing. If this is a defined benefit plan (you don't specify but most government plans are), buying past service will increase the pension you receive at retirement, perhaps by a significant amount. Ask the plan administrator for the numbers. The income is guaranteed. Since it is a government plan, you don't have to worry about the shortfall problems that are bedevilling some private plans at present.

Perhaps investing the money on your own would produce a better result, but you cannot be certain of that. When it comes to retirement income, I prefer to err on the side of caution.

Income Security Programs

Scratching for Money

Q: I am 67 years old. I have $8,000 cash in a savings account and no other investments. I receive $1,200 per month from Canada Pension Plan and Old Age Security. Any advice would be most helpful. —D.J.B.

A: It sounds like you are really scratching for income. It must be hard to live on only $1,200 a month. However, I have one suggestion that might help ease matters a little. It appears from what you say that you are eligible for the federal government's Guaranteed Income Supplement (GIS), which is available to those 65 and over who qualify as lower-income Canadians. The maximum income you can receive to be eligible is $13,464 a year (2005 figure), not including Old Age Security payments. Your income totals $14,400, but with OAS taken off you should be well under the threshold.

The maximum monthly GIS payment in the second quarter of 2005 was $562.93 for a single person. The amount is adjusted quarterly for inflation.

To find out more, visit the government's Income Security Programs website at **www.sdc.gc.ca/en/gateways/nav/top_nav/program/isp.shtml**. If you qualify, I'm sure the extra income will help a lot.

When to Draw CPP?

Q: I have taken an early retirement at age 55 to start a home renovation business. I have a federal superannuation pension which will be reduced at age 65 to compensate for the CPP payment. I have two questions:

1. Should I start collecting CPP at 60 years or wait until my 65th birthday?
2. Can I collect CPP at age 60 if I am self-employed?

—H.D., Grimsby, Ontario

A: The response to the second question may make the first one redundant. No, you cannot start to draw CPP at age 60 if you are self-employed. The rules say that you must be "substantially retired." However, there is a loophole. The definition of that term is that you have completely stopped working *or* that any employment income (including self-employment) that you receive during the month before the pension begins and the first month of eligibility does not exceed the maximum amount payable at that time ($828.75 in 2005). So if you can limit your income to less than that during the two-month period, you can qualify. After that you can go back to earning as much as you want.

When you should begin is a difficult question. If you start to collect at age 60, your pension will be 30 percent less than it will be at 65. But if you need the money, that probably won't matter. Other factors to consider include life expectancy, taxes, and whether your CPP might actually be reduced by waiting because of the complex pensionable earnings formula. The best advice I can give is that if you don't need the money and have no reason to think you have a shortened life expectancy, wait until you are 65.

Wants to Avoid OAS Clawback

Q: My husband and I are both retired. Our RRSPs did poorly for many years but by working very hard on our own through a discount broker and with the help of your recommendations the situation has improved. In 2007, my husband will be 69 and will have to wind up his RRSPs. He has currently $77,000 in RRSPs of which $13,700 is in a spousal RRSP. We are both receiving Old Age Security. What plan could we use so that we do not offset our OAS by having to pay the clawback tax and how can we minimize our income from the RRSPs? —G.M.

A: Unless you are receiving very healthy pensions, you probably don't need to worry about the OAS clawback. The special tax does not kick in unless your net income exceeds $60,806 (per person, not jointly) and that figure will be somewhat higher in 2007 because it is adjusted annually for inflation.

Once the RRSPs are wound up, they can be converted to RRIFs. The minimum amount you can take out each year is set by the federal government. At age 70, it will be 5 percent of the value of the plan on January 1 of that year. The money that comes out of the spousal RRSP is taxable in your hands, not his. So his personal RRSP is currently worth about $63,000. The amount that would have to be withdrawn from a RRIF at age 70 would be a little more than $3,000, probably not enough to cause a lot of concern from a tax perspective.

It might be a good idea to consider withdrawing the cash from the spousal RRSP when you reach the point at which the plan must be wound up, especially if your income is low. It will be treated as taxable income in the year received, of course, but carrying such a small amount into a RRIF won't make a lot of sense in relation to the cost involved. In fact, if you can close out the plan earlier you might do so. Just be sure that your husband has not made any new contributions to the plan within the three years prior to withdrawing the money.

Sharing CPP Payments

Q: I'm 57 and retired on a schoolteacher's pension. My wife is 55 and has been a homemaker for most of her life. I'm planning on taking out my

Canada Pension when I'm 60 and splitting it with my wife since her pension income will be quite small at 65. Can I do that if she is still under 60? If she dies before me, could I get that half back? —W.C.

A: You cannot split your CPP payments until both of you are age 60. After that, the way it works is that your CPP entitlement and your wife's are added together and then divided between you according to a formula. If your wife has no CPP entitlement, then your pension would be split between the two of you.

The formula takes into account the number of years you were together while you paid into the CPP. So, for example, if you have been married for 25 years the combined pension you both earned over that period would be added together and then divided between you. Pension credits earned prior to the marriage would stay with each individual.

If one spouse dies, the amount of the CPP payment reverts to what it would have been had there been no pension-splitting arrangement. So you would get your full CPP payment back, but your wife would get little or nothing as a retirement pension if you were to predecease her because of the short time she spent in the workforce. She would, however, be eligible to claim a survivor's benefit.

You can find more details at **www.sdc.gc.ca/en/isp/pub/factsheets/ retire.shtml#e** and at **www.sdc.gc.ca/en/isp/cpp/survivor.shtml**.

Leveraging

Borrow to Invest?

Q: My husband is age 52 with a small pension. We are financially secure with no mortgage etc. and have the maximum in both of our RRSPs. My question is: Would you recommend borrowing an amount of money for investment purposes now and paying it back over the next five years, or just depositing $20,000 into a non-registered plan for five years to help offset his pension shortage? —I.J.

A: I would certainly *not* recommend borrowing. You say you are financially secure. Why would you jeopardize that by taking on debt when you don't need to? Think about what happened to the folks who did that back in 1999, just before the bear market hit. The consequences were pretty dreadful in some cases. The preferred course would be to invest the $20,000 in a portfolio of income-generating securities with low to medium risk and regular payments. Or you might consider a conservatively managed monthly income fund such as those offered by the major banks.

Retiring Allowances

Worried about Severance Transfer

Q: I am planning to retire at the end of 2005 from employment with the Ontario government for 36 years. I will receive severance pay of approximately $42,000. My pension will be approximately $55,000 per year.

If I take the severance as a lump sum, I will be taxed at approximately 30 percent and have EI and CPP deductions as well. I have been advised to roll it over into an RRSP and no tax will be deducted until I withdraw the money. The problem here is that, although the tax savings look good, I want to roll it over into a type of RRSP where I can soon start to withdraw a monthly amount to supplement my pension income.

What should I do? Will I save any income tax? It seems that I cannot find anyone that can give me a straight answer. —E.T., Pembroke, Ontario

A: Your severance is technically known as a retiring allowance. In your case, you can transfer all of the money into an RRSP and save tax. You are allowed to roll over $2,000 for every year or part-year of service prior to 1996 into an RRSP. You say you have been with the employer for 36 years, so that means you should have 26 years of eligibility. Multiplying that by $2,000 gives you a rollover allowance of $52,000, which will cover the full amount of the lump-sum payment.

There is no restriction on the type of RRSP that you use so there is nothing to prevent you from making monthly withdrawals on the basis of your plan.

RRIFs and Annuities

Wants to Balance RRIFs

Q: I have two RRIFs. One is my own while the other is a spousal RRIF. Question: Is it possible to transfer an amount from the larger RRIF to the smaller RRIF to effect a rebalancing of both? —G.G.

A: No, you can't do it. A RRIF, like an RRSP, is considered to be personal property and non-transferable. The only way a transfer could take place is through marriage breakdown or death.

RRSP or RRIF?

Q: I am 65 and need to withdraw money. Would it be smarter taxwise to withdraw from my RRSP or to convert it to a RRIF? —G.N.

A: The effect is the same no matter which you do—the money from the plan will be taxed in your hands at your marginal rate in the year it is received. However, switching to a RRIF before you need to do so reduces your flexibility. You cannot make contributions to a RRIF and you must take out at least the minimum withdrawal amount each year, whether you need it or not. That's why in most cases I suggest that people leave their RRSPs intact until age 69.

However, there is one tax angle you can play. Those 65 and older are eligible for the pension tax credit on payments from a RRIF. This means that the first $1,000 withdrawn is taxed at a lower rate (or at a zero rate if you are in the lowest tax bracket). To take advantage of this, set up a small RRIF now and make $1,000 annual withdrawals. There will be some tax withheld at source, but that will be refunded at tax filing time if the withholding tax was too much.

Switch from RRIF to Annuity?

Q: My husband, recently deceased, had a RRIF. My question is should I change it to an annuity or leave it as a RRIF? I am going to have to be very careful with my finances. I already have a RRIF, but my husband had no private pension. —R.T.

A: The advantage of switching to an annuity is that your income would be guaranteed (assuming the issuing company stays solvent) and you would not run the risk of loss within the RRIF portfolio. The disadvantage is that when interest rates are low, you will get an inferior return on the money with the annuity.

An alternative to consider would be to invest the money in your husband's RRIF in very safe securities, such as short-term bonds or GICs. That would protect the capital. When interest rates rise, that would be the time to consider switching to an annuity.

Sources of Information

If you're looking for more information on some of the subjects covered in this book, the following sources may prove helpful.

1: The Retirement Time Bomb

PUBLICATIONS

Commission on the Future of Health Care in Canada, *Final Report* (2002). Available online at **www.hc-sc.gc.ca/english/care/romanow/ hcc0023.html**

WEBSITES

U.S. health care cost projections: Centers for Medicare and Medicaid Services, *Health Accounts,* **www.cms.hhs.gov/statistics/nhe**

3: The Pension Mess

PUBLICATIONS

The Conference Board of Canada, *Is There a Pension Crisis? The Perspectives, Reactions and Strategies of Canadian CFOs,* November 2004

WEBSITES

CGA report *Addressing the Pensions Dilemma in Canada:* **www.cga-online.org/servlet/portal/serve/Library/Advocacy+and+Research/CGACanada+Key+Areas+of+Interest/Pensions/ca_pensions_report.pdf**

Conference Board of Canada: **www.conferenceboard.ca**

Statistics Canada: **www.statcan.ca/start.html**

4: Take the Offensive

PUBLICATIONS

Canada Revenue Agency: *Pension Adjustment Guide*

Canada Revenue Agency: *Retirement Compensation Arrangements Guide*

Canada Revenue Agency: *RRSPs and Other Registered Plans for Retirement*

WEBSITES

Canada Revenue Agency: **www.cra-arc.gc.ca**

Investor Education Fund: **www.investored.ca**

SEI, *DC Pension Plan Member Study:* **www.seic.ca/individuals/General_Press_Releases.asp**

5: Your Life Stages

PUBLICATIONS

Twenty-first Actuarial Report of the Canada Pension Plan, tabled in the House of Commons on Dec. 8, 2004; available at **www.osfi-bsif.gc.ca/app/DocRepository/1/eng/oca/reports/21/CPP2104_e.pdf**

WEBSITES

Income Security Programs—CPP, OAS, GIS: **www.sdc.gc.ca/en/gateways/nav/top_nav/program/isp.shtml**

Office of the Superintendent of Financial Institutions: **www.osfi-bsif.gc.ca**

Quebec Pension Plan: **www.rrq.gouv.qc.ca/an/rente/11.htm**

Social Development Canada: **www.sdc.gc.ca**

6: The Secrets of Success

PUBLICATIONS

AXA Retirement Scope, **www.retirement-scope.axa.com**

AXA Financial, The Canadian segment of AXA Retirement Scope:
  **www.axa.ca/axainternetwebapp/client/en/index.jsp?current=
  infoPress/a7_1.jsp**
Net worth calculator (click on Your Net Worth): **www.buildingwealth.ca**
Retirement calculators: See the Money section at **www.50plus.com**

8: Sources of Income

PUBLICATIONS
Decima Research CPP Awareness Poll (press release): **www.decima.com/
  en/pdf/news_releases/050301E.pdf**

9: Building an Investment Portfolio

WEBSITES
Bank of Canada currency converter: **www.bankofcanada.ca/en/
  exchform.htm**

10: RRSPs for Everyone?

PUBLICATIONS
Richard Shillington, *New Poverty Traps: Means-Testing and Modest-Income
  Seniors,* published by the C.D. Howe Institute, April 2003; available
  for downloading at **www.cdhowe.org/pdf/backgrounder_65.pdf**
FP Equities: Preferreds and Derivatives: Published annually by the
  Financial Post

WEBSITES
Canada RSP: **www.cis-pec.gc.ca/eng/bonds_crsp.asp**
GIS calculation tables: **www.sdc.gc.ca/en/isp/oas/tabrates/tab
  main.shtml#using**
Dominion Bond Rating Service: **www.dbrs.com**
Standard & Poor's Canada: **www2.standardandpoors.com/servlet/
  Satellite?pagename=sp/Page/HomePg&r=3&l=EN**

11: Understanding Income Trusts

WEBSITES
Canadian Association of Income Funds: **www.caif.ca**

12: Exchange-Traded Funds

WEBSITES

Closed-End Fund Association: **www.cefa.com**

iShares: **www.ishares.com**

iUnits: **www.iunits.com**

13: The Role of Bonds

PUBLICATIONS

FP Bonds: Corporate: Published annually by *Financial Post*

WEBSITES

CBID Markets (selected bond prices): **www.cbidmarkets.com**

14: GICs and Guaranteed Securities

WEBSITES

Royal Bank GIC rates: **www.rbcroyalbank.com/rates/rateadv.html**

Royal Bank Market-Linked GIC Return Calculator:

   www.rbcroyalbank.com/cgi-bin/gic/rates/gic_return.cgi

16: Mutual Funds—Battered but Unbowed

PUBLICATIONS

Report on Mutual Funds: Published annually by *The Globe and Mail*

WEBSITES

Globefund: **www.globefund.com**

Morningstar Canada: **www.morningstar.ca**

Sedar: **www.sedar.com**

The Fund Library: **www.fundlibrary.com**

18: Getting at Locked-in Money

WEBSITES

Alberta Department of Finance—Pensions: **www.finance.gov.ab.ca/ business/pensions**

Financial Services Commission of Ontario: **www.fsco.gov.on.ca**

Office of the Superintendent of Financial Institutions: **www.osfi-bsif.gc.ca**

19: Claiming Your Rewards

PUBLICATIONS

Canadian Life and Health Insurance Association, *Retirement as You'd Like It*

WEBSITES

Canadian Life and Health Insurance Association: **www.clhia.ca**

Cannex Canada (annuities): **www.cannex.com/canada/english**

20: Effective Tax Planning

WEBSITES

Canada Revenue Agency: **www.cra-arc.gc.ca/menu-e.html**

21: Alternative Income Sources

WEBSITES

Allowance program, Social Development Canada: **www.sdc.gc.ca/asp/ gateway.asp?hr=en/isp/pub/oas/allowance.shtml&hs=ozs**

Canadian Home Income Plan (CHIP): **www.chip.ca**

RBC Group retirement report: **www.rbc.com/newsroom/pdf/ RetireesSlides.pdf**

22: Living in the Sun

U.S.: PUBLICATIONS

Canada Revenue Agency, *Canadian Residents Going Down South;* available online at **www.cra-arc.gc.ca/E/pub/tg/p151/README.html**

MEXICO: WEBSITES

General information from ExpatExchange: **www.expatexchange.com/ rspgennet.cfm?rid=64&answerid=479&networkid=159**

Foreign Affairs Canada, *México: ¿Qué Pasa? A Guide for Canadian Visitors:* **www.voyage.gc.ca/main/pubs/mexico-en.asp**

Canada Department of Foreign Affairs, Mexican FAQs: **www.dfait-maeci.gc.ca/mexico-city/consular/faq-en.asp**

Real estate: Mexperience, **www.mexperience.com/property/default.htm**; Mexonline, **www.mexonline.com/propmex.htm**; The People's Guide to Mexico, **www.peoplesguide.com/1pages/retire/house/buy/aj-realestate.html**

Tax information: Solutions Abroad, **www.solutionsabroad.com/ a_mexicantaxes.asp**

Visas: Consulate General of Mexico, **www.consulmexny.org/eng/ visas_fm3.htm**; Mexico Connect, **www.mexconnect.com/mex_/ immigration.html**

The Government's View of Retirement Savings

When Finance Minister Ralph Goodale tabled his 2005 budget in the House of Commons in February, there was no mention in the document of tax-prepaid savings plans (TPSPs). This came as something of a surprise since the subject had been addressed in the two prior budgets with comments that the plan was being studied.

The 2005 budget proposed raising the dollar contribution limits for RRSPs to $22,000 by 2010, prompting criticism that this would benefit higher-income people while doing nothing for middle-income Canadians.

Following the budget's being tabled, I submitted a series of questions on the government's retirement planning policies to the Department of Finance. Here are the replies they provided.

Q: Is Budget 2005 the last word on savings for a while?

A: In December 2003, Department of Finance officials consulted with interested groups, experts, and academics on ways to improve the tax treatment of savings, including the introduction of TPSPs.

After reviewing the views brought forward and examining a number of important issues, it was determined that increasing the registered pension plan (RPP) and registered retirement savings plan (RRSP) limits is the most efficient, proven, and effective way to improve the tax treatment of savings at this time.

We will continue to examine potential improvements to the tax treatment of savings on an ongoing basis.

Q: Does this mean that TPSPs are now off the table for good?

A: No. However, our examination of TPSPs raised a number of issues.

First, the introduction of a new savings vehicle with a new set of rules and limits would impose administrative costs and additional complexity on financial institutions, governments, and individuals.

Second, a difficult issue is how TPSP investment income would be treated for income-tested benefits and credits, such as the Guaranteed Income Supplement (GIS). Many proponents of TPSPs suggested that some or all TPSP investment income be disregarded for this purpose. However, this would create inequities vis-à-vis other types of income, would mean that these benefits and credits would be less effectively targeted to those who need them most, and could significantly increase the costs of TPSPs.

Q: Is the department actively considering new ways to encourage low-income Canadians to save?

A: It is important that the tax system continue to provide effective mechanisms to support saving. We will continue to examine potential improvements to the tax treatment of savings on an ongoing basis. The effects of any potential improvements on savers at different income levels would of course be considered.

Q: What about low-income Canadians? Don't they face disincentives to save? Isn't RRSP saving unattractive for them?

A: It is important to recognize that public pensions alone—OAS/GIS and C/QPP—replace a significant portion of pre-retirement earnings for low-income Canadians: from about 75 percent to over 100 percent for those with pre-retirement earnings of $20,000 or less.

The support provided by public pensions means that low-income individuals have much less need and incentive to allocate income to saving—income that they may well need for current living purposes. It also means that rate of return considerations—such as the effect of the GIS reduction rate on the return to RRSP saving—are secondary for many low-income Canadians.

Of course, individuals will be better off in retirement the more they save. As pre-retirement earnings levels increase, public pensions replace a declining portion of those earnings, meaning that private savings needs rise. The deferral of tax provided on pension and RRSP savings assists and encourages individuals to save for retirement.

The best saving strategy for a particular individual or couple will depend on a number of factors, including: pre-retirement earnings levels, the desired level of retirement income, expected retirement age, the marginal tax rates faced before and after retirement and the corresponding rate of return to saving.

Thus, it is important for individuals to plan for their retirement needs carefully, including seeking professional financial advice to ensure that they make the best decisions possible about what savings strategies and vehicles will best meet their needs.

INDEX